Praise for *In Borrowed Houses*

Beautifully written, with plenty of humor and just the right amount of detail, this book tells the story of an American missionary who, with her husband and their colleagues, lived through the violent civil war in Lebanon and made a highly significant contribution to the life and witness of the Christian community. Was it really possible to establish a Christian publishing house producing relevant and good quality literature while bombs were falling and the country was being torn apart, and to establish such deep and enriching relationships with Lebanese of all kinds? Having lived through some of the same events, I can vouch for the fact that this is what they really did achieve. Charles Malik is quoted here as expressing in 1985 his fears that Christianity was facing extinction in the Middle East. If recent events in the region since the Arab Spring have revived these fears, western Christians and Middle Eastern Christians need to read this story which is full of remarkable perceptiveness and genuine hope.

—Colin Chapman, formerly Director of Lebanon Inter-Varsity Fellowship and lecturer in Islamic Studies at the Near East School of Theology, Beirut; author of *Whose Promised Land?*

With *The Chameleon's Wedding Day: Stories Out of Lebanon,* Fuller established herself as a marvelous and compelling storyteller; now she brings all her narrative skill to bear on *In Borrowed Houses.* Full of vivid and complex people, this extraordinary book is a page-turner as well as a profound spiritual memoir. While the horrors of war intensify, the Fullers and their friends grow stronger in spirit and in love. With bombs exploding around them, they grieve and cry, comfort each other and pray, but they also laugh, crack jokes, and play games. In her funny and compassionate true story, Fuller thanks God for tangible blessings, in borrowed houses and borrowed time: she is healed, safe from bullets, and her loved ones thrive. But she shows us that there is also mercy at times of illness and devastation, when God is with us.

—Aliki Barnstone, Professor of English and Creative Writing at the University of Missouri, author of *Dear God, Dear Dr. Heartbreak: New and Selected Poems* (Sheep Meadow Press, 2009)

In BORROWED Houses

A True Story

by

Frances Fuller

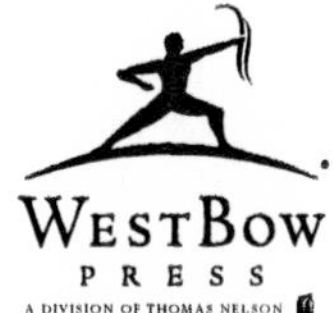
WestBow Press
A Division of Thomas Nelson

Cover Design by Julia Hanuliakova.

WestBow Press books may be ordered through booksellers or by contacting:

WestBow Press
A Division of Thomas Nelson
1663 Liberty Drive
Bloomington, IN 47403
www.westbowpress.com
1 (866) 928-1240

ISBN: 978-1-4908-1609-8 (sc)
ISBN: 978-1-4908-1608-1 (hc)
ISBN: 978-1-4908-1610-4 (e)

Library of Congress Control Number: 2013921091

Printed in the United States of America.

WestBow Press rev. date: 12/17/2013

Contents

Foreword ... vii
Preface ... ix
Introduction ... xiii

A House in a Village ... 1

An Abandoned House — A Normal Way to Live — Imagining a House — Protection Money — The Decision — The Mule Goes and Comes Again and Goes and... — Messages — Enormous Changes in a Hurry — The Hard Truth

Invasions ... 21

The Camel's Nose in My Tent — A Goat in the Sitting Room — The Neighbor Before the House — The House that Wayne Found — Locked Out — Better and Lasting Possessions — Georgette — A New Floor and a New Idea — While The Earth Trembled — Dress Warmly, Bring Food

Neighbors and Aliens ... 58

Stringing Beads — Something New Under the Sun — Now Where Were We? — Promises — A Diary of Peace — Wasta — The Problem with Peace — Moving — Getting Taller — Home — General Security — Mary, the Dragon-Slayer — The Occupation Army — Neighbors — Tours

Big Decisions and Narrow Escapes ... 103

The Oldest Man — A Missed Appointment — Afterwards — Measure Twice, Cut Once — Twenty-four Crazy Hours — Finding a Way

Houses on Battlefields 120

From My Seat in the Front Row — Scary Saturday — A Prayer for Sodom — War and Words — Patience — Reality Check — Nightmares and Ceasefires — Losses — John and Elena — Getting to Know John — Are You Lonesome Tonight? — Mastering Life — Only Spectators — Two Ways of Thinking — Letters — A Tough Question

Strategies and Damages 158

Dinner Music — Writing Day — Things That Had to Be Said — The Highest Price — Dense Fog — Clinging to the Deck — Akram Delivers the Swing — Leaders Leading — Lots of Refrigerators — 20 Rules for Surviving Civil War — Playing Games — Indispensable Friends — Nine Years

Intervals of Peace 211

Rendezvous in Larnaca — Pictures in My Head — Finding What Was Lost — A Place to Be Together — A Designer Shelter — A Small, Momentous Decision — Going Slow — Rejoice with Those Who Rejoice — Raising a Child

Houses of Clay 230

A Sorrowful New Year — Sharp Eyes — Ugly Suspicions — To the Edge and Back — Healing Our Diseases — Explosions of Grief — Explosions of Happiness — It's a Miracle — Compromises — Affirmation and Warning — Becoming Citizens

Exiled 264

Epilogue 283
Acknowledgements 287
About the Author 289

Foreword

When I first visited Lebanon over 40 years ago I was struck by the beauty and elegance of Beirut. At that time it was a country at peace with a thriving economy, and its inner conflicts presented themselves as simply a colorful set of cultural contrasts. But the serenity did not last.

Within a few years of that memorable first visit, the country was in turmoil and the scars of war were everywhere. Even the magnificent Phoenicia Intercontinental Hotel where I had stayed showed its wounds from gunfire and the neighborhood around it was badly damaged. It was in such an environment that I first met Frances and Wayne Fuller, a delightful American couple, whose love for the Lebanese people, their appreciation of the Arabic language and the culture and history of the region, impacted many.

My purpose for being in Lebanon—and that of the Fullers—was to encourage the publishing of local Christian Arab writers in their own language. I picked up quickly that Wayne and Frances were dedicated to excellence in everything that was done, and brought to their work a remarkable sensitivity to the Lebanese people and their values.

That was the beginning of a deep friendship that has stretched for more than 35 years. During several visits, sometimes with my wife, Peggy, I would arrive in Lebanon with anticipation and hunger for the stories that Frances, a captivating storyteller, would share – and which she shares through her memoir, *In Borrowed Houses.*

These are the stories we first heard when we sat with her—about people such as Georgette and Maria, about the scary trip from Beirut to Cyprus on a freighter circled by warplanes and gunboats, and being shot at by a sniper on the way to a print shop. Here, too, we could say is the love story behind all the other stories – the love that so motivated the Fullers that bullets and warnings and even the kidnapping of Americans did not persuade them to leave their "borrowed" home in Lebanon.

The stories we enjoyed in Beirut have, in the pages of this book, become the rich canvas of Frances's writing. Above all, in today's continuing warfare and conflict in the Middle East, they are the stories that take us behind the scenes into the heart of a region of which we in the West have so little knowledge or understanding. I am so thankful Frances has had the courage to write her personal journey here. I am confident that any reader who opens the pages of her book will, through her experiences and insights, her love and her faith, enjoy the rich experience of having their eyes opened.

Robert B. Reekie
Co-Founder, Media Associates International, Inc.
August 15, 2013

Preface: Remembering the Truth

In Borrowed Houses is a piece of my life as I remember it.

I have written with awareness that my memory is not one hundred percent reliable. For this reason I have used whatever documentation was available to me: histories, news reports, the fragments of diaries I sometimes kept and letters I wrote. Sometimes these documents helped me to recall associated experiences that they did not even mention. In a couple of instances they proved my memory to be slightly skewed, prompting me to change a detail.

During the years covered in this memoir I was separated most of the time from five of the most important people in my life, my children. They were young adults. They knew Lebanon; they cared about what was happening to Lebanon and to us. It was not easy or useful or acceptable in our relationship to lie to them. So I wrote them long letters in which I told the truth, though sometimes, I admit, not all of it. In a way these letters saved my life, because all five of those faithful people kept files or boxes full of these letters through the years and offered them to me later as references and reminders.

Even my tendency to tell stories helped to preserve them. At the dinner table other people eat, and I tell stories. The food, casual remarks, everything reminds me of a story. Consequently, many of the experiences recorded here I first related orally. Sometimes I did this soon after the events, when they were fresh in my mind, and later when I began to write, that previous telling was an asset. In some cases, what I had told appeared to almost take the place in my memory of the original experience, but it constituted a valuable recording, since I knew I had shared honestly.

Most of the stories within my story involve other people who are likely to remember these events somewhat differently. Yet recent conversations with some of them have given me confidence that when they read what I have written, they will recognize the truth.

In Borrowed Houses is my own story, not anyone else's. A great deal of it is not forgettable. It is part of me. My memories, after all, are the baggage and blessing that I carry around within myself, things that hurt or please or disappoint and, added together, create sense out of my life. I can know my story is true, because I know what living it did to me.

Frances Fuller
August, 2013

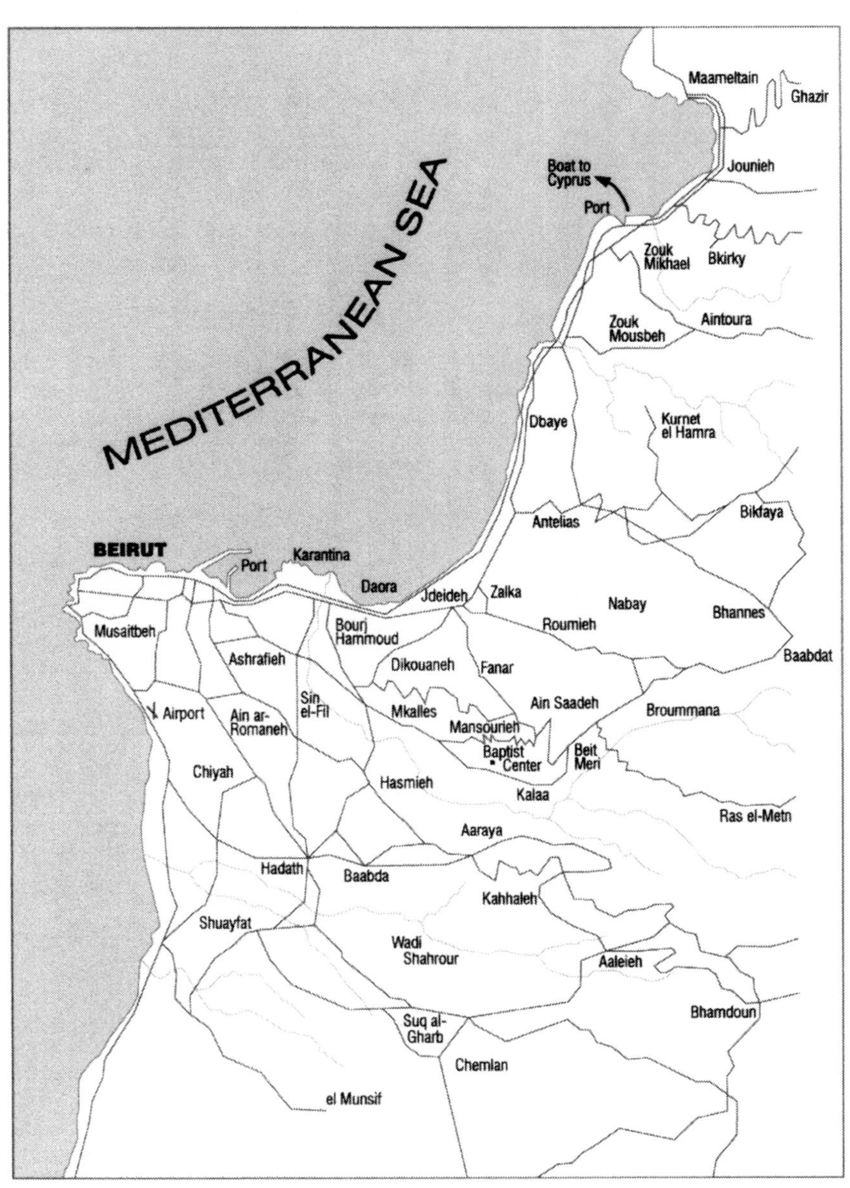

Beirut and vicinity (Map by Michel Makhoul)

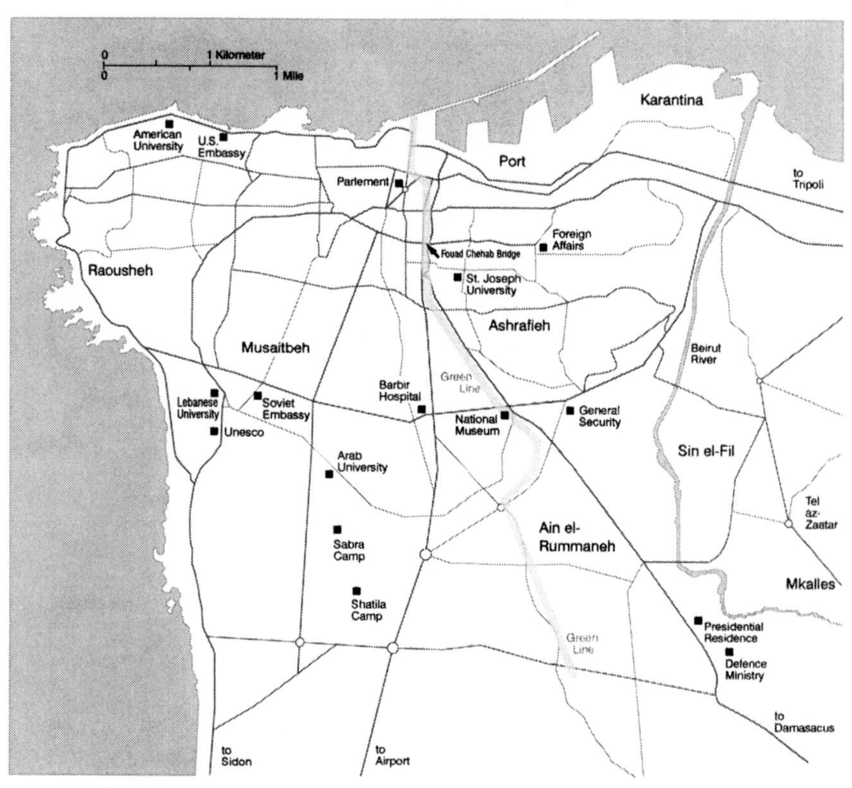

City of Beirut and suburbs (Map by Michel Makhoul)

Introduction

For thirty years of our adult lives Wayne and I lived in the Middle East, mostly in Lebanon. For twenty-four of those years I ran a small publishing house with an international purpose, creating Christian literature in the Arabic language. This task, along with raising five children in a foreign land, was challenge enough, and living in Lebanon was exciting and fun.

Then Lebanon was dragged down and backward into a long and dreadful war, not a war really but several wars. Pressured from the outside and tortured on the inside, invaded, occupied and abused, Lebanon splintered into chaos.

It started, or appeared to start, in the spring of 1975, the tenth year of our sojourn in the Middle East, while we were living and working in West Beirut. Small fights broke out, bursts of gunfire, advancing explosions, a lot of running and confusion and emptying streets, and then it seemed that someone had struck a match and thrown it into dry grass. The Paris of the Middle East was embarrassed to find her skirt on fire. We asked a series of neighbors what was going on. They lifted the shoulders of their shirts in their fingers, shook them and said, "Believe me. I don't know."

It was not our war, so understanding it was not our problem, just doing our jobs in spite of it, though of course, we could have opted out, like the thousands of other foreigners who got on planes and left Beirut at the sound of gunfire. The reasons we didn't are complicated.

At first our staying contained elements of false hope and misunderstanding. This fighting was silly and would not last long, we thought. The Lebanese were fun-loving, materialistic and tolerant people. They were looking for anything but war. So when the first artillery battle fizzled out, silenced by a thunderstorm, we were sure that no one was willing to get cold or dirty or bloody for this cause, whatever it was.

We were wrong, of course, along with stubborn. In 1963 we had accepted a lifetime appointment from the Southern Baptist Foreign Mission Board. We had volunteered to be sent on a mission, and we had chosen the Middle East. Publishing in this setting was both vital and exciting, especially because of the dearth of Christian literature in the Arabic language. We were creating a Christian library for a world basically without one. That was worth considerable inconvenience, and Beirut was still the best place in the world do to that.

I admit, however, that Wayne and I never asked ourselves if we could cope with fifteen years of extreme stress. Why would we imagine that the ordeal could last so long? Day by day we adjusted, found ways to work, accepted new goals and dreams, and collected friends so dear that walking away in a time of trouble would have felt like abandonment. Remembering who we were, we tried to be as neutral as God, but neutrality is hard when people you know and love are hurting.

A civilian on a battlefield is a kind of alien I had never thought about before. We had no voice, no power over the situation, usually not even good information, but in this we were just like most of our friends and neighbors. All we, or they, could do was to go about our business, while trying to protect ourselves and sometimes one another. And on those wonderful occasions when we foreigners could leave the battlefield and escape to America, I experienced the worst alienation of all and rushed back to the place where I understood the causes of my status.

In case all of this sounds like a mild form of insanity, I should point out that the war was not continuous. Days of noise and smoke and grief and an occasional panic were relieved by days of wonder and happiness. When shells were falling, we found it impractical to leave the house, much less the country. Afterwards, in the ecstasy of surviving, we were again overcome with hope. Finally, on the worst day of our lives, we lost the right to decide.

No one could live through such an experience without being scarred or transformed or at least educated. So we paid a price and received a reward, while getting damaged and changed. We learned things, including some I didn't want to know: about the Middle East, about America too, about war and surviving it, about being useful and being useless, broken hearted and happy, making a home and being homeless, walking with one's destiny and falling over a cliff.

But what I write here is not a lesson or even an explanation. It is a story. The whole story is too much to tell, so I have limited my tale to the years between 1980 and 1987, when we lived in Beit Meri, a town on the beautiful mountain above Beirut, because it was there in 1980 that Wayne found the house of his dreams.

A House in a Village

An Abandoned House

It could not rightly be called a house. Only in Wayne's imagination was it a house. In reality it was a heap of rocks, a landslide, a stable with a mule in the inner room, a one- hundred-and-fifty-year-old ruin, clumsily revised.

It stood tipsily too near the edge of the cliff, its front wall buckling. The front door was accessible only to goats and sure-footed shepherds—and Wayne, who pulled me up the hill, conquering the steepness by following a stony zigzag he claimed was a path. We had to stop more than once to extricate my skirt from giant thorns.

The wooden door—weathered and gray—sagged against the stone threshold, its hasp dangling. Wayne took time to check the condition of the top hinge—I could see his impulse to repair it on the spot—before he dragged the door open, and we stepped into a cold, dim room, its stone walls dark, a dirty color, its floor just earth and manure. A stingy light leaked through two dusty windows. Animal odors pierced my sinuses.

Simultaneously I saw the boulder and the arch and the mule. The huge rock protruded from the floor just inside the arch, and the mule stood beside it, his tail toward us.

"What's he doing in here?"

"Don't worry," Wayne said. "He'll go."

The stone, of course, was there because it wouldn't go. It was four feet wide and might have been sitting there since God separated the sea and the dry land. When I pointed this out, Wayne insisted in Arabic that it was a small matter. "*Baseeta.*"

The arch, however, was big in every way, wide and powerful, drawing a pleasing frame around our view of the mule and the stone. I admit that I liked the idea of a house with an Arab arch. There is something grand about an arched doorway, something magical about the way the keystone holds it all together, but this arch didn't look like it belonged in a palace; the big stones were rough and dirty. And a curved doorway in the middle of a stable doesn't make me want to move in.

Afraid of the mule's heels, we couldn't enter the room, and that was O.K. with me. I thought I could see enough. The floor in there was earth, not hard-packed earth but black, spongy dirt, the level of it higher than the front room, attained by a rough slope under the archway. The stones of the back wall had been blackened by maybe a century of fires.

Wayne said, "Beautiful, beautiful." He was looking up at the ceiling, the crudest possible ceiling—a few bare beams, just logs actually, with smaller trees and limbs laid across them, the kind of ceiling people make when snatching shelter out of a wilderness. All I could see was the dark crevices between the limbs, sure they were full of spiders.

In our family, everyone knew that Wayne had wished a long time for an old-fashioned Lebanese house. He liked the traditional architecture, he said. He also liked antiques, such as crude farm implements and ancient scales. Even more, he liked taking something broken and fixing it, something no one else wanted and making it valuable—a new washing machine from two broken ones, a usable car from pieces in a junk yard.

Once when the children and I had been Christmas shopping in Ras Beirut on a street reminiscent of Paris, we peeked down an alley at a dilapidated stone house, part of its roof gone, weeds growing inside its broken walls, and hatched a plot to buy it for Wayne. Then we walked on, smiling over our joke.

Wayne wasn't joking. He had found himself an old house in the village and wanted me to see all of it before I started getting negative. I humored him by looking at it.

From the front room we stumbled over a couple of flat stones into a vast room made of concrete blocks, as raw inside as out.

"This is where they had the cows," he said.

We counted eleven places, marked by cement feeding troughs.

"We could do anything we wanted with this room," he told me.

"Like planting flowers in the troughs."

Though I had meant to make fun, he said, "Now you're thinking."

The stairs to the upper level were outside and had no handrail; I hugged the rough stones for safety. The walls up there were a foot thick, like those below, but plastered inside. The plaster thickened and bulged in spots. In fact this whole part of the house might have been fashioned of clay by the hands of a child. The two rooms were nowhere straight or square or smooth, and various layers of paint showed here and there—green under a thin white, a hint of pink under the green. In the far back corner, one water spigot stood against the wall.

"Modern plumbing," I said, "but no closet."

"No problem," he said.

We walked out of the larger room onto the flat roof, into the welcome sunshine, and looked down on other flat roofs. Goats grazed in the field across the road, a field that was winter green, like the terraces and the forests. I heard chickens and the chatter of children.

This was The Hara, the old part of Beit Meri. It clung to the mountainside, with a few roads circling the slope—narrow asphalt lanes that might have evolved from donkey trails. Houses on one side of the road were above it and those on the other side below it, and lengthy flights of steps ran up or down to houses not on a road at all. The long, snowy summit of Mt. Sunnin dominated the skyline, and below the mountain the foothills divided, opening a steep canyon with a little river in the bottom. We could see here and there on top of the opposite mountain the flat line of the road to Damascus and the big stone buildings of Bhamdoun beside it.

Because The Hara was so low on the canyon wall, I felt surrounded by the mountains, which were taller and closer than they seemed from our modern apartment on top of the hill, straight up from where we stood. Living in The Hara would be like living in a bowl, looking up at the horizon.

Wayne sat on the wall surrounding the roof and hung his feet over. An old man with a hoe over his shoulder, trudged across the field past the goats. He waved and shouted at us. "*Ahlan.*" (Welcome.)

Wayne said, "We'll like the people down here. The neighbor before the house, you know." Another thing Wayne likes is old Arab proverbs. His speech, in English or Arabic, is full of them.

I couldn't even imagine myself in this country village. Weren't those people on another roof down the road looking at us right now and wondering who we were? And didn't I look strange—too tall and blond and foreign to be anything but a curiosity, standing here on the roof of this awkward, derelict house?

I said, "You sound like we're planning to live here."

He said nothing. He usually gets very quiet when we disagree. A hard man to argue with.

Descending to the road, I dodged the thorns—purple starbursts, beautiful but vicious—and wobbled on one unstable rock and then another, with Wayne gripping my arm. I said, "The first problem you would have here would be how to get your wife in and out of the house." I meant this to sound a little less stubborn than my last remark.

He said, "Oh, no. We could fix that."

Standing by the car, we looked up at the house while Wayne described the triangular shape of the lot, with sweeping arm motions. But I was wondering why this house had such a closed and secretive bearing. Maybe it was its windows, so small and few, implying a lack of interest in the world. Iron grilles over them, saying, "Keep out!" And the way the door didn't face the road but turned toward the terraces. At the same time there was a careless air about it. The long retaining walls of the terraces stretched out, like extensions of the house, like an over-grown root system—the same stones, the same haphazard style, but they were nearly lost in that jungle of weeds and wild blackberry vines and thorns masquerading as flowers.

I admitted to myself that the place was interesting. It would catch my eye if I were driving past. It had a graceless beauty, like driftwood and old weathered barns. Hammaoui could make a watercolor of it that I would be happy to hang on the wall in my painted modern apartment. But live in this stable? How could Wayne even think of it?

A Normal Way to Live

It seems absurd now that we were house hunting—after days and nights in the stairwell during artillery battles, after the sniper's bullets made little puffs of smoke as they struck the pavement around my speeding car, after staring into the black barrel of a gun, without breathing, until an incredulous militiaman lowered it and said, "I almost killed you!"

Thirty thousand Syrian soldiers were occupying Lebanon—bivouacked under pine trees along mountain roads and in confiscated, battle-scarred apartments on city streets, controlling all movement with their roadblocks and rifles and tanks. In 1976 they had intervened in the fighting between Lebanese militias and aliens camped in Lebanese territory, rescuing the Kata'ib-led forces that had been nearly overwhelmed by the Palestinians. Then they had settled down, claiming to be peacekeepers, and since then we couldn't leave home without encountering them, slouched in the middle of the road, beside little huts decorated with their black, white and green flag and pictures of Hafez al-Assad. With bored faces and lazy gestures, they obstructed traffic, cost us valuable time, made everybody angry. They had become the butt of all the best jokes, though they could shoot us or make us disappear.

My work could not be done just sitting in an office. It could not even be done staying on the mountain where both my home and office were located. Frequently I had to go down the hill to Beirut. Keeping safe on this or any trip required up-to-date information, because a drive of a few miles would take me, not just past the Syrians but through the turf of several armies or militias.

Beirut's one million souls crammed into about seventeen square miles, depending on where the lines were drawn through the suburbs. A more complex city would have been hard to find. Some of its maps named seventy communities within its roughly rectangular space. These areas were like villages, with cultures and accents and vocabularies that distinguished them from one another.

The streets were not laid out for the comfort of strangers. They angled across one another, plunging into bewildering intersections with no lights and no lanes or losing themselves in clogged traffic circles. Sometimes they split into one-way alleys lined with parked cars and peddlers' carts, and often they curved around hills or cemeteries or old structures that stood in their way.

Back in the lovely days of the early seventies these streets fascinated me. It was interesting to cross a street and find another language or religion or political persuasion. In the atmosphere of war these same streets terrified me, their slashing patterns and manifold divisions expressing the political milieu. One could cross the street and suddenly be in enemy territory. Added to all that, a scary no-man's land stretched through the middle of the city, dividing West and East Beirut. The Lebanese called this the fire line; the western press called it the Green Line. I saw a lot of fire there, but green was scarce. Some areas of the no-man's land were reduced to gray piles of stone. In others the buildings were standing but riddled and gutted, empty like skulls, black inside, but still holding the heart-stopping memory of beauty and life. It was a barrier, a buffer, and a desert in the middle of the city. I got a knot in my stomach every time I drove through it.

Mostly, Beirut was a rowdy city, with shouts and loud bartering, music with stirring rhythms, and laughter and clanging and screeching and beeping—constant beeping, along with color and jaywalking and sudden dangerous disobedience of the rules—a child chasing a soccer ball, a car double-parked or pushing upstream against the traffic. And abruptly there was the Green Line with its scary absence of all this commotion.

On the way to the press, I drove past the magnificent houses of Ashrafieh, with their tall pointed windows and decorative iron grilles, their gardens enclosed by stone walls. Big trees sheltered the street that narrowed and curved, and then the traffic dropped away and I was in a quiet, lonely place. Up ahead huge metal containers, stacked one on top of another formed a wall, shielding this East Beirut street from the West.

One day two young men with guns stood in that part of the street, lifting their hands to stop me. These were Kata'ib militiamen, Christian boys, cordial and concerned, and I felt glad to see them. I told them I was going to Calfat Press and asked, "Is it O.K.?"

One of them said, "Yes, but don't go any farther. If you go three meters past the door of the print shop you may get shot."

I took time to think about that, because this was a one-way street and usually I would return by making a right turn around the next corner and drive for a hundred meters just beside the Boulevard Fouad Chehab.

"Come back on this street," the boy told me, pointing at the ground under his feet.

"A sniper," the other one explained, and gestured to show me the approximate location of the gunman. By that time I was more afraid of a sniper than I was of big artillery. Sniper fire could be very personal.

I parked in front of the press, and had a good view of Fouad Chehab, a wide divided road, a big city thoroughfare, empty, controlled perhaps by just one man with a gun.

Stepping within two meters of the sniper's vision, still protected by the building across the street, I entered the shop and its distinctive atmosphere, its waves of warmth and energy, its smell of sweat and metal and ink, its tinkling and clacking and roaring and thudding and the crunching of the big trimmer through five hundred sheets of paper. All these busy men had gotten there the same way I had. Edmon, the shop foreman, looked up and greeted me without surprise, convincing me that the world was in order and I was not crazy.

Edmon used a roller to ink a galley of type and then pressed a piece of paper against it. I checked the proof, drank a cup of coffee with Mr. Calfat, asked about his children, answered questions about mine, got the latest estimate on when my work would be ready and came out again.

As soon as I shut the door the whomp and clack of the presses were gone, and a few meters to my right the wide road was empty and the city as quiet as death. For an instant the true state of the world was a surprise, a terrifying surprise, and I froze, staring at the faces of the buildings in front of me, flat and gray like the pavement, their windows shuttered. In the whole visible world nobody was home. With my skin prickling, I got into my car, backed away from the curb, turned around in the narrow street and drove toward Sassine Square against the pointing arrow, as the militiamen had instructed me. They waved at me as I passed.

I wrote it all down, though not in a letter home. One had to protect people who were far away and not equipped to understand that this could be a normal way to live and, like anywhere else, one had to find a suitable house.

Imagining a House

I agreed to walk through the house with Wayne one more time, promising myself to think positively, to act nice. On the way I said, "I do like this little road." The road into The Hara had a steep hillside rising at its left edge with boulders and weeds and red poppies protruding from it *hi yalla,* as we say in Arabic. Helter-skelter might be a good translation. On the right, though, the land sloped away toward the wadi and *snobar* trees stood around, like a crowd of villagers—very tall ones—come to see who was passing.

Snobars are pine trees, usually towering and spindly with an umbrella shape encouraged by cropping. Throughout most of Lebanon they stood along the summits of distant hills with sky showing under their branches. Their round tops made the slopes green. And they were useful, producing the tiny pine nut common to Lebanese foods. Here on the road to the village they made shade but left spaces between themselves for views of the towns across the canyon and in the distance Jabal Sunnin with a little cloud above its head.

But the way into The Hara was so charming it made arrival disappointing. Those gentle curves and graceful trees and lovely hovering mountains suggested something better at the end than square gray concrete houses and old tumbling walls. The Hara was very poor.

This time, when I looked up at the house, I noticed how the concrete addition violated the character of the old stones. The stone walls themselves were crude—big stones and little stones, square, round, and flat stones, stacked up in a way that could never have been planned. That walls had actually been achieved in this manner seemed miraculous. But the stones had a nice golden color, and it was plain tacky to add gray concrete blocks.

Again Wayne pulled me up the hill. We went first to the upper level of the house, tramping through the weeds on the east side of the house this time, instead of taking the stairs. The space behind the house—between the wall and the hillside—was only a few feet wide, rough and gravelly. With our backs to the rear door we would see only the bank of the hill, but we could turn the corner to our left and walk onto the roof.

Inside, the first room was an outlandish dimension, probably three times longer than deep and looked so forlorn with that water faucet rising from the floor at the end—four feet high, on a pipe that leaned about ten degrees. But Wayne led me through this area and showed me first where he would build a wall to divide the other, bigger room. A closet would be part of the wall, and he proved to me, tape measure in hand, that there was space. The east side would be our bedroom, and the smaller portion on the other side would be his study.

"And mine?"

"Just stick with me now. One thing at a time."

The end of that long, narrow room with the water spigot was spacious enough for a big bathroom, with cupboards and a dressing table. Again the tape measure proved this. He showed me where the new wall would be, and that left the rest as an entrance hall, wide enough and perfectly shaped to accommodate another cupboard with shelves. All we had to do was build frames and hang doors.

Below, in the huge room where the cows used to be, he visualized amazing things. First, he would use the space against the inside stone wall to make a stairway to the upper hall. This would create under the stairs a perfect place for a furnace room.

A furnace? I had imagined being cold.

Sure. The ceilings were so high, he could easily leave space for heating ducts under the floors.

"What kind of floors?"

"What would you like?"

He would build another wall along the back of the kitchen to enclose a walk-in pantry, and in the far corner we could have a small bathroom, just for convenience. And still there would be space for cooking and eating. He talked about an island and cupboards.

Would I like to have a desk here, from the same material as the cupboards? Just a small one with space for a typewriter, a few books, my personal correspondence?

I didn't mind that idea, but all the time the stench of manure filled my head. Would the smell ever go? And the place where the mule lived harbored unsolved problems. What about those black, ugly walls? What crawled around in that ceiling? What would we do with the Rock of Gibraltar rising from the floor?

Wayne admitted then that the stone could not be moved. It was part of the rock on which the house was built. It was too thick and hard to chisel away, and dynamite would bring down the house first.

And another thing. Beside the front door, at a right angle to it, a portion of an old wall protruded uselessly. I had not paid attention to it before. These obsolete stones descended—ceiling to floor—in a jagged line, extending into the room farther at the bottom, where they formed a little ledge about knee high. Wayne explained that the front wall of the house must have been there once, and someone had knocked it down to enlarge the room. (Silently I thought, *It fell.*) The remaining stones were anchored to the outside wall and had to stay. "Part of the decor," he told me.

Protection Money

However sure a foreigner in Lebanon might be that she was supposed to be there, moments of doubt would sneak through her mind. When she needed to explain it to someone else and didn't want to use any pious words, or if shells fell while she was all alone, or if she made a mistake and a sniper almost got her, a suspicion might arise, like a smooth-talking devil, and say, "You're crazy, you know."

Often we were saved from these doubts by seeing our colleagues, or even thinking of them. Then we would know suddenly that we were still sane and reasonable, because we were part of the Near East Baptist Mission, a sane and reasonable group of people, who had already passed up forty official warnings and three hundred opportunities to leave Lebanon.

In 1980 most of us had been in Lebanon a long time. There had once been more of us, and we were the stubborn ones who didn't hear a call to some other place when the shooting started. This doesn't mean that we were right and the others wrong, or vice versa. It just means that we were the ones who felt chosen and said yes. For sure no one forced us; we volunteered for this assignment.

There were no cowards in our mission and no heroes, either. We had agreed about that. In the heat of battle anybody who wanted could take his family and leave; the others would help them get transportation and tickets. And, if or when they came back, they could count on a welcome. There would be no judgment for leaving or for staying. Our home office supported us in this, assuming that the people in danger understood the situation better than anyone else, and they left such decisions to individuals and families.

The forces that pulled Lebanon apart often separated people in mountain towns like Monsourieh and Beit Meri from those in West Beirut. For weeks at a time we might not see each other, though the trip between the Baptist school in Musaitbeh and the seminary campus in Monsourieh would take no more than half an hour without battles, roadblocks or traffic jams. Sometimes the crossing points on the Green Line would close or dangers would prevent us from leaving our area. Often the telephones didn't even work. All of us were so busy, too, and some were hopelessly single-minded. Jim and Leola Ragland, for instance, refused to be distracted from running the Beirut Baptist School. And why should they?

Looking from the outside in, it appeared that the Raglands spent their lives shut behind the wall surrounding the school and their house. Seeing things from the inside, one knew that there was a whole world, a big one that came and went through those gates. This school, with the respect it had commanded from the country and the love it had inspired in Muslims and Christians alike, was the best platform for personal influence that any of us ever had in Lebanon. And it was one of the slender threads holding the torn fabric of Lebanon together.

Leola, a chubby, motherly woman, supervised little kids on the playground. She made a special point of taking care of runny noses, because someone else, someone long since gone from Lebanon, had announced that she was not called to wipe noses. That's when Leola decided to accept this duty, as from the Lord. That's in her New Testament—the second mile, the other cheek and runny noses.

Jim was an administrator with all the headaches involved: the normal problems of running a school, and the abnormal problems of doing it in West Beirut.

One day when the phones didn't work I drove down to Musaitbeh to talk with Jim. I think I wanted him to do something, though I can't remember anymore what it was. I must have thought it was important, though, to make a special trip.

His secretary behaved oddly. Without saying a word, she motioned for me to sit down. I did, and she went on working—shuffling papers around, rolling a sheet in and out of her typewriter—though I had the impression that she had one ear and half her mind focused on Jim's office. The door to the office stood ajar just a crack, and through this narrow opening I could see Jim's long, slender face and hear him talking to another person whom I could not see. The secretary, at her desk across the room from me, could not see into the office.

Jim sat behind his desk, arguing in his quiet way with another male voice, a loud one. They both spoke in Arabic. I can't recall any of their exact words, though I remember the meaning clearly.

The visitor demanded money, a specific and large sum of money. He said that once he had received the money the school would be safe. Jim replied that he did not have such an amount of money. The other voice professed to know that he did have it. Jim said that the school belonged to God and any money that the school had also belonged to God, so he could not touch it. The visitor's voice began to show serious frustration. It expressed surprise that Dr. Ragland could be so unconcerned about the safety of the school. Jim told him that he relied on God to keep the school safe.

At that point a man's hand reached across the desk, and I saw first a flicker of fear in Jim's face, not actually a change in his expression, just a blanching, a fading of his skin. Then I saw that the hand laid a pistol on the desk. The voice said, "Pick up this gun. It would be easy to kill me." And I realized with horror that he meant the reverse—"It would be easy for me to kill you."

Jim stared across the desk. He never looked at the gun. He said, "That wouldn't change anything. I have no money to give you."

Whatever I meant to talk to Jim about—the thing that was so urgent I had driven through the traffic to Musaitbeh—now seemed so trivial that I decided to leave. There was nothing I could do to help Jim, and it crossed my mind that I didn't want to see that man's face or have him see mine. I never wanted to meet him on the street and recognize him or have him recognize me.

I stood and lifted my hand to the secretary. She understood and nodded agreement that I should leave. I drove up the hill to Monsourieh and went to Bill Trimble's office to tell him, "We need to pray for Jim Ragland."

The Near East Baptist Mission was made up of such people—people so sane that they looked simple and odd and anomalous in a world full of corruption and brutality. I drew confidence and courage from belonging to this group.

The Decision

I gave in. Unconvinced, scared, I told Wayne, "O.K." Considering the fact that I am often stubborn and disagreeable, this needs explanation. It mostly came down to trusting him to see both the problems and the solutions. If he really made the old house convenient and charming as he thought he could, it would not be the first time he had turned a dump into a house I liked. And he wanted this house so much that I was afraid of feeling guilty later, seeing him disappointed.

But the decision was not wholly ours, of course, because the house would not be ours. The matter had to be presented in a mission meeting where the group had to consider board policy, questions about the location and a required engineer's report. Undaunted when the report advised us to tear down the house and start over, Emmett Barnes took Wayne's side, declaring that this would be a beautiful and comfortable house. Finally, a colleague who usually didn't say anything in business meetings spoke up, her voice carrying both reticence and urgency. "Well... I would like to ask Frances a question." She turned her small brown eyes toward me. "Do you really want to live in this house?"

Immediately I said, "No," which caused a few faces to look startled, so that I added, "but Wayne does, and I do want to live with Wayne."

The Mule Goes and Comes Again and Goes and...

Somebody did take the mule. Not exactly when they said they would, but then neither did we start remodeling our house exactly when we said we would. We just went down to the house to measure the rooms and start drawing plans for reconstructing walls and a kitchen, found him gone and thought that things had turned out well enough.

The day was cool and brilliant with big white clouds floating past. Red poppies bloomed among the weeds on the terraces, and for the first time I noticed the prickly pear, four or five big ones—great complicated cactuses with a hundred thorny faces—on the hill, along the back perimeter of the property. They were putting out green knobs of fruit. I like to eat prickly pear (if someone else peels it for me), and I suddenly thought, *Hey, those are my prickly pears.*

Wayne stood near the house, among the flowers and weeds and said, "I'm going to put a grapevine right here. Emmett will give me some cuttings off those vines at the seminary."

As he moved down the length of a terrace, his feet making swishing, tearing sounds in the weeds, he said, "What a garden this will make!"

I couldn't understand what had come over him. He was a builder, not a farmer. He'd never been willing to cut grass, much less plant anything.

Now that the mule was gone, we could walk into the inner room, which we did, our shoes sinking into the muck. Immediately, we dubbed this room "the cave," because the back wall was mostly against the earth and looked as casual and rough as the terrace walls. Given a little sunlight, clumps of grass would sprout from the crevices. The room had one window in its short outside wall—actually just an irregular kind of opening between the stones, a little higher than head level inside and ground level outside. Wayne guessed that it had been a place for the chickens to go in and out, and the size was appropriate for that.

Standing there in two inches of manure, we tried to figure out what had to be done first. Two little boys joined us and started asking questions. They thought we were very funny creatures when they discovered that we could speak Arabic but not French and that we planned to live in this old house. I was resigned already to being funny.

The first change in our old stable-hoping-to-become-a-house was the installation of a new door. The reason was that a storm had ripped the old one off its last hinge. Then the mule came back again and reoccupied the house. "The *bugal*," Wayne called this animal. (Sometimes I couldn't get him to speak English.) He realized that superior intelligence might be his only weapon against this *bugal*. He left the door off until the animal went out to chew the grass, then he nailed the door shut. At that point we realized that the opening was unusually wide, so Wayne ordered a custom-made door in two parts—a simple door, made of planks, appropriate to a modest dwelling. While waiting for it to be finished, he found the *bugal* waiting also—standing at the threshold. That *bugal* was stubborn as a mule, whatever we called him.

Wayne painted the new door white, mounted it and secured the padlock.

In the next few weeks he braced the front wall and made it straight, saving it from falling over the cliff. This was not a simple task. Wayne dug a trench inside the house, next to the buckling wall, about three feet deep and twelve inches wide. Then he placed reinforcing iron in this trench, mixed concrete by hand and filled the trough, creating a footing twelve inches thick, below floor level. According to him, this moved the center of gravity uphill, toward the middle of the house. Above this footing, he then poured a thinner layer of concrete, against the stone wall, two feet at a time, until it reached the ceiling—all of it reinforced with iron rods. Wayne assured me, then, "This house is not going over the cliff, not ever—" He paused and then added, "—unless it goes all in one piece."

Messages

Mother always wrote to me on blue air letter forms. Sometimes I blamed her omissions on the lack of space. After she told me who had given her "a mess of turnip greens," and how hot it was in Louisiana, she didn't have space to mention things like births and deaths and divorces. But every letter told me reasons why I should not be in Lebanon. "I worry about you and can't stand to watch the news." "I pray you'll get out of there before it's too late." "It's not fair to your children."

Lately the theme had been, "Your Daddy is going to die with you on the other side of the world."

With all my heart I did not want this to happen. But Daddy had already been in bed for more than two years, lacking the breath required to sit up, wasting away from emphysema after a lifetime of smoking. I did not know how to be there for this long dying.

Around the first of June, I received one of those urgent blue letters. Daddy's breathing was worse. He choked more. She got up at night and used the suction machine. She wanted me to know that she would probably have to call for me.

My concern was mostly for Mother. How long could a woman in her seventies live like that? So I wrote to say that I really wanted to give her some help, but there was no way I could come again before August 9, the planned departure date for our coming furlough.

Mother had never been to Lebanon, and nothing had prepared her to imagine my life there or the work I did. Sometimes I wrote a lot of silly detailed explanations, and sometimes I resorted to being superficial. This time I explained that the last two months before a furlough were the busiest time in my life. I had to pack up my house, while finishing a dozen projects at the office and preparing my staff to finish others without me. I told her about the conference that our Middle East director was holding in Cyprus for certain key people, missionary and national, and why the speech I had to make there was so important. The meeting would be in Cyprus, the last week of July.

I didn't bother to mention how hard this speech was going to be, that I had to tell them, too, something they didn't want to hear.

Sending a survey to Arab church leaders in Lebanon, Jordan, Egypt, Israel and Gaza had been a great idea, but it had given me a figurative and a genuine headache. I had asked a lot of questions inviting evaluation of what the publishing house had done so far, and I asked the leaders what they most wanted us to do in the future. A majority of them bothered to fill out the form and send it back, and I transcribed their answers to a kind of score sheet I had devised. They were happy with us, frankly. We had made history, giving them the *Greek and Arabic Concordance of the New Testament*. The Bible had been in the Arabic language for a thousand years, but no one had made a concordance. We had given them in full color the *Picture Bible for All Ages*, a translation of the David C. Cook cartoon Bible. There was no other book in the Arab world so attractive and desired. But Sunday School literature! The thought took my breath away, though I should not have been surprised.

Sunday School happened every week in every church in the Arab world. In most of them Sunday School attendance was several times bigger than the church membership, and yet the churches had almost no teaching materials. Each week the teachers, often young and untrained, had to create the next lesson—choose the scripture, figure out how to present it, collect materials. This resulted, naturally, in a lack of comprehensive study, the repetition of favorite themes and the neglect of others, and poor teaching methods. The pastors knew and the teachers knew that they needed help. They had told me plainly.

And though I owed my spiritual life to a loving Sunday School and well-written books, I had to stand up and tell them that I couldn't give them what they needed. Making them understand would not be any easier than telling Mother that I could not come home, not even if my Daddy was dying.

Enormous Changes in a Hurry

Our son Dwight came to Lebanon—a taller, more muscular version of the kid we had sent off to college—excited about helping his Daddy rebuild a house. One by one we had sent away five young Fullers to study in their own country, Dwight being the fourth. He had just finished his junior year, studying math at Furman University in South Carolina. Every missionary kid was entitled to one trip back home as a gift from the mission board, and this was Dwight's trip. It was what we called in Lebanon a "hot summer," meaning that we couldn't let Dwight go anywhere, not to the cedars or downtown to a movie or to our old apartment in West Beirut or the American Community

School, because life was so dangerous. But, anyway, he had come to work, Dwight said.

Truthfully the others envied him, but Tim, our eldest, had graduated from college and was working as a technical writer in San Francisco. Jan was in Yale Divinity School on her way to becoming a university chaplain, and Jim had finished technical school and was working in construction in Minneapolis. Cynthia, the youngest, had gone off to Cal Poly to become an aeronautical engineer.

Every night Dwight and Wayne pored over the drawings Wayne had made and talked details. In the day, while we were at the office, Dwight dismantled the feeding troughs in the cow stalls—a job that needed brute strength—and piled up the chunks of concrete, so he could start digging a trench—from the space where the furnace would be all the way to the front room. Then he and Wayne lay two sets of pipes, one for heat and one for the cold air return. Eventually the floor and the new indoor stairs would cover these pipes. They worked together in the late afternoons and on Saturdays and came home to our apartment dirty and starved.

Those two were itching to do all the work themselves, but time was short before our departure for furlough, and when we came back we would be homeless, so Wayne hired a contractor who brought a crew of men. They built dividing walls, did a neat job of indoor stairs, curved off the crude doorway between the living room and the dining-kitchen area, plastered, installed new window frames and bright new glass, put in a septic tank, ran pipes to two new bathrooms, tiled the kitchen floor, and stuccoed the outside of the concrete block room in a color like the stone of the other walls.

My work at the office was so heavy that I barely had time to think about the house. I was merely dropping in to see the progress, always late in the day, and liked what I was seeing. The house would have a few quirks to live with, but I had lived in worse places, as well as better.

With only a couple small assignments to complete, the contractor really wanted to lay floor in the living room while we were away, but I was reluctant to let him. I had no time to choose the tiles and was afraid he would drop plaster on the new floor, walk in it and leave the mess there for a year while we were away. So we asked him to finish certain things already begun and then leave.

Piece by piece, we dismantled our lovely, familiar apartment, and the men carried the furniture away for storage. Most of our smaller belongings we stuffed into boxes and moved them also to the big corner room of Baptist Publications' floor in the seminary building. We would unpack them again in the little stone house in The Hara. Even while we did all this, we prepared a set of suitcases to be opened in the U.S. and another with things we would need at the conference in Cyprus. The day before we flew out to Larnaca, we moved into the seminary's guest apartment to spend the night.

That's where we were when the word came—my Daddy was gone.

The Hard Truth

At the conference I tried now and then to rehearse my speech but lost interest in the middle. My mother's prediction had come true. My Daddy had died with me on the other side of the world. The others were together, and I was here, wondering if maybe there were stray pieces of my life that didn't fit anywhere. On day four, in the last hour before lunch, my turn came. I was tired and shaky from too much coffee and a carbohydrate breakfast.

I stood at the podium and explained as best I could—that BP was too small for the task they wanted to lay on us. We lacked the writers, the editors, the artists, the sheer manpower, the expertise in education, the biblical scholarship, the time, the money. I told them that BP didn't have these things because the community did not have these things. I illustrated my point with a piece of cloth—clashing colors in a wild design. It had amused me when I chose it. It amused them, in spite of the lackluster presentation. "This is the Baptist community," I told them. Then I tore off a corner and held up the fragment. "This is BP. We are just a small part of you."

Showing them a Sunday School book from America, I described its creation. I told them that the publisher in America hired editors and writers, Bible scholars, graphic artists, illustrators, layout designers, and production staff to create and print 30,000 copies of the book. Then I asked, "If we publish only 100 copies for our churches in the Middle East, what will we need?"

The group looked at me, their faces saying, You tell us. So I told them. "It would require exactly the same personnel, the same amount of work – only less paper and ink. That's all." Their jaws dropped.

I tried not to leave them without hope. I said that we, all of us, would have to grow—study, develop skills, multiply in numbers—and become a community of people who could produce their own literature.

They sat up on the edges of their chairs to listen, and when the picture became clear they let out their breath collectively and sank backward.

Invasions

The Camel's Nose in My Tent

I could say a lot about borrowed houses. Altogether, I have lived for years in other people's spaces, with other people's possessions. Each time I have been thankful for the option but spent half of my time looking for something that I must have been just remembering from some other house.

At the end of our furlough Wayne and I had faced a conflict of responsibilities and made a difficult decision. Two of our boys needed their parents, or at least one parent, preferably their dad, and the publishing house desperately needed us on the job, at least one of us, preferably me. So Wayne stayed in Oklahoma with the boys, and I returned to Lebanon. Because the little rock house was not quite ready for occupancy and all my possessions were stored in the publishing office, I was fortunate to have the use of Emmett and LaNell Barnes' house for a few months while they took a furlough. It was on the seminary campus, near friends and about ninety seconds from my office.

With the Barnes' house I got a dog named Thumper, a white poodle with vim, vigor and personality when the Barnes were there, but when his family left and I moved in Thumper crawled under a bed and wouldn't come out. I couldn't coax him out with food or drag him out by force. I knew he was alive, because I could see his eyes under there and because he scrambled out and dashed to a window anytime he heard a car in the driveway, but each time he saw that the Barnes had not come, he put his tail down and returned to his hiding place. I was so afraid he would die under there that I asked Abu John to come over. Abu John was the seminary's cook and caretaker and guard and, basically, all things to all people in the community. He would kill a snake for you or roast a sheep or tell you how to harvest olives. He came when I called and spent a lot of time talking with me and to the dog under the bed, but Thumper refused counseling.

The Barnes also had a cat that hated me. She appeared at the back door morning and evening, arrived angry, and scratched me while I was trying to put the food into her dish. Because I happen to like cats, her attitude hurt my feelings.

The Barnes were such sane, balanced people; I was really surprised to find their pets so maladjusted.

This was the fall of 1981 and Lebanon had visibly deteriorated. Refugees were streaming into Beirut, fleeing war in the South where Israel was using a right-wing Lebanese militia to create a buffer between herself and her enemies. I drove down to Musaitbeh where we once lived and discovered a crush of people on the streets, a crowd similar to that in the covered *suq* (market) in Damascus. I found that West Beirut had become a gangland; the lack of security interfered with services, and the best streets stunk with garbage. Even in the mountains life had deteriorated. On my first trip up to Beit Meri to buy food I was surprised to find trash by the road, sandbags at storefronts and much higher prices than I had seen before. Then when I put my groceries down in the Barnes' empty house, I lost my appetite. Forlorn and depressed, I welcomed a mountain of work.

As a natural consequence of our year in America and inadequate staff, editorial projects were piled up and international sales had languished. During the day I met with staff and committees and visitors, ran to the presses and made long lists labeled "To-Do-Immediately." At noon I usually ate peanuts and an apple at my desk, while writing a business letter on my very old electric typewriter. I went shopping, too, and bought a little press and a plate maker to go with it, using money given by a church in America; these were for small projects that would be feasible if we could do them in-house. Since our substitute bookkeeper had already gone and Wayne, our regular accountant, was still in Oklahoma, I had to make rudimentary accounts as I went, recording expenditures and income and sales. The reading I needed to do looked like a full-time occupation in itself, so I took it home and usually fell asleep with a book or manuscript on my chest.

As soon as I felt I had all our publishing projects moving, I traveled to Cairo and spent several days with people who sold our books there, talking about their market, taking orders, and alerting them about materials they could expect from us soon. A trip to Cairo always included a lot of walking, partly because one could lose a lot of time trying to get a taxi, and partly because riding past the fascinations of Cairo seemed also to be a great waste. It was a long, long walk from the little hotel where I always stayed, near the Nile, and the humble office of Dar al-Thaqafa, the Coptic Evangelical publishing house, off the street in an alley. Here and there along the way little drifts of sand lay against the buildings, as though the desert might reclaim the city, and thirst overtook me quickly. Still, I loved being part of the crowd on the sidewalk, and I liked being able to drop into an unknown bookstore and look at teetering stacks of books, trying to read the titles and notice popular subjects and prices.

Sam Habib, the director of Dar al-Thaqafa, was the busiest man in Egypt but always took time for me, and as we talked he always scribbled on little squares of paper, tucking them into his shirt pocket. Sam and I worked together well, agreeing, "You do this, and I will do that, and we will buy from one another."

Back in Lebanon, I would lie down to sleep, and Egyptian faces, the color of coffee with milk, kept passing in front of me. Then I had to help Abu Issam, our stock and shipping clerk, with the huge job of packing boxes and shipping off all the books I had sold. Sundays I spent with Lebanese friends, often going home with someone who spontaneously invited me for lunch.

All this time violence punctuated our lives—each day a bloody explosion, each day in a different area, on a different street, sirens always screaming. In our early morning devotional meetings, the staff would compare notes on where we all had been in relation to yesterday's car bomb: Frances passed the spot an hour before, Abu Issam and Abu Sleiman five minutes before. We would tell our stories and then pray. On the way to Hadath once, I drove up to a Syrian checkpoint. Instead of asking for an ID or just waving me on, the soldier said the Arabic equivalent of,

"Get out of here as fast as you can." I obeyed. A few minutes later a battle erupted at the checkpoint between the Syrians and a Christian militia.

My phone rang in the middle of the night. A young man who had once worked for me was down at the Green Line, wounded. He was not a fighter, just a boy who had been born a Muslim and chosen to follow Jesus. This was not the first time he had been attacked. We had wars inside of wars. Feeling angry and motherly, I drove through the spooky night and found him where he said he would be, with stab wounds in his back.

Occasionally I thought about my house, that heap of rocks that Wayne was going to turn into a little mansion, but seeing it was not a high priority. Besides that, I realized that I didn't know where we had left the key.

Then one day a man came to see me in the office, introducing himself as Hashim. He behaved with courtesy, sat down across from me after shaking hands, and asked about our welfare. He wore a working man's clothes, was scrubbed and combed. He looked to me like a man trying hard to make a favorable impression.

Hashim asked permission to put some machines in our house to get them in out of the weather. "I will just put them in the room that has no floor," he said.

A little caution flag waved in my head and I entertained the useless thought that I could use a husband right now. I told Hashim that we would need the house on the first day of February.

"Whenever you come I will leave," he said, maybe a little too quickly.

"It will be winter," I reminded him, "and where will you put the machines?"

"I am making a place for them in Monsourieh. I just need a couple of months to get it finished."

"I'm not sure," I said. "I wish I had a chance to talk with my husband about it. In fact, I have to ask somebody where the key is. I don't know."

"I have the key," he said.

At first I was so stunned I didn't know what to say. Finally, I managed to ask him, "Where did you get the key?"

"The contractor gave it to me."

"Why did the contractor give you the key to my house?"

He shrugged and said, "*Haik.*" (It's like that.)

Later I realized that I could have said, "Then please bring me the key," but I didn't. Sure that he had already occupied my house, I said, "O.K., you can put your machines inside, only in the room with no floor, and only until February first. We are coming on that day, and we will begin work on the house. We have to live in it."

He shook hands, smiled, and left looking very satisfied.

A Goat in the Sitting Room

A few weeks after Hashim's visit, having located a key that we had left with the mission, I went up to Beit Meri to measure the windows so I could buy curtains. It was December, and I was going to the States for Christmas. Wayne would come back with me.

When I opened the door a horrendous smell assaulted me. Immediately I saw the goat, a dingy little white goat standing on top of the big stone just inside the arch. I stood still, feeling like I was having a familiar bad dream with only a minor detail changed. The machines were not in the living room—the room with no floor—where I told Hashim he could put them, though rows of aluminum window sashes leaned against the walls. I found the machines in my dining room on the new tiles. The tiles were covered with aluminum shavings, tools, nails, screws, dirt, footprints.

The smell was even stronger in the kitchen and odd, something more than a goat. In the walk-in pantry I found birdcages hanging, an astonishing number of birds fluttering and scattering their food and droppings all over the floors and walls. I climbed the stairs then and found the same thing. Birds, maybe a dozen cages or more, hanging high on the walls in both rooms. The new bathroom fixtures were unbelievably filthy. The toilet had been used and never flushed. Rust stains covered the bottom of the lavatory and the new tub.

Somebody had trashed my house. I would never get it clean again. Even with these thoughts going through my head, I tried not to be upset, since I was leaving the next day and there was nothing I could do. I started measuring the windows in the upper rooms. Hearing footsteps and voices, I opened the opaque glass on the door leading to the roof, which also functioned as the bedroom balcony. Five or six people were strolling around (on *my* roof), looking at the view. I greeted them. Then I looked directly at a young woman, the one who seemed surprised to see me, and said, "Whose birds are these?"

"Mine," she said.

"And those machines downstairs?"

"Hashim's."

I wanted to say that Hashim had asked if he could put his machines in the house to get them out of the weather, not if he could open a workshop, but I said only, "Please, take your birds and please tell Hashim that he has to take his machines by February 1, as we agreed. When we get here we want to start working. We have to use the house."

I turned back to my work, and I could hear them talking out there. Someone was saying, "What did she say?" And another, "She said they are going to use the house now." I could hear disappointment in her voice.

Fuming inside, I stretched my tape across the window again and scribbled the figures on the little pad I'd brought. Then I thought the number was wrong and measured again. It was right, but I was a fool. First the contractor had betrayed us, then Hashim had tricked me, and his wife had taken advantage. On top of that, she was hoping I would never come and take my house. She wanted to raise birds in it. Was she one of our neighbors? I hoped not.

On the way out I saw the goat, still perched on the stone, his four little hooves close together, his tail toward me. When I stopped to stare at him, he turned his head and stared back. He had small horns and yellowing shaggy hair on his underbelly. If I had seen him in the field across the road, I might have thought he was cute, but I didn't like his smug complacency about occupying my space.

The Neighbor Before the House

During the Christmas vacation our colleague David King went up and put a message on the door, saying that we were coming and everything had to be removed from the house. But in February we found everything exactly as I last saw it: goat, machines, window sashes, shavings, tools, dirt, stains, birds, droppings, smells. We went over to Um Elias' house, having learned that it was her daughter who owned the birds and her son-in-law who was running a window sash factory in our house.

Nothing but a rocky path separated our house from hers, and though the route up from the road was steep, it was possible to step from the roof of our house onto this path and then directly onto her doorstep, which led first to a patio. This was what we did. A bare vine twisted through a network of strings above the patio, and small plants in assorted tin cans stood in rows around the concrete block banister. Um Elias met us there, welcoming us effusively, "*Ahlan, ahlan, tfaddthalu.*" Welcome, welcome, come in.

She was a large woman with plump cheeks and always wore shapeless dresses and sandals and a pleasant expression. Her narrow sitting room contained only a knotty couch with an iron frame, a straight chair and a small television. We sat on the couch against the wall to the right of the door, facing the tiny kitchen where she made coffee for us.

While she boiled the coffee she asked us all the routine questions. How are you? How was your trip to America? How are your children? And if any moment of silence occurred she filled it with another "*Ahla wa sahla.*"

I tried my best to appear comfortable, sitting there in my coat, but the tile floor emanated cold, and a draft came in through the open door. I wondered how cold her feet were in those sandals.

We learned that she and Abu Elias had a thirteen year-old son as well as several married daughters. We expressed a wish to know all of them.

"Of course. We will be neighbors," she said.

We explained to her that we needed our house, that we were living temporarily in a friend's house and had a lot of work to do before we could move into ours. Wayne said, "Please tell Hashim that everything has to be taken out of the house immediately."

"Of course," she said.

A week later everything was the same. Wayne happened to see the thirteen-year-old, chatted with him a bit and then said, "Tell Hashim that I am coming next week, and everything has to be taken out of the house."

The next week came and nothing had happened.

The contractor came to the office to visit us, looking for work. He wanted to know if we were ready to lay the floors.

I asked him, "Why did you give the neighbors the key to our house?"

He said, "They wanted to use it for a shelter in case of an attack. It's safer than their house."

We told him about my agreement with Hashim, about the goat and the birds and the machines and the expired deadlines.

And after all that he said, "Don't worry; they are good people. They won't give you any trouble."

We went to see Um Elias again. This time we set a deadline one week in the future and told her that if the things were still in the house when we came on that day, we would remove them ourselves.

She said, "Of course. The truth is with you."

The House that Wayne Found

We were still living in the Barnes' big house. Cold weather and rain continued, and we didn't dare turn on the furnace because of the fearful cost of kerosene. For warmth we had two gas heaters, the cook stove and an electric blanket. To save on heating expense we lived in the kitchen and the bedroom, and I ran if I had to pass through the hall. Wayne suggested that I wear gloves when I read in bed, but they made turning pages rather difficult.

At the office we had materials ready to run on our new press, but couldn't set up the printer because our personal possessions filled the workroom, and we couldn't move them to our house. The situation made a "House That Jack Built" kind of story:

This is the house that Wayne found.
This is the goat that lives in the house that Wayne found.
This is Hashim who owns the goat and took the house that Wayne found.
This is the man who will lay a floor when...

On the last Saturday in February the goat, the birds, the aluminum and the machines were still in our house. We had so much work to do yet before we could use the house, and we needed to be in it by July, because the Barnes were coming back.

"O.K. here we go," Wayne said. He took the goat outside and tied him to a little bush.

I went next door and told Um Elias, "We have waited a long time; we have tried to be patient. Now, *khallas*, finish. It's our house, and we have to have it."

"The truth is with you," she said, and she came over and started helping me move the birdcages. I was carrying them out quickly and setting them on the roof. I wanted to illustrate the urgency, and I couldn't wait to get rid of the stink.

"Wait," she said. "I have to hang them up, because the cats will get them."

So I went out to the terrace and started raking and let her carry birdcages. She hung some of them around the edges of her porch roof. Later she came over with a pot of coffee, and we sat down on the edge of the terrace, hanging our feet over the wall, and drank with her.

I never exactly figured out Um Elias. She always said and did the right things in our presence, but if she was really on our side she had no influence at all. It seemed best to accept her neighborly gestures as sincere and not think about the rest. I did suspect that while the stone house stood empty, so close to their own front patio, the whole family had used it freely—the roof certainly. It was larger than their patio and had an unobstructed view of Jabal Sunnin, which they lacked. And later I observed that her grown children and her sons-in-law could be an unruly bunch, and when the village women got together to drink coffee or to pick greens Um Elias was never among them.

Our friend and colleague, Pete Dunn, came and we planted grape vines, using cuttings that Abu John got for us from the Barnes' back yard. Wayne shoveled the mule manure and goat droppings out of the cave and the living room. (Some people just rent an apartment and move in.) Wayne and Pete carried the machines to the living room where there was no floor yet, along with the many pieces of aluminum, and the tools. I thought they should put them out of doors, but Wayne doesn't like to be nasty. Hashim had nailed boards to the tops of small tables to increase their work area, and Wayne and Pete had to break these off to get the tables through the doorway. With my dining room empty, I swept the tiles and found that only a couple had been chipped. Wayne changed all the locks on the doors before we left. It was a good day's work, and we felt satisfied.

A few days later Hashim and another man, came to the office looking for Wayne. They were visibly upset. They said, "We need just ten more days." It was March already, and they had promised to leave by February 1.

Wayne said, "You can have ten more days to come and get your machinery, but you can't use it in my house."

Hashim's face turned red. They left without shaking hands.

Locked Out

On the Saturday following the visit of Hashim and his partner we found we could not enter the front door of our house. The key didn't work. The wood around the lock had been broken, and a new lock installed. The church young people stood with us outside the door, cleaning tools in hand.

Wayne and Naji, Abu John's son, a stout personality in a stout body, forced their way in, prying the door open. The machines were where we left them and surrounded with shavings. The goat was in the cave again. A trail of droppings climbed the stairs, but they looked like that of another animal, not a goat.

I said, "O.K., let's throw these machines outdoors."

Wayne said, "We better think about it first."

Naji said, "Let's go get the Kata'ib." This was a reasonable suggestion, since the militia was the closest thing we had to a police force.

He and Wayne left after Wayne gave the other young people instructions about how to scrape the floor of the cave and level it. Nadia and I took a five-gallon container of water upstairs and cleaned the bathroom. A product called Flash took off the rust stains, and I was so relieved.

The fellows came back and said, "*Khallas,* the Kata'ib is after them now."

Wayne had bought a new lock and began working on the door.

In a little while Naji's dad and some other friends of ours arrived. They took a manila folder and wrote on it and tacked it to the door. The note said that anyone who wanted to enter the house would have to go to the *ra'is al-Kata'ib* in Monsourieh for the key. Wayne had already installed a new lock, and he gave one of the two keys to Naji for the *ra'is.*

"That fixed them," Wayne said.

While some of the young people helped Wayne scrape the floor of the cave, others helped me clean the terraces. We just piled up all the debris, two or three piles on each terrace for picking up and hauling off another day.

Then we sat down on the edges of the terraces, with our feet dangling, and ate the lunch I had packed—bread and *zaatar* (thyme), cheese, salami, oranges, cookies, and Pepsi... We talked, while we ate, about the parties we would have on the terraces and the roof in summers, and in the cave by the fire in winter. The young people had big plans for this house; I could see we were not going to be lonely in it. Najat was the most enthusiastic. She kept saying it was going to be beautiful and not like anybody else's, but she was worried about where all of our kids would sleep when they came, and twice she suggested that we could build another room on the roof.

We all left, leaving the goat outside on a short leash.

* * *

On Monday Hashim and the other man came again to our office. They talked with Abu John and Wayne. From my office I could hear them talking, something about fifteen more days, and I heard Wayne protest and then more talk. It got quiet down there, and then Wayne came to my office and said, "The *ra'is* said we should give them 'til the end of the month, and Abu John says this is the way we need to handle it."

I felt like screaming. I did scream. "Why? Why is this the way to handle it?"

Wayne tried to keep me calm. He said, "Look, this is Lebanon. We can't afford to be nasty."

I said, "What's the matter with the Kata'ib? Are they scared of these guys?"

"No, of course not."

"What did we do? Give our house to the Kata'ib? Now the *ra'is al-Kata'ib* has the key to our house and the right to tell people they can stay in it. They can move in next."

We sat there. A bell rang. The students would soon be going to the dining hall.

Didn't I have a bad feeling about this house from the beginning? Thinking this, I said, "You know, don't you, that they won't leave at the end of the month."

"Well, wait and see."

"O.K. But why should they? If we can't make them leave now, we can't make them leave then."

"Did you forget that we're invited to the Nicholases for lunch?"

I had forgotten, but I didn't want to change the subject.

I said, "It's my house. I need it. I want to put my own things in a house and be at home. I want to get our furniture out of that corner room, so we can set up the press. I can't do anything at home or anything at the office, because they need to use their machines and don't have a place to put them. It's impossible that they need the house worse than we do. Anyway, it's our house. Doesn't that mean anything?"

In the car on the way to Nicholases' house, Wayne finally gave me the crucial bit of information. "The *ra'is al-Kata'ib* is Hashim's relative. His brother-in-law."

This news was like a dash of ice water on my face. I felt suddenly more awake. So that was it.

When we got up to the main road, I realized that it was good to be changing scenery. I needed to stop raving. Wayne needed me to stop raving. But I certainly didn't feel hungry.

There were other people at lunch, and Wayne and I managed to act half sane and cordial. David King asked what had happened about our house and Wayne told him in a few words. I tried hard to keep quiet. Everyone expressed sympathy and that gave me courage to admit finally that I had wanted to throw the machines outside, but Wayne had been nice.

Anne said, "Just this week I've been writing a Bible study on how to solve problems without getting angry."

I said, "I need to read that one."

Better and Lasting Possessions

I sat in the Barnes' house with my cold feet on the open oven door and tried to think of reasons to be thankful that we were still unable to claim our house. The scripture says, "In everything give thanks," and I was trying hard.

I wrote down my thoughts:

1. *It's going to make an interesting story. I can call it "A Goat in the Living Room."* Actually, that was the second title I wrote. I drew a line through the first, because it was unfair.
2. *The situation is an opportunity to show a Christian attitude, to learn patience and self-control, to be angry and not sin, to suffer injustice and not repay, to become good neighbors to those who have been bad neighbors.* So far, I realized, I had missed this opportunity all the way.
3. *All things work together for good to those who love God.* This was one of my favorite promises from the scripture, and I had ample evidence in my life that God's purposes are not deterred by obstacles and interruptions and that nothing in my life would

> be wasted. But I was upset and frustrated and could see nothing worthwhile in the confiscation of my house. Hoping was the best I could do, and hoping, I would assume that Romans 8:28 was true. I do this sometimes, when my faith is in trouble. I believe for the moment, to test it, because I prefer to believe. This turns out to be much more instructive than not believing.

Finally, I realized that there was nothing unique in our situation. All over Lebanon people were "borrowing" houses. I had seen refugees knocking down the doors of empty buildings or apartments to get their families out of the cold rain. I felt that I might have done the same. Refugees, of course, were homesick people, who would usually go back to their own place when they had the opportunity. Hashim was not a refugee. And sometimes even refugees grew to like a place or depend on it and refused to leave. The Lebanese way was to pay them to leave, though no judge or lawyer had ever been able to explain this to the satisfaction of an American.

This was not the first time my house had been borrowed. In 1976 we had a place in Musaitbeh at Mafraq Sharouq on Mar Elias Street, on the fourth floor of an apartment building. While we were away on furlough, a shell hit the building in the middle of the night. In our landlady's apartment on the seventh and top floor, her daughter and grandchild were sleeping in the back bedroom, the child against the outside wall, his mother across the room. Early in the night the child, a boy about four years old, woke and went to his mother's bed. She pulled him under the covers, and they went back to sleep. The shell blew away the outside wall and the corner of the room, without hurting the mother or the boy. In the light of morning they saw the child's empty bed in the parking lot, seven floors down.

When I went back to West Beirut that summer to pay the rent and renew our lease, I found the landlady and her family living in our apartment. She did not want the money; she wanted the house. So I hired a truck and four men and moved our possessions to a borrowed space in a damp basement until I could find another place to live.

That apartment had brought us all the benefits and drawbacks of living in the city. Two benefits were Mustapha's store around the corner, and a bakery just across Mar Elias. I used to put eggs in the pan and then send somebody for hot bread. If I didn't have time to cook, Wayne could go downstairs and bring up a chicken, hot and garlicky, roasted on a rotisserie, wrapped in the soft, thin bread that we called mountain bread. Shouting vendors pushed carts of vegetables and fruits down the street; from our balconies we could look down on these bright patches of green and yellow and red, and run down to choose what we wanted. Across the way Lebanese women in their nightclothes would just yell for a kilo of *kusa,* drop down a basket with the money and lift up the squash.

As for drawbacks, we learned there that 1800 square feet in a building crowded by other buildings is not like 1800 feet with a lawn around it. Our girls had to keep their bedroom curtains drawn, otherwise they would find that men on balconies next door would be looking at them while they were still in their beds in the morning. When our neighbors made long distance phone calls with poor connections, we had to listen to their shouted one-sided conversations. We could tune our television to the channel someone else was watching and turn off the sound.

We used to escape, late on summer days, over to the point of Ras Beirut where the land dropped precipitously into the water. There we would join the crowds strolling along the wide walkway between the ring road, called the Corniche, and the cliff—breathing salty, fishy smells, cooling our skin, listening to the waves smash against the Pigeon Rocks and absorbing the peace that seemed to rise out of the sea.

Like others we would stop at a little stall and buy ears of corn, boiled and then roasted. The corn was tough and gummy; it stuck to our teeth. Wayne always told us, "In Minnesota we would feed this to the pigs," but smelling it and not eating any was torture, so we always ate it. And we bought *ki'ke,* a kind of bread that the Lebanese baked in a comical but practical shape resembling a pouch with a handle. We bought the bread from a man on a bicycle with strings of it hung from the handlebars. He had a voice hoarse from shouting "*Ki'ke*!", a word whose middle sound—a consonant which I have represented with the apostrophe—has to be dragged through the throat. With the bread came a handful of seasoning—thyme and salt, folded into a scrap of newspaper. We were supposed to tear a hole in the pouch—it was crusty and covered with sesame seeds—and sprinkle the spice inside on the spongy soft part of the bread. *Ki'ke* and roasted corn, eaten by the sea while mingling with families and barefoot fishermen and youths in the latest fashions, never lost its appeal to our kids and made dinner in a hot apartment unnecessary.

Leaning on a rail or sitting on the sea wall to stare out across the water was always part of the ritual. Everybody did it. The sun would paint a golden path and at the end of it sink under the water. People stared at the disappearing sun as though wishing to follow it. I decided then that there was no way to understand the Lebanese without thinking about the sea. It was not a barrier, but a road—a wide, wide road running west.

We were there at Mafraq Sharouq during the initial stages of the civil war when hardly anybody knew what was happening. We learned to shove bookcases against the windows and sleep on the floors.

The fighting followed a pattern, stopping in the early morning and starting again in the late afternoon. At night the whole neighborhood was voluntarily blacked out and we couldn't do much, except sit in the dark and listen and talk. We became lax about putting the bookcases back where they belonged and picking up the beds. It seemed like useless work to all but Cynthia. One day while I was on the phone, trying to find out what had happened to our friends during the night, she lost patience with her siblings and raised her voice, "Just because there's a war is no excuse for this house to be a wreck." I covered the mouthpiece and told the boys to help her straighten the house. We came to accept the truth she had discovered, that we shouldn't let chaos in the streets invade our house. We still sometimes say it. "War is no excuse."

We lost the good with the bad, even friends whom we never found again. When I left all my possessions in that basement, I went to a two-room apartment where I slept and ate and did my work and cried only once because I was alone. Even Baptist Publications was homeless, an enormous problem that I had solved temporarily by borrowing a place. Emmett Barnes had just been named president of the Arab Baptist Theological Seminary in Monsourieh, and I had put him under pressure the way Hashim later put me under pressure. I requested permission to move into the main building of the seminary, which like BP had not functioned that year. Unsure that he was doing the wise thing (he also knew about camels that might gradually occupy a tent), Emmett let me take over the basement as a storeroom and establish offices on the upper floor that housed the single men's dorm and the small guest apartment. Emmett kept one wing on that floor of the U-shaped building, and when the seminary reopened BP shared the space with students.

In the spring of 1982 this temporary arrangement had already lasted five years. BP was growing, adding projects and staff, approaching fast the limits of our space, and the seminary had run out of dorm rooms for young men.

I often remembered that we were working in borrowed space, that Emmett had a right to come upstairs and ask us to leave. I knew that the seminary administration struggled with problems that could have been alleviated by taking back a few rooms, but they were patient with us, knowing that our board hesitated to finance another office building in such an unpredictable situation.

More fundamental to my life than any of this was the truth that I had in a sense borrowed Lebanon. No Lebanese had asked me to come and to love it and put down roots. To some I was an alien, endured the way Lebanon had always endured aliens. (They borrowed right back from intruders—Turkish coffee, French words, American movies.) To others I was a guest, welcomed because the Lebanese are welcoming people. Annually I had to go to General Security and renew my permit to live in the country. Whenever the government decided not to want me I would have to go.

Long before Wayne found the old house in The Hara, I had dreamed one night about a stone house. From the beginning the dream was ambiguously threatening. I was walking on a beach at night, struggling through the soft sand, with fog rolling in from the sea. There I encountered a Lebanese couple who invited me to bring my family and take a vacation in their house on the beach—a fine stone house, old-fashioned with arched windows and a tile roof, standing near the beach in a swirling fog.

They were going away, they said, and why should it stand empty? When I protested, they insisted, because "it will make us happy."

After we moved in, one of our daughters, only a child in this scene, discovered a dead man in a bedroom. I saw him myself and instructed her to shut the door. "He was there when we came, and he is not our business."

The images and words of this dream haunted me for many months, and eventually the borrowed house in my dream became to me a metaphor for Lebanon, a land of elegant beauty, a gracious, hospitable country with something dead in it. This dream had left me pondering the question of my responsibility as an alien witness of horrors.

In the dream the impact of the house on us was unexpected and perceived as unintentional or accidental. The house in The Hara had become a great deal more trouble than we had guessed it would, just as Lebanon had cost us more grief than we had imagined when we came. On the other hand, Lebanon had blessed us in unpredictable ways too, and the story of our house was not finished. Anyway, for better or worse, we were inextricably tangled with this house and this country.

All of this I thought, sitting there in the Barnes' kitchen with my feet on the oven door, reading the book of Hebrews. Again. I had often read about the faithful of past generations who admitted they were aliens and strangers on earth, people who were looking for a home, for a country, people who died without receiving the promises they believed in and without losing hope. God was not ashamed to be called their God. But that day in the spring of 1982 verse 34 of chapter 10 really stunned me: "You sympathized with those in prison and joyfully accepted the confiscation of your property, because you knew that you yourselves had better and lasting possessions."

Never before had I noticed what a hard saying this was, nor had I actually related the spirit of the early Christians under persecution to myself or tried to adopt their attitude. In fact, I had not noticed that, like most Americans, I was super-sensitive about my rights. So I struggled with all that and finally understood that in having my own house seized unjustly, I tasted, only tasted, like merely touching my tongue to it, the bitterness of a host of people—Palestinians who lost both house and country, citizens of Beirut who had aided refugees and then been victimized by them, Lebanese in the grip of a foreign army, the Jews of Europe dragged from their homes to death camps, Christian Armenians massacred by the Turks, the Native Americans who were killed or pushed off their lands, Africans carried away into slavery, old ladies whose small, loved corners were sacrificed for a new freeway, and long lists of people down through history who were victimized by tyrants or invaders or thieves or arsonists.

Most of these victims had lost much, much more than a house, much more than I was equipped to understand. (I once asked a refugee what he had lost in Palestine, and he replied, "I lost my dignity.") Now I saw that unlike some of these I had reason to be patient, knowing already that I had better and lasting possessions.

Finally I admitted that getting my house taken could do me some good. Maybe I would grow enough to get out of what my teacher-friend Nancie Wingo would call "the slow learning group."

Georgette

When Wayne and I drove over to Nabay to see Georgette, it was as fine a Sunday afternoon as I've seen anywhere, the temperature just right for a sweater, new leaves pushing out among the overblown blossoms of flowering trees, the mountain villages all basking in the sun, the sea bright and clear all the way out to the edge of the world. Everybody in Lebanon was out of doors, playing soccer, picnicking, picking flowers, holding hands, singing while driving recklessly around corners. In Broummana groups of boys lolled in the sidewalk cafes to watch the girls tricking along by the road in the latest knee-length trousers and high heels. I wanted to take a picture of a mule eating daisies, but a Kata'ib truck got in my way.

Georgette was alone at Boutique Tewfik, sitting behind the counter, surrounded by too much merchandise—dresses hanging on a rack, shirts stacked on shelves, cheap hair ornaments, kitchen utensils, toys. She jumped up to kiss us, asking questions immediately. Georgette was forty-six, so small she made me feel like a giant and so gaunt I felt like a young athlete, though I was fifty-three.

"*Keef* Tim? How is Tim?" she wanted to know, then "*Keef* Jan?" and on through our list of children. We gave five reports and each time assured her that our kids thought of her and sent greetings.

She looked more tired than usual. Her hands were red and swollen, and when she touched me I noticed that they were cold. She said that her feet were the same and she didn't know why.

We scolded her. "Georgette, why are you working? It's a beautiful day, it's Sunday. Everybody else in the world is having fun."

"True. But somebody needs to be here. I don't want to make Aziza work. She is with her friends."

"Close the store," I told her. "Stay home. You need rest like everybody else."

And in a teasing tone, Wayne told her, "Georgette, it's in the Bible. In six days you should do all your work; then rest."

"True," she said, "but in Nabay, closing the store doesn't help. People come to my house to say, 'I need a scarf,' or 'my kid lost his shoes.' Then I have to go. It's easier to stay in the store."

Because we loved her, we scolded. And every time I saw her in the store, I felt so proud of her.

We didn't have in Lebanon a friend dearer than Georgette, whom we had known for about twelve years. When we lived in Musaitbeh, she worked as a maid, coming down to Beirut by public transportation five days a week. I was trying to learn how to run a publishing house and still take care of my house and my children, and having Georgette made it possible. I gave her a key to our apartment and twice a week she came, arriving after I left for the office and often leaving before I returned. She kept the tile floors shining, the bathroom clean, the ironing done. She brought wild flowers from the village and decorated my house, and after doing the work as though for love, she accepted her salary as though it were a gift.

We forbade her to do any chores that were the children's responsibility, like making their beds or putting away their messes. She complied, knowing that children must learn to work. In summers our kids were often in the house when she was there, and she humored them by making treats, like a bowl of *tabbouli* for dinner. Tim asked her to teach him to make the Lebanese dips, and once she told me that his *hommus* was better than hers. Sometimes she took Cynthia home with her to spend the night with her girls, and many a Sunday we had lunch in her house in the village.

After lunch other people in the community would show up, walking in the open door unannounced, and the room would be full of people chattering and drinking coffee. Unless the weather was really cold, the balcony doors, like the front door, would stand open, and breezes off the sea would flow through the little house. We got to know half the population of Nabay in Georgette's living room. We felt at home there, like everybody else.

Georgette's husband, a cordial man, always nice to us, had a crippled hand, no marketable skills and little initiative. His name was Andraous. He worked at small jobs here and there, mostly in the fields and orchards around Nabay, but he often gambled away the money he made. Even in his own house, he never took charge of anything, not the fire in the stove, not hospitality. One could spend a day in their house and mistake him for a visitor.

Georgette and I rarely had time to sit down and share secrets and feelings as women like to do, but sometimes an event would cause her to tell me something revealing of her inner self. When their eldest daughter Ilham married Sami, I discovered that Georgette hated weddings. She would not go to a wedding if she could avoid it, not even the wedding of her own daughter.

Ilham and Sami had eloped. We assumed this meant that they had surprised everyone, even their families, but sitting in Georgette's living room, we learned otherwise. Everyone knew that Ilham and Sami were getting married, but no one except their witnesses went with them to the priest. While the rest of the family explained it to us, in excited voices, mentioning details of plot and time and place and transportation, Georgette sat beside me on the couch, muttering quiet asides, telling me, "I didn't go, because I didn't like to go… I would cry… No, Sami is fine... but marriage…" She left this sentence hanging, then said, "Weddings I hate."

Georgette had two sons who did not even look like brothers. Tony, slender and dark-skinned like Georgette, suffered from a brain disorder that made him unpredictable. On some days the problem endowed him with superhuman strength. He once walked from Nabay to our house in Beit Meri, an uphill route that needs half an hour in the car. He arrived flushed and sweaty, sat down for a few minutes, drank a glass of lemonade and started home again. On such days his sisters were afraid of him. On other days he was gentle and quiet.

Tewfik, the younger boy, was stocky and fair, happy, inclined to be religious, with a strong desire to be a good person. When Tewfik was a young adolescent, Georgette had for a while been worried to the point of tears about Tewfik. She came to work one day with a cloud over her head and told us that he wouldn't get out of bed in the mornings and refused to go to school. She said he wouldn't talk to her; maybe he needed to talk to a man. Wayne drove to Nabay and found him, as she had said, in bed in an otherwise empty house. He talked. His problem was a small thing, unless you were a kid and didn't understand it. In an hour Wayne had him smiling and on his way to school. Many years later I could see the special bond between Wayne and Tewfik and assumed they shared some manly secret.

All of Georgette's children were well-behaved, hard-working kids, courteous and loyal to both of their parents. Once when we visited them on a Sunday, having been invited for lunch, Andraous never showed up. Tewfik, perhaps twenty already, said, "I apologize for my father. Someone wanted to buy the country, and he went to discuss the deal."

We all smiled, seeing that Tewfik had a twinkle in his pale eyes and intended no disrespect.

During the first year of the war when we were stuck in California, I worried about Georgette, fearing that she was stranded in Nabay without work. Once I dreamed that I was in Lebanon, that I opened our door in answer to a ring, and there stood Georgette, older, with the skin drawn tight over the bones of her face, and the luster gone from her black eyes. "Praise God for your safety," I said in Arabic, and she answered, "Praise God you came back."

When I saw her next, realizing that I had dreamed the truth, I gave Georgette most of the money I had, thinking that she would buy food for her family. She didn't. Traveling by a series of cars for hire she made a dangerous trip to Beirut where she bought things that people in the village needed but not badly enough to risk their lives for them—needles and thread and copy books and pencils and cheap shoes for the kids. She sold these things from her living room and made a profit. Then her brother-in-law gave her a gift equal to mine and she used it to increase her working capital. Her business prospered, because Nabay needed it.

Then Tewfik came home from his job in Saudi Arabia and gave her money to get the tiny space on the main road through town. When she opened this shop, her enterprise had become Boutique Tewfik, and I had been so proud of her.

That sunny Sunday afternoon in March, after we scolded her, Georgette saw a little girl about ten walking up the street and asked her to go for Pepsis and cookies. A few customers came in and out, while we sat on the porch in the sun, a few feet from the street, and drank the Pepsis. A neighbor woman came over and sat with us, a witty lady who liked to laugh. Georgette would go in to help her customers and rush out again, urging all of us to eat cookies, though she never ate one. She told us that Jumana, her youngest—a beautiful girl, endowed with a practical intelligence, sensitive to other people's feelings—had failed the first baccalaureate exam and then dropped out of school. Tony had to take medicine all the time, and sometimes he slept for a week or two.

Georgette wondered if any of our kids were coming in summer. We told her maybe Cynthia, calling her Sass, because Georgette always did.

"If there isn't war in Lebanon," Wayne said.

The women agreed that there were lots of rumors and nobody could know anything about what he would do in summer.

We said, "Down in Beirut, people are afraid."

They said, "Here, too, everybody is afraid."

We couldn't stay long, because Wayne had to be at the church for a choir practice, but Georgette didn't let us leave until she had invited us for a Sunday lunch and we had written it on our calendar.

People who live abroad as aliens—people like us—have to live knowing that one day they will kiss their friends goodbye and maybe never come back. Most of the time they just live without thinking about this. But that afternoon I kissed Georgette on both cheeks, and when we were driving along the road between the tall trees, with a breeze blowing through the windows, passing a few lovely stone houses in the forest, hearing the pesky buzz of the remote-control airplane somebody was flying, I realized how much I loved my selfless, stubborn friend and remembered that I was one of those aliens. The thought stunned me like bad news, like a diagnosis of a terminal illness that would cut short my only life.

A New Floor and a New Idea

To my surprise and relief Hashim did leave our house at the end of the month of March. After that Wayne spent as much time as he could working on the renovations. We still had mud floors in two rooms and unpainted walls and no cupboards, but the little house was about to undergo a dazzling transformation—from mud to marble, white marble.

Reluctantly I had chosen the large marble tiles, quietly imagining the naturalness of wood. But I could only dream of a hardwood floor, since in all the Middle East wood was a luxury. Marble was more affordable and, of course, beautiful, but it would be hard and slippery and cold and difficult to protect from stains.

Anxious for a perfect job, Wayne helped the tilers cut the blocks, shaping them to fit them around the rock in the floor. I had a brainstorm myself about how to use this obtrusive boulder. I surprised myself. It came to me while I was wondering what kind of furniture I would put in the cave and couldn't think of any couch or chair that would not be out of place. If a room looks like a cave, it doesn't need modern furniture or even American Country.

I suggested that we create a seat, a built-in couch, starting with the big stone, and then use other stones, smaller ones, to build up a base along the whole end of the room, a base that we would top with the white marble and then with cushions. We could put cushions to lean on, as well, and cushions on the floor. Wayne liked the idea of the stone bench and immediately said that he would make another to match it against the back wall at the other end of the room.

The floor was amazing—glossy and rich—fit for a palace. I loved the two marble steps that took us from the living room into our cave.

But the cave was still a primitive room with a hundred and fifty years of smoke on its walls and nothing but dirt between its stones. And one day when we arrived we scared a big tarantula that scurried across the white floor and disappeared. Wayne said, "They must get in through this hole to the outside. I've got to have a window made for it."

After talking with numerous workers about the false ceiling we wanted, with fiberglass insulation above it, Wayne decided to do it himself. The installation of this new ceiling in the kitchen alone took weeks, but it erased the cold look and feel of concrete and made me forget those cows. Then in the front room the old wooden beams with the suspicious spaces behind them disappeared, too, replaced by a white ceiling, creating a lighter, cozier and more modern room. We decided to keep the original rustic ceiling in the cave, where even I recognized its appropriateness.

When Wayne started building kitchen cupboards, we began talking about doing the essentials for living and finishing little by little after we moved in. Though I dreaded that, I felt that being home at last might be worth the hassle.

In summer I would be traveling for a few weeks. I had been invited to teach a seminar in the Wheaton College summer program. Our mission really wanted me to accept, and I could take this opportunity and also be present for Cynthia's graduation from California Polytechnic University in June, all within a one-month trip.

Cynthia had taken the five-year course in aeronautical engineering in four years from pure impatience. She already had a job. From numerous offers, she had chosen to work on the space shuttle main engine at the Rocketdyne plant on the north side of Los Angeles. However, she had asked to delay her first day of work so that she could come to Lebanon. Wayne wrote a letter to help her get a visa.

Since he would be working while I was away, Wayne thought that he could move our possessions, and I could come back to my own house, bringing Cynthia with me. This plan was making me very happy.

While The Earth Trembled

In my borrowed office I always sat with my back to the window. Though the glare was minimal, because of the balcony and its overhanging roof, the view from our hillside location was fascinating and distracting. Below us on the slope, trucks and graders worked ceaselessly, making the ground level and raw, and steel girders, seven or eight stories high, rose from the spaces they prepared. Beyond this activity, the whole city of Beirut lay in front of me—a triangle with its nose in the sea and covered with a mass of concrete structures. Most American cities, seen from above, have a center where the skyscrapers gather, and from there the cities flatten and thin out into industrial districts with sprawling parking lots and residential areas enhanced by tree-lined streets and parks and the roofs of one-family dwellings.

Compared to this model, Beirut looks like one massive downtown. Its several concentrations of skyscrapers do not rise to spectacular heights like those of New York or Chicago, but neither are they exaggerated by the falling away of the structures around them, because—except for the camps of refugee huts near the airport—it is a city of apartment buildings. The "suburbs" are no escape from city living.

Beirut is beautiful in the early morning light when it glows in the sun and the lines of its buildings and streets are sharp, and the sea is blue around it. And sometimes it is beautiful again at the end of the day when the tall buildings of Ras Beirut stand up against an orange sunset and the rest of the city is sinking into shadows.

My office windows offered all of this, plus ships gliding in and out of the port and planes taking off or descending toward runways and sometimes sudden towers of smoke from car bombs. Often there were arching tracers across the Green Line and full-blown battles to watch instead of working.

In April that year I was sitting there with my back to the view, editing a stirring piece of literature, when the day erupted into a storm of explosions and the roar of jets and the stuttering of anti-aircraft fire. Israeli planes were bombing the two refugee camps, Sabra and Shatila, as well as surrounding parts of the city. My staff and I gathered on my balcony to watch (downhill from us the graders and trucks kept roaring and moving) until we noticed that anti-aircraft shells, which must come down somewhere, were exploding around us.

This went on for a couple of hours and suddenly ceased, except for the smoke that kept rising from the city, and we gathered our jangled nerves and went home for the day.

All the month of May Israel made incursions into south Lebanon. In quiet parts of our cloudless day we could hear distant thunder, and every day hundreds of people fled up the coastal highway into Beirut. (This too had happened before.) Then on the fourth of June, Friday afternoon, I sat down at my desk to write a nice apologetic letter to my high school class, the Wynne, Arkansas class of 1947, to say that I could not attend our reunion because I had to go to Chicago and then to San Luis Obispo for my daughter's college graduation, after which she would come out for a visit. This effort was interrupted by warplanes swooping down on Beirut, screeching and roaring and rattling the windowpanes.

Again we had a grandstand seat, as a part of the southern suburbs blew up in flames and dust. Wave after wave of jets came in; fire streaked out of the bellies of planes and rockets crashed into targets unknown to us. Waleed, one of our editors, paced the floor and made frantic phone calls and gestured and talked: "I can't find my mother; she should be home." And two hours later, "It's too much. Really, it's too much." Abu Sleiman, a Palestinian who lived just beyond the place where the bombs were falling, said almost nothing but went home, though I tried to stop him. Too tired and grieved to write anything, I decided that the "Dear Classmates" letter made no sense anyway.

The Israeli invasion really began the next day, though we couldn't know that, because until then everything that was happening had happened many times. The only difference was that now some of the people fleeing South Lebanon were dying on the way. People who lived along the coast were in the way. A school bus taking children home was blown off the road by a bomb dropped from a plane, and when the children scrambled off and started running for cover, a second bomb killed most of them.

The Israeli ambassador in London had been shot, and the Israelis were saying that their attacks on Lebanon were retaliation for this shooting, but the men being held in London for the crime were Jordanian, Syrian and Iraqi.

For the next few days, several times each day, the airport closed because of conflicting activity in the air, then opened again long enough for a few planes to take off. Israeli gunboats and planes pounded the coast to the south, and we could hear the noise. On Sunday afternoon I finally succeeded in writing the letter to my class and told them that all plans of any human being were in suspense and I might not get to Cynthia's graduation or to Chicago either. While I wrote, the earth trembled almost constantly, and occasionally an explosion bigger or closer than the others shook the windowpanes.

I was scheduled to leave on Thursday morning, and if I left two hours later than planned I would miss the graduation, because I would miss my connection in Paris. The chances that I would make it out were obviously dim, and while I really wanted to be with Cynthia on her graduation day and to fulfill the responsibility I had accepted at Wheaton, I did not know if I should leave Lebanon and Wayne, my colleagues and friends at such a traumatic and uncertain moment. For indefinable reasons, this didn't feel right.

Then the pounding of West Beirut began, and we knew the Israeli Army was coming, advancing up the coastal highway. Refugees, fleeing in the only possible direction, were running toward a city under siege and being overtaken on the road by tanks. Syrian planes went up and clashed with Israeli planes in the air above our heads. Horrendous noises shocked our nerves. I tried to make a meal in the Barnes' kitchen, while explosions in the air banged against the roof, and I could hear debris falling. A plane made screaming noises, louder and louder as it fell, and I held my breath until it exploded against the earth, shaking the mountain.

I drove to Broummana to send a telex to the mission board—I was press representative, and Baptists would want to know that their missionaries were safe—and as I passed up along the Beit Meri road something fell below it, making a thud and a tremor.

I had other work to do—a book was ready to print, except that I still had the corrected proof of the last few pages. I wouldn't want to leave the country with it still on my desk. When I called the printer, he insisted that I should not be on the road. He would send someone to pick up the proof. The shop foreman came, and we talked about some layout details. He said they had electricity and wanted to keep working while they could. (Months later I discovered that one of us had made a mental mistake. It was probably me. A picture that I had wanted at the end of the book was missing.)

After the printer left, I cleaned up my desk, wrote a note to myself about where to begin when I got back, and put the note in the top drawer. In the back of my mind, I was remembering. We had been in Jordan during the six-day war in June, 1967. When that Israeli invasion ended, every inch the Israeli army had put their feet on had been subtracted from Jordan, and those who fled the fighting had never gone back. I was now worried about all those people who were fleeing from the South. Maybe Israel would occupy their land and not leave it.

We listened to the noise and then to interpretations of it on the radio. For a while the Israelis were saying that their army would stop short of the city of Beirut, but there were no signs that they would. A Kata'ib militiaman told me that they wouldn't. "They will keep coming and finish the problem of the Palestinians." Then President Reagan spoke angrily, telling the Israelis to turn back. I was pleased with this at first, knowing that the invasion violated Israel's agreement with the United States concerning the use of American weapons, and knowing that everybody knew it. The Lebanese knew it; the Arabs knew it. But the advance continued, and Reagan's face was black. America's face was black.

Then the planes dropped leaflets on West Beirut, warning the Lebanese population to flee the city, providing maps and telling them which streets to travel. Things to feel bad about multiplied by the hour. We ate little, and I woke frequently at night, hearing the thunder of battle.

The airport closed, making my reservations useless. I no longer wanted to go anyway, and at the same time I desperately wanted to go. We were imagining what our kids were experiencing, watching the news. Wayne wanted me out, and he wanted me there with our family. Yet we knew that, except for the two events that I was scheduled to attend, I would not even be thinking of leaving now.

Wayne proposed to put me on the Russian hydrofoil to Cyprus, then learned that it was not going to run. The management told him something really odd. They had received orders several weeks earlier that the boat should not run for a while, beginning on June 8. They had not understood it, they said, and no reason had been given to them. Wayne kept saying to me, "Did the Russians know the date of this invasion? Who else knew?"

I thought of going to Amman, through Syria, and on to California from there. Wayne didn't like the idea of my traveling overland, because of reports of strong anti-American reactions in Syria, but I called a taxi driver who went daily to Damascus. Maybe his opinion would be helpful. The man told me that for the first time in his life he was afraid to go. He feared that Israeli and Syrian forces would clash along the highway.

No passenger boat, no plane, no taxi to Damascus added up to: no way out. I thought I should go back to Broummana and send a message to Wheaton to tell them that I would not be there. Wayne said, "They probably assume that by now."

Dress Warmly, Bring Food

On the ninth of June, acting on a suggestion from a friend, we went to the office of a shipping company in Monsourieh to ask if there was any chance of my getting on a freighter to Cyprus. The manager, cordial and understanding, explained that they had a ship in the Beirut port that would embark that afternoon whenever they got their load on board, sooner if "anything happened." The freighters did not normally take passengers, since there was no place for them, but he had already told an Italian businessman that he could go. The Greek owner and his family would also be on board.

"For this reason I can send you. I would not put a lady alone on a ship with only men." He told me I should dress warmly, because I would have to sit on the deck all night, and I should take my own food. He could not sell me a ticket but I should give the captain one hundred dollars.

Suddenly I was going. Maybe. Nothing in the world was sure, not even my intentions. I scanned the list of items I needed to pack and started stuffing them into my suitcase—the materials I had prepared for teaching the course at Wheaton, skirts and blouses, a dress for the graduation, dress shoes, walking shoes. What would the weather be like in California? In Illinois? What if I couldn't come back in a month? Now there was a question I had not considered. What if?

Wayne remembered that I was always sick on boats and said, "Do you have Dramamine?" I didn't, so he went to the pharmacy.

At noon we walked down the hill past the pomegranate tree and the tennis court and the tangerine trees and across the small parking lot to the seminary dining room. We could hear bombs exploding down the coast, booming against a steady drone of airplanes. Abu and Um John were serving lunch to the seminary students and faculty, whose faces and abnormally soft voices revealed an awed suspense.

Um John wanted to fill a plate for me, but I refused it. "*La, shukran*, Um John. I only came to say goodbye." Actually, my stomach felt like a tiny twisting tornado.

To my surprise Um John began to cry and to mutter something like, "You don't know what will happen to that boat, and you won't get any dinner, and none of us know what will happen to us, and we don't know when you'll get home or when you'll be back, and you need to eat."

I knew she wasn't really crying over my lack of appetite, but I took the plate of hot food and sat down and ate what I could.

When we arrived at the port area, we went directly to the general security office in a small building near the port to check me out of the country. We found no one there. My reaction to the empty office and locked door was that I would not be able to leave; Wayne's reaction was that nobody cared who left. As we drove to the pier I told him that leaving without a stamp in my passport must be illegal; maybe there would be consequences when I came back. But he dismissed the whole problem with a word, "*Baseeta*!" His favorite word.

After he put me and my luggage on board the freighter, he went to arrange new plane tickets for me out of Cyprus. We both knew that he might not find a travel agent to sell him a ticket and that the ship could leave before he got back. If he returned without a ticket that was O.K. I had dollars and could buy one in Cyprus, but as soon as he left, I knew I would be very upset if he didn't come before we sailed. I stood around on the deck, amid all the tangled ropes and the tangled unknowns, watching a crane lowering crates into the hole and porters struggling up the ramp from the pier with boxes on their backs. I paced, keeping an eye on my suitcase and what I called my "carry-on" bag, my mind and heart in a muddle. I wanted to go. Our children would be comforted if someone got out of Lebanon. Cynthia wanted me at her graduation. I had a commitment to Wheaton College. And probably Wayne would feel better if I were gone. But I had no idea whether or not it was right to be on this ship. I was responsible for so much. Maybe I had forgotten some detail that I needed to take care of at the office. Maybe Wayne would need me. Also, I wanted to stay. I wanted to be a witness to whatever happened next, though at the same time I felt like hiding. For the first time I acknowledged to myself that I could not bear to watch the Israelis pound Lebanon. That they would actually ride into the streets of Beirut in their tanks was unthinkable. Another army trampling Lebanon!

The tall and handsome man strolling on the deck had to be the Italian businessman. He spoke to me in fluent, polished English and explained how he had come to Beirut to sell his products and had gotten stuck. He expressed extreme relief to be on board. I asked if he had given his money to the captain yet. He said yes and pointed him out to me—a big fair-skinned man with soiled hands, helping the crew with their duties. No one on board was wearing any kind of uniform.

I wondered if the captain even knew that I was on board, so when I found him alone I spoke and tried to put my one hundred dollar bill into his hand. He lifted both big hands and showed me his palms, saying "No," and something I didn't understand, except the words, "do good." I was baffled. He spoke Greek to one of the younger men who then came and got my suitcase, showing me where he was putting it, inside the control room of the ship. Before dropping my smaller bag there with it, I took out my water bottle and swallowed my seasickness pill.

A lot of time passed. The sailors fastened things down, winding up ropes, doing the kinds of things that might signal an imminent departure.

What if Wayne didn't come? What if something happened to him, and he was helpless to come? Anything seemed possible. I felt ready to jump ship. And then I saw him. He ran up the ramp, clutching a small paper, and immediately pressed it into my hand. "A ticket to London and on to L.A. Sorry, I couldn't get any reservations."

"They don't have a place for me?"

"They don't know; they have no contact with Cyprus or London. But if they don't get you on one plane, they will get you on another."

I could feel the engines running, the deck vibrating under my feet.

"Maybe I shouldn't do this. It's not too late to get off."

He said, "No way! You have to go. For Sass you have to go. You have to be there for both of us."

A sailor came and made motions to tell us that the ship was moving out. Wayne kissed me, said, "I'm glad you can go," loped down the ramp, waved and hurried toward the car. I watched the Peugeot back out of a space on the sea side of the road and disappear toward the desolation of the Green Line. West Beirut, shapeless like an unplanned happening, looked shabby and gorgeous in the afternoon sun.

The water between the ship and the shore was only a few hundred yards wide when Israeli planes swooped down, all the sound behind them, so that I didn't look until they had passed and were over the city. The world shook from their power and then from the rumble of explosions. Smoke began to rise in the direction of the refugee camps, as the expanse of water behind us grew fast.

This picture is burned into my brain. Hanging in a gallery it might be called "Running Away." The boat in the harbor faces the sea, churning water behind it; the city is burning. The lone figure on the aft deck leans toward the land. Just remembering muddles my heart, makes the earth shiver under my feet, and arouses my pity for the Palestinians and my love for Lebanon.

Again the planes came, their engines screaming, while I cowered against the wall of the little room that seemed to be the ship's command center. The deck heaved up and down under my feet, and suddenly a brisk wind, shockingly cold, hit me, snatching at my scarf and the tail of my coat.

One of the planes peeled out of the attack line and appeared to circle our ship in a big loop. It came back, making the loop again, and then again. I wondered if it would attack a Greek freighter. This seemed conceivable. I tried to hide, leaning against the wall, shivering. Already I knew that the warmest coat I owned would not be enough.

A sailor brought me a chair, placing it in the semi-shelter of the cabin, and I sat down, grateful, pushing my hands into the sleeves of my coat, then taking them out to cover my ears. Gloves had not occurred to me until now. We were ploughing across the water, with Lebanon receding faster than seemed possible. I could no longer see the mountains at all, just the tip of Ras Beirut floating in the haze like a tattered ghost. It was forever too late to go back.

Tired already, my limbs heavy from the medicine, I wondered how I could be sleepy when I was so cold. What could I think about all night, to keep myself upright and sane? I could pray, of course. There was plenty to pray about.

The sound of the ship's engines shifted into a lower key, like a voice recording played too slowly, then the noise of it died completely, and we began to wallow in the waves, rising, tipping and sinking. Something was wrong. I tried to look at the horizon so I wouldn't be sick.

The Italian gentleman appeared and said that the captain wanted me to come inside. I went gladly. The room felt warm and safe. A youthful but corpulent man, the owner of the ship, stood beside the captain looking out at the sea. He offered me a seat on a plastic bench against the wall and then asked for my passport. His wife was sitting on a bench, too, holding on to a stroller by its handle. I kept looking at the child in the stroller, thinking that his face was beautiful beyond forgetting, with his thick, dark hair and curling eyelashes. His father, I realized, must have looked like that once. His mother had a blank, lazy look. Maybe she had taken Dramamine, too. Then the man read my name and other information into the ship's radio. Though the words were distorted a bit by his accent, I heard him say my mother's maiden name and the place where I was born.

When he had finished, I asked, "What was that about?"

He said, "The Israelis want names, everybody."

"The Israelis?"

"Look," he said.

Finally, I saw a gray boat to the west, small and almost invisible on the gray sea.

"Israeli gunboat. They order us stop. They ask what we have in the ship, and who."

Shortly the engine roared to life, the horizon steadied, we began to push through the water again, and I returned to my chair on the deck. The Italian came with me. He was wearing a smart looking woolen overcoat, and I wondered how he had happened to have it in Beirut in the month of June. He sat on a capstan, an iron spool with rope wrapped around it, and we tried to converse, shouting above the noise of the engine and the roar of the wind and the water washing the sides of the ship.

I liked the ease with which he sat there, as though he had practiced sitting on the decks of ships whipped by the wind. Certainly he had cultivated other graces as well, and practiced the English language. I felt glad that he was there.

The hours ahead of us looked long and miserable. I began to think of all the things I should have done to prepare. For instance, I wished I had brought an old blanket, one I could have discarded, and I realized that a sleepless night in the cold would require more food than I had brought. The cold, boiled egg in my bag seemed inappropriate and pitiful.

The ship pushed through the waves with an up and down motion, its engine humming loudly. Our wake spread out like a wide white V in the black water, and darkness had enveloped the ship, when a sailor came and invited us to supper. The Italian interpreted for me; obviously he knew Greek, too. As the sailor escorted us into a small dining room, I thought this the happiest surprise imaginable. We sat at two oblong tables with ten or twelve crewmen, the owner of the ship and his family. Each place at the table had a big chunk cut from a round loaf of bread, a green salad and an empty bowl. A warm, homey smell filled the room. Two men served us from steaming pots, ladling a thick, fragrant soup into the bowls—a fish soup. It was perfect. I got warm from the inside and happy and began to feel hopeful that I could survive the night on the deck.

After dinner the owner spoke with his two passengers and showed us a place where we could sit out of the cold, in a small lounge with plastic benches around the walls. The Italian chose a bench and said, "This is fine. I think I'll stretch out right here."

I felt a little awkward, thinking of lying down in this room with a strange man, but he was a nice man, after all, and this was a lot better than the deck. Just as I was trying to figure a way to get both my body and my mind comfortable, a sailor came and spoke to me in Greek. The Italian translated. "He is inviting you to sleep in his bunk room."

I tried to imagine this and then asked, "Where will he be?"

"He has duty and won't need his cabin until five a.m."

"Should I do it?"

"Why not?"

When I didn't answer, he added, "I'm sure you can trust him."

The room was tiny, the light dim, the bed rumpled. Pictures of curvaceous half-dressed girls decorated the wall and the closet door. As I lay down, still wearing my coat and my shoes, I felt suddenly that I could not have stayed erect another minute.

The next thing I knew the sailor was at the door, pointing at his watch. Whatever he said sounded like an apology. Still lying on my back, still dressed for the out-of-doors, I struggled to understand where I was and to move my arms. On the stairs my legs weighed a ton each, and up on deck I felt awful for a few minutes. The Italian stood by the rail, with his hair combed and his tie straight. I needed the routine things: a splash of cold water on my face, a cup of hot coffee. Meanwhile the sky grew light behind us, and the boat floated so quietly and smoothly that the island of Cyprus seemed to be the thing that moved, bringing toward us a city strung out along the sea front.

"What are your plans now?" my companion asked.

"I have to get to the airport and then on a plane to London."

"Me, too, except I'm going to Rome. But we are in trouble, you know."

"Why?"

"We're docking in Limassol, not Larnaca."

"Oh, no. How far is it to the airport?"

"More than an hour, I expect. Shall we share a taxi?"

It seemed a good idea.

A sailor walked out on deck with a tray and offered us small cups of Greek coffee, thick and bitter-sweet. This lifted my spirits considerably.

Then I saw the man who had given me his bunk. He was busy with ropes, but I went over and handed him $25.00 in American bills, saying "Thank you," as I pressed it into his hand. His smile was reserved, but his eyes lighted, and with a nod that was almost a bow, he said, "*Efkharisto.*"

I added this word to its synonyms in my vocabulary. *Efkharisto, gracias, merci, shukran,* thanks. I offered them up together to God for my mysterious good fortune. Somehow I had slipped out of the noise and chaos, and I was on my way to America to be with my children. A feeling of relief overtook me, and at least for a moment I discarded guilt and uncertainty to lean on the rail and breathe the beauty and quiet of morning, as the freighter glided slowly toward the dock, making small cranking noises and now and then a clank. A few sea gulls came to meet us, squawking, dipping and careening, white wings flashing in the clean light. The rising sun poured wonderful soft colors on the surface of the water—pink and gold and blue. These colors surprised me, like the captain refusing my money, like hot fish soup and a bed to sleep in and coffee on the deck at sunrise, and I thought that I would always remember those gentle colors and the smooth water and the loveliness of this dawn on the Mediterranean.

Neighbors and Aliens

Stringing Beads

The Greek freighter was the last ship to leave Lebanon for many weeks. Unimaginable things happened during those weeks. Twenty thousand Lebanese died, most only because they were in the way. No one counted the Palestinians, who were the target.

A youthful Bechir Gemayel was elected president. The PLO guerrillas left Beirut, making victory signs, while their women screamed and wept and American Marines stood guard. I saw the show on television. It was melodramatic and foolish, like an opera without the music. The Israelis promised that the remaining refugees would be safe. America guaranteed these promises. Diplomats made simplistic speeches about how the departure of Arafat and his men was step one in the solution to the Middle East conflict.

Doubting and afraid, I experienced an inordinate desire to be alone, knowing that if anyone asked me the wrong questions or made me remember the tension and the thunder, I would be in trouble. The one time I spoke in a church, I concluded that living in Lebanon was never so difficult as being in America and needing to explain Lebanon.

When the worst was over, Dr. Isam Ballenger, Middle East director of the Foreign Mission Board traveled to Lebanon and made the decision that every missionary needed a rest—outside of Lebanon. And so, Wayne came home, too.

Bechir Gemayel died in the rubble of his militia headquarters. Knowing he had many enemies, I was still incredulous. Does the protagonist die in the second chapter of the novel? Then the news trickled out—a massacre in the refugee camps. Hundreds dead at the hands of Christian militiamen. The Israeli Army had stood guard while it happened. So much for their promises. So much for America's guarantees.

Before most of this happened, I attended Cynthia's graduation, a lovely, orderly event, in a football stadium overlooked by peaceful hills, in sight of a calm sea. I remember best the very end, when all the graduates shouted, threw their caps into the air and ran to find families and give them hugs, except one section, Cynthia's section, the engineers. Ignoring the celebration, they marched out in perfect file. Why? I guessed just because they were engineers. I went on to Chicago and shared in teaching a course on mission publishing at Wheaton and then I joined Wayne at a cabin on Lake Eufaula in Oklahoma and heard his stories about the strangeness of Israeli troops camped so near his bedroom window that he could hear them chatting in their tent.

The good thing that happened to me was that I had time to think. When had I ever had time to think? I spent hours writing paraphrases of the Psalms, and getting in touch with God and my stunned and confused self. My life, it appeared to me, kept getting disrupted, divided, scattered. I saw it in fragments—segments of time, stages of development, geographies and houses, incompatible roles, incomplete projects, interrupted relationships, disparate loyalties.

Under a clothesline stretched from tree to tree, my wet sheets limp, Eufaula Lake shimmering, the forest looking burned by summer, I perceived that my life with God was the one continuous element in it all, an invisible string holding everything together, the way the string of a necklace holds beads in a pattern. If the string breaks, the necklace falls apart and becomes nothing but a scattering of beads. I picked up my empty plastic pan, seeing clearly that without my faith—a link with ultimate reality even when tenuous and neglected—nothing made any sense.

We left our children again, scattered from coast to coast—Tim working in San Francisco, Jan in Baptist student ministry at Yale, Jim building houses on Lake Eufaula, Dwight in graduate school at UCLA preparing to be a math teacher, Cynthia testing developmental engines for the space shuttle. Because of the invasion she had missed her chance to come to Lebanon.

I flew first to Germany where I attended the Frankfurt Book Fair and then a conference on relations with Muslims at a retreat center nearby. Having a whole week between these two events, I spent it reading the book of Proverbs and stringing beads. Whatever I thought I wrote, and because I was searching, the words evolved into a story that was searching for its own meaning. I didn't know until the end that it was about giving in to the impulse to love, about giving up the temptation to ignore the world's pain and just enjoy life.

The day the conference ended, Middle East Airlines promised me that "tomorrow" the Beirut airport would be open, and I could get a seat on a plane. Suddenly I felt I had been gone a year and was overwhelmed with homesickness. All my thinking and studying and reading and waiting had led to this—that Lebanon was where I belonged, whatever army was in the streets, whatever disaster was coming next, and wherever I put my head at night.

Something New Under the Sun

Jean BouChebl was a small, dynamic man, always meticulously groomed, always intense. He came to see me in my office, not long after I came back to Lebanon. I did not yet know him well, only that he was from Bikfaya and a member of the Baptist church there. Jean had been Director of Food and Beverage at the elegant Phoenicia Intercontinental Hotel—long ago devastated in the fighting—and after that he had worked outside of Lebanon for several years, returning shortly before the Israeli invasion.

Jean—his name is the French form of John and pronounced the same—welcomed me home, accepted a seat and then came straight to his subject.

"Mrs. Fuller, I want to share something with you." Jean's English was excellent; he enunciated every syllable and this seemed to be part of his earnestness, his nature.

I stopped him, offering to go and make coffee for us, but he said, "No, thank you, I'm drinking very little coffee these days."

I could see that he meant it, that coffee would be just an interruption he didn't want.

"After this massacre in the refugee camps," he said, "some of us felt so bad. We felt like nobody has shown any love for these people. Maybe they have been considered our enemies, but you know, they came here mistreated and grieved, and now they are mistreated again, and after all, the Lord did tell us to love our enemies."

This was not something I had expected to hear, having learned already that loving our enemies is not easy when they live next door and have machine guns. Jean sat with his elbows on the arms of the chair and his fingers intertwined, in a way that showed, not nervousness but Jean's characteristic intensity. His shirt collar was perfectly white, his shoes polished like mirrors.

"Brother Sami Dagher talked with me about an idea. He said the door is open now and the time is good to go in to the Palestinian camps and maybe show some love. The Italian troops are in charge there now, and it is possible to go in and out. And I thought that now while I am still looking for a job in Lebanon, I can do this."

I knew Sami Dagher. He was pastor of the National Alliance Church in Beirut—a man with a warm heart for the Muslims and for the poor.

"So," Jean explained, "I started going just to see what we could do, and for several months I went alone and now Brother Edgar Trabulsi goes with me. At the beginning we didn't know exactly how to approach them, but Brother Dagher and I decided that I ought to take refreshments with me, in case people invited me in, so I went with tea and cookies. At each little house, I said to whomever was there, I am a Lebanese Christian, and I have come to hear your story. And I sat down and listened."

Now I was genuinely surprised. Bikfaya was the hometown of the Gemayel family and considered the capital of the Maronites. The Gemayels were founders and leaders of the Kata'ib militia. As homeless aliens the Palestinians were their natural enemy. Wasn't it the Kata'ib that perpetrated the massacre? And now this son of Bikfaya could go to the refugee camps? Alone with all those angry people?

I searched for the right question to ask. "How did they respond?"

"They screamed at me. They shouted. They cried. The women told me about the men in their families being forced to leave Lebanon, and now they don't know where they are. They told me about the massacre, about people who tried to escape and were caught, about family members killed in front of their eyes."

"It was as bad as we heard?"

"Yes. Maybe worse." Jean's voice grew husky.

I asked him, "What are their living conditions now?"

"Terrible. Holes in the walls, no glass in the windows. The rain coming in. Mud everywhere.

"I saw they appreciated the visits, that they needed somebody really. They started to trust me. After three or four months people started to say to me, 'You know, I told you my name is Ahmad but really it's Maher.' They decided they could tell me the truth. And when Brother Edgar heard about it—he's in my Sunday School class—he wanted to go with me, so we are keeping on with these visits.

"After their stories we always suggest that we have tea together, and we bring out the little bag of tea and a few cookies. The woman of the house will jump up and make the tea, and after we drink with them, we always ask their permission to read a few words from the Bible and to pray for them. And, Mrs. Fuller, no one has refused. Every house we approached has opened the door to us, and no house refused to hear the Word and let us pray for them. As we leave, they hold our hands and often they have tears in their eyes."

"Jean, that's... that's... wonderful. I'm so glad to hear about this."

"Everyone there knows us now. When we arrive the children start following us. We get this train of kids all saying, 'Give me a cookie.'"

"Who pays for all these cookies?"

He saw my intent and said, "Thank you, Mrs. Fuller, we have cookies, but I do need something from you. You can help us. Since everyone has let us read the Bible, I want now to start leaving New Testaments with them, if they want, and I need something for the children, something like a little book."

Immediately I thought of our story leaflets. Each one was just a folded sheet of glossy paper, with a colored picture on the front and a Bible story inside.

We talked about how many he needed, and he told me that he went four times a week and might see forty or fifty children each time. "When we go to a house, lots of other people come in, you know. Neighbor women and their kids."

So I called Abu Issam up from the storeroom and told him to give Jean an assortment of the leaflets, two hundred altogether.

"Where's the invoice?" Abu Issam said, just doing his job right. So I wrote an invoice to myself, and Abu Issam brought up two small packages.

I told Jean, "Try these. If they seem to be what you need, we can get more."

"Thank you, Mrs. Fuller. God bless you. I knew I could count on you."

* * *

After he left, I stood at the window looking down on the camps, remembering those days when the Israeli planes swooped down dropping bombs. I could almost see again the flashes of fire on the ground and hear the thunderous explosions. Now a quiet rain was falling on Shatila and Sabra. During the invasion I had feared something like the massacre, but it had not occurred to me that anything good could come of it. What an amazing turn of events! Christians from Bikfaya visiting their enemies, bringing tea and cookies! I felt like running around to spread the news that Christians were acting like Christians.

Now Where Were We?

Because of the invasion, Wayne had not been able to work on the house. We were homeless still, camping out in the seminary's guest apartment. While picking up the pieces of our publishing work, we started going up to Beit Meri el-Hara to sit on the marble steps under the arch and talk about the fastest way to get our place livable.

Kitchen cupboards were a must, and Wayne felt he had to do them with his own hands. He had started, in fact, and had ordered some beautiful oak that was being shipped to Lebanon. This was for the doors only. Couldn't I live without the doors for a while? I guessed it was better than living without a house.

And then there was the pointing to do. Wayne had to teach me this word, the way builders use it. All these stones had to be pointed. Every crevice had to be filled with "*kahli*," he said.

"*Kahli*! That's eye makeup."

"Yeah, same word."

Strange, a hundred words for a lion, and just one for both eye makeup and mortar to holds stones together. Wayne said he would do this work himself. "Pointing has to be done first. Then we clean them."

"How?"

"We'll try brushes, I guess. Then maybe soap and water."

While preparing to do the pointing, whisking trash and dust out of a million spaces, Wayne found an old i.d. card, slightly crumpled and dirty, which had been pushed into a crevice. It had expired nearly twenty years earlier. The owner was an Armenian, a taxi driver. I stared at it, intrigued. People don't throw away their own i.d. cards. Or hide them. Questions started racing through my head. I said, "I'll ask Um Elias if any Armenians ever lived here."

Wayne said, "Why risk opening a can of worms?"

The answer was that I love a mystery, but I didn't mention it. I just said, "Could something have happened to this man? Here in this room?"

Wayne said, "If it did, I don't want to know about it."

What he really meant was, "I don't want you to know about it." So I didn't conduct the investigation I had in mind, though I never quit wondering why that i.d. card was hidden between the stones inside our house.

There was another mystery, though, and I didn't like it. We still had tarantulas. And some other creature that ate them and left their crooked, hairy legs scattered around on the marble floor.

When Wayne saw them, he said, "Oh, yeah, that window," and he put it on a list of things to do. It would be the craziest window anyone had ever seen, taller on one side than on the other. It would even open, swinging inward, and would have a screen on it. That was one of the really nice things about living in Lebanon. Anything could be made to order—a one-of-a-kind lampshade or an asymmetrical window in a preposterous size.

Wayne stood on a ladder, squatted on his heels, crouched in corners. He was a rubber-gloved artist, doing a mural—a mound of golden putty on his palette. Drawing with his right forefinger, he filled cracks, defined the irregular shapes of the stones, created strength, made order out of chaos. Day after day, he worked, from ceiling to floor, from door to corner, corner to corner, around the room, across the arch.

And then we began the cleaning. The caveman who built this wall had not been concerned about a little soil clinging to his rocks. Nor, apparently, had anyone since. For years—maybe for a century and then half of another one—it had been solidifying, and smoke and soot had collected over it, hiding the stones under more and more layers of carbon and dust. Cleaning was an act of discovery.

First we swept the wall from top to bottom, and after we picked up dustpans full of fine debris, we knew there was more. We tried brushing with a stiff brush and then vacuuming; we clogged the filter of our vacuum cleaner and dumped it and did it all again. We poured water from a watering can, holding the can above the target area until my arms hurt, and attacking the dirt with a steel brush. The water ran black onto the white floor.

In the final stage, we brought in a hose, forced water hard against the stones and let rivers flow over the steps in a lavish waterfall into the living room. I swept the water out the front door. It was great fun.

Gradually we found that wall—a clumsy jigsaw puzzle of sizes and shapes, in multiple shades of yellow and brown and rust and pink and gray and flecks of black and flashes of crystal. But the shapes fit together in the end, and the colors blended into one mellow shade, like honey in the comb. An amazing wall, unique among all the world's walls, a beautiful accident, pure grace.

Promises

Hardly more than a week after his visit Jean came again, smiling broadly. "Mrs. Fuller, now the children follow us saying, 'Give me a story. Give me a story.' Those leaflets are so popular they forgot about cookies. And you said I could come for more."

While Abu Issam brought the leaflets, Jean told me, "Now we are leaving New Testaments with them, and I want you to pray with me especially for a man named Fadi who is reading the scripture and asking questions. I can just feel how his heart is hungry."

"There are still men there?"

"Oh, yes. A few. Men who didn't fight, I guess.

I promised to pray for Fadi.

Then he said, "I want one more thing from you, Mrs. Fuller. I want you to go to the camp and visit some of the women. Fadi's mother, Um Na'im, for instance. These women have stories to tell, and they have a right to be heard. Could you go and listen and maybe even write some of their stories?"

So I promised to go to the camp, and Jean said he would mention to Um Na'im that I was coming.

Standing in the door of my office with his new packages of story leaflets in his arms, Jean—this man who had served the rich and now served the poor—said, "Mrs. Fuller, for the first time I understand how missionaries can leave their homes and go to a foreign country. If I didn't have a wife and two children to take care of, I would leave Bikfaya and go and live in Sabra with the Palestinians."

Jean disappeared from my door and left me standing there speechless, trying to absorb this astonishing statement. Until now nothing else I ever heard from a Lebanese Christian surprised or encouraged me like those words.

A Diary of Peace

One early evening, after a hard day's work in our house, I walked outside and found our little world amazing. The sky was black and strewn with stars, and the hills blacker, with sparkling villages scattered across them, and the great hush of a rural evening spread over hills and houses and fields. I stood still listening to the silence. It felt like some positive force, a vesperal benediction, and I thought, *this is Lebanon the way it should always be.*

There was no more beautiful spot on the face of the earth than right there on that hillside, and I was going to live there in an old relic of a house, a wonder in itself. This thought gave me a little dream of peace. We would sit on the roof at the end of the day and watch the moon rise over the mountain, maybe even invite friends and cook outdoors. We would watch the lights come on in all the villages and love our neighbors and not be afraid of anyone.

But over there across the canyon were two rival militias, not to mention both the Syrian and Israeli armies. We understood that in the Bhamdoun area the Syrians had Russian technicians with them, probably three or four hundred meters from Israeli positions. Scary stuff. Often we heard shooting, and journalists had written that the new occupation army was bringing Israeli Druze into the Shouf—surely a trouble-making move. We knew two people who had witnessed this. In the middle of my dream of peace, the prospects of more war made my heart sink from dread, and I heard myself say, "Please"—an involuntary prayer.

The fact was that I had stopped praying for peace. This too had been unintentional, as well as gradual and unnoted. I wanted peace, I thought God must, too, and I believed in prayer. I believed in it, knowing that praying for peace in Lebanon was asking for the rocks to melt. According to Jesus I had a vote that counted—odd since God didn't need any advice. It must be important, I concluded, to express a preference, to cast a vote for what seemed right and good. But after stuffing the box for years, I sort of let it go and waited. I prayed for other things—for the protection of my friends, for the opportunity to do my work and a chance to sleep. Sometimes I asked only to be one of God's people, whatever happened. But after the traumas of the invasion and the massacre and assassinations and signs of a new beginning, I had begun to long for peace intensely, maybe because I hoped its opportunity had come or maybe because the alternatives were getting worse and worse.

I was keeping a secret diary that I had boldly given the title, "A Diary of Peace." I was learning from it. Sometimes an image or an idea of peace—like the quiet over the mountains now—would present itself, and I would write it in my journal. Jean's visits to the camps were in there, but mostly my diary was not very exciting. Peace could be really ho-hum. It rarely made me run to the window to watch it happen.

Wasta

A certain young man whose family I knew was in big trouble. He was in so much trouble that it challenged one of my long-standing policies.

I will call the young man Adeeb, because that is not his name. Adeeb was brilliant and ambitious, also aggressive and energetic—the kind of young man who goes after what he wants, the kind who can't sit still without getting restless. His fascination was computer technology, and he felt desperate to study in some university with a strong computer science department. Adeeb was also stateless, one of those many thousands who were born in Lebanon with a Syrian father and a Lebanese mother. Moving around the country was perilous, every roadblock a trap. At a roadblock one needed an identity card. He had never owned a Lebanese i.d, and his Syrian card had expired. A trip to Damascus to renew it would land him in jail or the army—an enemy's army. And traveling to any other country was impossible, with no passport.

Then one day a family friend went to Adeeb's home and told him and his parents that he knew a way to get Adeeb a Lebanese passport. They would need to tell a lie, a "small" lie. Adeeb and his mother should go to the bureau of statistics and register Adeeb as her illegitimate child, writing on the application that his father was unknown. This was a shocking idea, a hard requirement that hurt everyone's pride, but suddenly Adeeb envisioned flying away from his trap and studying in America. His mother, with his father's consent, decided to swallow all her dignity and do what she could. They told the lie, and even while they waited for the statistics bureau to do its work, Adeeb scrambled for college applications.

Once his mother had obtained this legal registration, their friend took it to the Lebanese Amin el-Am (General Security) and brought Adeeb his passport. Adeeb could hardly believe his good luck. There he was, holding the little folder with the cedar tree on the front, an actual passport with his picture in it, the government stamps in place, as well as the stamp of the *mukhtar*—a local official whose stamp meant that he knew the person in the picture.

Wild with ecstasy and impatience, Adeeb went straight to the American embassy and presented his passport, acceptance papers from an American university and a request for a student visa.

The consul put the passport under his magical blue lamp and informed Adeeb, "Bringing me a false passport is a criminal offense. I am putting your name on a list that will go to every embassy in the world. You will never travel to any place."

The same day his family came to me for help.

Many years earlier we had decided not to intervene for people at the American Embassy. Helping people go to the U.S. did not fulfill any of our purposes. And too many people wanted visas; if once we helped someone we were bound to be besieged with requests, especially since Middle Easterners like to do everything through *wasta*—a middle man with some kind of power or helpful relationship. I always just told people that *wasta* didn't work with Americans; it was not our way.

The gravity of Adeeb's situation and my interest in his family drove me to set aside my policy. I told them, "I doubt that I can do anything," but I went to the embassy.

I told Adeeb's story first to Joseph Karam, the consul's Lebanese assistant. He was a slightly built man in his forties, an approachable man who for years had been solving problems for the American community while consuls came and went. He had a plain unmemorable face, with a complexion common to people who spend their lives mostly indoors, but it was an open, friendly face. What I liked was his attentiveness and efficiency. When Joseph said he would take care of a matter, he took care of it with dispatch, and he remembered people, along with their names.

Joseph acted glad to see me, said I had not been in for a long time, and asked what he could do for me. I told him the story about Adeeb. While

I talked, his face revealed nothing except his understanding, and finally he said, "I will have to call the consul." I stood in front of the high counter waiting for them. Behind the counter were several file cabinets, a couple of desks with typewriters on them and some cubbyholes full of things like application blanks. A Lebanese woman was rearranging a stack of papers beside her typewriter. Through the broad windows on the opposite wall the sea sparkled, blue and lovely.

When they came back, Joseph introduced the consul and said to him, "This is Mrs. Fuller. She works with the Baptist mission." The man did not acknowledge the introduction.

I told him that I had come to talk with him about Adeeb's case, using his full name and adding, "He was here yesterday. I'm sure you remember him."

Immediately he fired a bullet at me. He said, "People with false passports are criminals. We give their names to Interpol."

If he meant to discourage me, he succeeded, but Joseph lifted my spirits a little when he said, "I have known Mrs. Fuller a long time, and this is the first time she has ever been here on behalf of anyone."

After that I was never sure the consul was listening. He tolerated me. He looked elsewhere—at the papers in his hand, at the corner of the room. Joseph stood beside him, backing me up with the right words at the right moment, speaking after me, like a translator. I thought this was gutsy behavior under the circumstances.

When I explained Adeeb's desperate situation as a non-citizen, Joseph said, "This is a true picture. Thousands of people in the country are in the same predicament."

I got the impression that the consul didn't know Lebanon very well. This seemed highly inappropriate but gave me courage to talk.

I said, "The boy didn't even suspect that his passport was illegal."

And Joseph told the consul, "This is plausible, because the process he followed was basically correct. Someone must have tricked him."

I said, "Adeeb and his family trusted both the friend who offered to help and the local *mukhtar*. They could not believe that the *mukhtar* would sign a counterfeit document. Besides that, when you buy an illegal document, you expect to pay dearly, and they didn't. They paid the normal fee."

Joseph said, "That is a significant point."

"Sir," I told him, "the reason I am bold enough to come here is that I know all of this boy's family. They are people of character." The consul almost looked at me then. I thought he was going to remind me that they had lied, but then he changed his mind.

I said, "They made a mistake, I know. A big mistake, but Adeeb is not a criminal and doesn't deserve to have his whole life ruined."

Joseph said, "Mrs. Fuller has been here a long time, and she knows the people well."

Finally, the consul spoke to me. "I have put his name on a list which will go out by courier. If the mailbag is still here, I will remove his name. If the bag has gone I can do nothing. I don't want to give you any hope."

"When will we know?"

"I will call you."

I thanked him, and Joseph said, "Mrs. Fuller, let me make sure we have the numbers where we can reach you."

Early the next morning the consul himself called. I was in the seminary guest apartment having breakfast. He came to the point without any pleasantries, and his words had the clipped off sharpness I had heard the day before. He said, "The mailbag was still here, and I have deleted his name." Before I could thank him he elaborated, "We can never give him a visa in this embassy, but if he ever has a valid passport and can ask somewhere else, there will be no record against him."

He gave me a chance to say, "I really appreciate what you have done." Then he hung up.

The Problem with Peace

Suddenly the government tried to function. For years the country had run quite well without it. Anybody who needed a new electrical service strung his own wire and spliced into the wires in the street or a neighbor's supply. The militias captured crooks and got rid of them the same week.

Drivers' licenses expired, but it didn't matter since nobody ever checked them. Foreigners failed to register or to renew visas and no one noticed. Whole departments of the government never opened their doors, on the assumption that they could not fulfill their purpose, and the happy employees of these departments got other jobs and drew two salaries.

Now, all at once, aliens without papers were being thrown into jail, drivers tested, illegal buildings bulldozed. There wouldn't for months be enough glass to replace what had been broken (Nancie Wingo, a teacher in the Baptist school, had none in her bedroom windows) nor for years, maybe, enough intact roofs to cover heads, and though none of the guns threatening our lives were being confiscated, time had run out for petty lawbreakers.

In my own little circles, publishers had produced books and magazines without proper permits. Now they were scurrying to see lawyers, to cover their tracks or to find out whether or not they were doing things right. Before I even knew about all this, our lawyer sent for me. And when I sat down in her dining room office, she said, "Frances, we have work to do." Mary Mathias loved work. That's why she was our lawyer.

'You and I always have work to do, Mary. So what's new?"

"The way this government is functioning. That's new. Everything is changing, Frances. There are new laws about everything. I'm staying up nights studying, trying to keep on top of it."

I could feel something bad coming.

She said, "We have new elements running the country now. They're after foreign organizations. I have studied the situation carefully, Frances. You have a problem, but it is easily solved, because, you see, the fault is not with Baptist Publications. The fault is with The Near East Baptist Mission."

"What...?"

"I will explain, Frances. They are now requiring that all organizations in the country must be legal societies. I have already organized so many of them—the Home of Onesiphorous, the Navigators..."

"Mary, what is a society?"

"The way a society is different from your mission is:" (I could hear the colon she put here) "its purposes must be declared to the Ministry of Interior, and it has a board of directors which must meet once a year to elect the officers and approve the general policies. A report on this meeting must go to the government. After that the mission will function the same as always."

"Why are you telling me, Mary, instead of the mission chairman?"

"Ah, good question. Because BP belongs to the mission. When the mission applies for status as a society, it will name the functions it intends to carry out: education, benevolent work, publishing, whatever. And from the society you will have the right to do all that you do. It makes everything easy. Otherwise, the government is starting to make everything hard for you."

"Mary, the mission is not going to like this."

"Frances, they must do it. There is a law. Every foreign organization *must* be a registered society."

"What about the old Ottoman law? Don't forget that the mission was here before the state of Lebanon."

"The law is changed, Frances. No matter how old the organization, every organization must register as a society."

Baptist Publication's legal status had been an ongoing debate between me and the Near East Baptist Mission for years. In 1970, just after becoming director of BP I investigated its legal standing. Having just come from Jordan, a country in which one had better take the law seriously, I wanted to verify our rights and limits before I made any mistakes. My predecessor and friend, Virginia Cobb, was dead, and I was in the dark about a number of things. BP's organized and efficient secretary knew nothing about any license to publish. When I asked the mission, Finlay Graham, our senior member, gave me the answer: missions, churches, even schools had a right to publish whatever they wished—a right enjoyed since the time of the Ottoman Empire. And he had explained the organization's special status under Lebanese law, the special status of those institutions that predated the Lebanese government.

Feeling miserably ignorant and not quite satisfied, I went to see the mission's lawyer. He listened with apparent amazement to my concern and asked me, "Did someone give you trouble?"

"No."

"Then I advise you not to ask for any."

I went away shaking my head. This did not sound like lawyerly advice to me. Later when I needed employee contracts and he did not help me, it came to my attention that this man took a retainer fee from the mission and did nothing to earn it.

Elias Moussa, a bright sensible young man who had become my assistant, told me about a lawyer he knew only by reputation, a woman who was really smart and would work, or fight if needed, for her client. Together we went to meet Mary Mathias, finding her office high up in a concrete edifice on a noisy thoroughfare in downtown Beirut. She was a colorful character in bright lipstick, with a flamboyant scarf flung back over her shoulder, but she was all business, asking questions faster than we could answer. We told her we were looking for someone who would keep us out of trouble.

After consideration on her part and ours, BP and Mary Mathias agreed that she would work for us, and she assured Elias and me that our publishing work did not require a license, unless we should decide to do a magazine.

Mary lived up to her reputation and served us well. After her office building was hit, then trapped in a no-man's land, she managed to get her files and stack them in her dining room, which became her office. I spent many hours in that room in Ashrafieh, facing those precarious stacks of files, talking with Mary, not bothered by her abrupt and nervous manner. Some clients said she lost things. I don't know. I did worry about how she found anything in that mountain of manila folders, but I'm sure she never lost anything from her head. She did have a visual problem, though. Her eyelids closed involuntarily, and she used to pry an eye open with one hand while holding a document in the other. Sitting at her ancient typewriter, she would hold her eyelids open for a moment to see what she had written, then let them fall and peck on the keys again. Walking with her somewhere, I discovered that she could not see the curb; I had to protect her from falling.

Mary often scheduled our work just before lunch, saying that I had to stay and eat with her. I discovered that cooking was not one of Mary's talents and that she needed a friend.

Eventually the mission also made Mary their lawyer, and she served the seminary and other mission institutions. In fact, most American groups in the country, especially Christian groups, used her, and she won many cases in which Lebanese landlords or business people were trying to win something from an American. She treated us with utmost respect and confronted our opponents with wrath and indignation. She could get angry with us, too, especially when we tried to handle sticky situations without her, because she trusted us on moral issues but never in official matters. We wanted to be fair even to our enemies; Mary wanted to bury them for us. And she wasn't afraid of anything.

Mary convinced me that Lebanese law had changed and sent a letter to the mission.

The mission was immovable. Somehow they still believed that the old laws applied to us and believed as well in the philosophy that if we didn't ask for it no one would give us trouble. Also, while the formation of a society might seem like a paper transaction with no real meaning, the full implications in our case were not clear. The Foreign Mission Board had policies for mission organizations and would not want anyone but the Baptist missionaries in Lebanon to elect officers or set policies for the mission.

When Mary received their answer, she was horrified. "You feel safe here," she told me, "but the day could come when someone would want to throw you out of the country. You are giving them the opportunity, by failing to comply with the law."

"Mary," I said, "where does that leave BP?"

"Out on a limb, Frances. If the mission is not registered, then BP must get a license like any publishing house."

"Mary, I can't change them. So you better tell me my alternatives."

And together we plotted. BP would have to register as a business like any local publisher. All we needed was a Lebanese partner. Mary explained the details to me and sent written materials for my local administrative committee.

The committee met and engaged in a long discussion of the pros and cons of the proposal. When the members realized that this route required registering with the Ministry of Finance and paying taxes, they objected.

Several people were adamantly opposed to this, on the reasonable basis that we were a non-profit organization. I agreed that it was not appropriate that we should pay taxes; the difference was that I was afraid.

After the committee said no and left, I sat at my desk, feeling like a failure. I thought I had done a decent job of publishing books and building an organization. But after all these years BP was a refugee, living in a borrowed office with no work permit. For a publisher that's what a license was—a permit to work.

A few days later I sent Abu Issam to the Naadi al-Thaqafa al-Arabi, the publishers' union, just to enter our name in the upcoming book fair, an annual affair in which we always participated. He came back saying that they wanted to see our license.

Moving

In mid-November we began to move our possessions slowly. Every evening, after a full day at the office and a quick supper, we threw a few things into the car and took them up the hill.

I arranged my pots and dishes on a pantry shelf, since our kitchen cupboards were not finished. We also put some canned foods on the shelves and brought a few clothes and hung them in the bedroom closet. The closet was simple but sufficient—two sections, each with one long shelf above a rod.

Wayne installed a small wood stove in the cave, a stove that he had seen in a home in the Biqaa and admired. I was afraid he had been rude when he offered to buy it from the man of the house, but the two of them had agreed immediately. We had an old music system, bought from someone who had upgraded to a real hi-fi, so we put that in the cave, too. We would have music while we sat around on the floor. I shopped for cloth and foam pads and gave them to an upholsterer with measurements for cushions.

On Lebanese Independence Day we had help, so we worked hard, but I took time to sit in the seminary kitchen with Um John and see the Independence Day celebration on television. Amin Gemayel, the new president and Bechir's brother, promised to get back every centimeter of Lebanese territory. Then the Army marched down the Corniche and crossed the Green Line, to prove that they could—that there was no line dividing Beirut. Both Um John and I wiped tears. I didn't know actually whether happiness or sadness provoked my tears. I was glad that for the first time in eight years Lebanon was celebrating its independence, but I was sad because the whole parade was the Army. I tried to imagine what a nationalistic parade would be like without soldiers and military machines, and I thought of wonderful things—orchestras, choirs, dancers, children on decorated bicycles, fine race horses and tough work horses, girls in elegant kaftans, floats carrying artisans at work, athletes running and jumping. *Maybe when there really is peace,* I thought, *if ever there is peace.*

Our helpers that day were the brawny kind and needed to be. They got our heavy pieces into the house—except the piano. Bringing the piano up the steep uneven path was a special challenge, and Wayne was still organizing the operation in his head.

The boys carried our bed up to the bedroom, then our chest of drawers and Wayne's desk. After hassling the refrigerator up the hill and plugging it in, they delivered the washer and dryer to their places upstairs in our big bathroom. They lugged up a lot of boxes and left them on the living room floor.

The dining table showed up in its place under the window—a perfect table for this spot, a rare table, designed for small houses. It appeared—when not in use—to be a mahogany cabinet. Our antique buffet came up in pieces—considerable assembly required.

After all our helpers left we built a fire in the stove. "Just to try it," Wayne said. He dragged up a couple of boxes so we could sit on them by the fire. The room was a bit dark, because we didn't have any light in there yet, and the little window was still boarded up.

"I'm too tired to move," I told him.

"Anything else we have to do before we go?"

"Well, I want to measure the couch and that chair. They're looking so shabby. Maybe we can afford to get them upholstered."

He jumped up and measured them. He always had energy for one more thing.

Sitting down again, he said, "It's already warmer here than down at the guest apartment."

"If we knew where the sheets are, we could sleep here. If we had any food."

"If we had any gas for the cook stove," he added.

"Or a bar of soap."

"It's a good thing we have another place to sleep."

Getting Taller

We named our magazine *Al-Manaa'ir,* a beautiful word for a shining image—a lampstand. *Al-Manaa'ir* is the Arabic word used in the book of Revelation, where the seven churches are called the seven golden lampstands. The suggestion came from Ghassan Khalaf, and once the editorial board had heard it, all other suggestions lost their appeal.

Nothing we had ever done had created so much energy and excitement among the young men of the Baptist community. A fine group of them had accepted the responsibility of serving on the editorial board. Each of these also wanted to write for the magazine and agreed to a process of reading one another's work and revising their articles in response to suggestions. Once a week we met in the evening, sometimes in our office and sometimes in Ras Beirut.

This board and the BP staff put all our hearts into the production of the first and trial issue. Ghassan wrote a comprehensive research article on Arabic translations of the Bible, and Waleed prepared a feature story on ministries to the garbage city in Cairo. Samuel Abd el-Shahid, hearing about our effort, wrote a letter from New Jersey telling us that such a magazine was his dearest dream for the Arab world, and he gave us a short piece of fiction. We even used his letter, placing it opposite my message introducing the magazine. We had an article about marriage, a page of helps for Sunday School teachers, a poem, an Easter sermon, book reviews, a section of news from churches in Arab countries, a Bible study, some puzzles and a story for children by a child. Black and white pictures or drawings illustrated every article and story. Michel Makhoul, the college boy who was our part-time artist, did the layout, and I paid a commercial artist to create a two-color cover design that could be used as a template.

Choosing our words carefully, we made it clear in the magazine that this was an occasional publication to be distributed only in Baptist churches. I hated this vagueness of schedule, because I wanted people to expect the magazine and look forward to it. I wanted them to contribute and take deadlines seriously, but I knew we could not legally publish a periodical. Anyway, the circumstances in Lebanon, the fact that we were using mostly volunteers to produce the magazine, and the overload our staff already carried made it doubtful that we could meet deadlines, so maybe it was better.

The first issue we delivered to the churches free—3000 copies to thirty churches in Lebanon, and a thousand each to Jordan and Egypt, with a request that they order specific numbers and pay for succeeding issues.

It was a triumph. The people loved it. On Monday morning, after the churches of Lebanon had received their copies on Sunday, our office was buzzing with reports. Each one of us had something to share. Then the phone calls started, oral and written messages were delivered, visitors popped into the office to say congratulations, to tell us how great it was, to ask when the next issue would come. Everybody on our staff got taller—Ghassan who had a right to celebrate; Michel who was still learning that his talent was useful; Jeannette who couldn't find a typo anywhere; Waleed who was shining as well as growing; Abu Issam, the most involved stock clerk in the history of publishing; a part time salesman who said, "I could sell this; too bad we can't sell this in stores." Even Abu Sleiman, who basically had just one calm, positive mood, no matter what happened.

Wayne said, "I helped; I paid the printing bill."

"Good job, Mr. Fuller," Waleed told him.

I had always enjoyed the support and affirmation of our international board of directors, but what happened in the June board meeting that year was unprecedented. Following my report to the board, the men began to comment on the magazine. Fowaz Ameish stated forcefully that it was the best Christian magazine in the Arabic language, and others said, "Of course, there's nothing close to it." And instead of the usual routine acceptance of my report, they voted to give BP a special commendation for the high quality of the materials we were producing and congratulations and thanks for *Al-Manaa'ir.*

Evidence of what the magazine could do for our community was the unsolicited materials that began to arrive. We got stories from a woman in the West Bank and from a teen-aged girl in South Lebanon. We received queries about ideas for articles. Suddenly every pew had somebody in it who wanted to write.

I was proud of the job we had done, and I loved the accolades, but it's hard to get taller with an axe hanging over your head.

Home

On Saturday morning, the fourth of December, Wayne moved the final few personal articles that we had in storage at the office. I stayed behind in the seminary guest apartment, to pick up small things and pack my clothes in suitcases; then I brought them up in the car. When I walked into the house, I sat down first and then declared that I had been running for months, no... years, and had arrived. It had been two and a half years since Wayne found this house, and we were finally in it.

After a big laugh and a hug and a little lunch, Wayne took a deserved break to play basketball with some other guys at the American Community School in West Beirut.

Totally energized, I scrubbed plaster from spots where it didn't belong, washed a window, lifted things I shouldn't have lifted, found sheets and made the bed, washed a few dishes and put them away, rinsed the bathtub, filled my chest of drawers, opened boxes of possessions I had forgotten I owned, put pretty things here and there and made a pot of lentil soup with onions and tomatoes.

When Wayne came home, we were both ravenous, and he declared the soup to be the best I had ever made. After supper, he built a fire in our wood stove, and we sat on the rug and played backgammon, the way we had imagined doing in this room. At bedtime we talked about missing our children and hoped they could come. They would love our house. I sighed and said I needed weeks to unpack all those boxes. Wayne said, "*Baseeta*," falling asleep. I feared it would be months before I had bathroom or kitchen cupboards. I tried to file my broken nails and found that each finger was sore.

On Sunday rain and sleet and snow fell all day, and the hills around us turned white—from a few kilometers up the road, all the way to the top of Mount Sunnin, and along the road to Damascus. Our house was oblivious to the cold.

General Security

I don't remember how the summons arrived in my office, only that it was a terse little note with official stamps on it. When I read it, I got cold, like a winter snowstorm had caught me in my summer clothes, but this lasted only an instant. After that I was calmer than I had been in years. If you've done everything you can to avoid a disaster and still it comes, the only thing left is just to walk through it.

I went to Ghassan Khalaf's office to tell him, "I have been summoned to General Security. Tomorrow morning. It's about *Al-Manaa'ir*."

Ghassan leaned back in his chair. I could see the little scar where the shrapnel had nicked him on the chin. He said, "What can I do, Mrs. Fuller?"

"Just go with me. I don't want them to think I'm alone in the world." Not only was Ghassan involved in the magazine but he was president of the Lebanese Baptist Convention. Besides that, he was calm. His presence would make me a lot stronger.

General Security was a place I associated with grimy floors on which men spit and then walked, chaotic cubicles where documents went astray, and long lines of anxious faces in front of impatient men whose scowls and scribbled words had enormous power. That morning, the eighth of July, however, Ghassan and I walked past all of this and were escorted up a flight of stairs and into a quiet, orderly office where the gentleman in charge of our case stood up and shook our hands. Ghassan said to him,

"God give you strength," because that's what we say in the Middle East to people who are working.

The man invited us to sit down in the two chairs facing his desk. His demeanor was courteous but definitely not cordial.

A copy of *Al-Manaa'ir* lay in the center of his desktop. I should have expected this, but I had not. The surprise shook me. Our dream-come-true magazine was about to be presented in evidence against me. He picked it up and looked at me. "Do you have a license to publish this?"

"No, sir, because I have been told that I don't need one."

"Who told you this?"

"A lawyer I consulted. He told me that a religious organization can publish anything that we distribute only in our churches, anything except a periodical, and this magazine is not a periodical. The lawyer gave me this number, the number of the law relevant to such materials."

I had to get up to place a piece of paper on his desk. He did not look at it.

In a cool, level voice, he said, "No one has a right to publish anything in Lebanon without a license. No one."

We stared at one another for a long moment. I said, "I wanted to obey Lebanese law; otherwise, I would not have gone to a lawyer."

He said nothing, but I could see that he understood my point of view.

Finally he said, "And who was this brilliant lawyer?"

I gave him the man's family name only. It was a famous name belonging to a lot of people.

"And where did he study law?"

"I didn't ask."

He said, "How many copies of the magazine do you still have?"

I gave him a number, around two hundred, as I remember. I told him that this number was not precise.

He instructed me to send them to him.

Then he asked for my passport and Lebanese residence permit and called a secretary to photocopy them. Not until she had carried them out of the room, did he explain that he was obliged to send a report to the Ministry of Information in case there was a penalty.

While we sat there, waiting for the girl to bring back my documents, I wasn't sure what to do with my eyes. I didn't want to look guilty. Neither did I want to act defiant. Ghassan found a way to break the tension. He asked the man, "Do you have other offenders or are we the only ones to make this mistake?"

"Many organizations are publishing illegally," he said. "They are poisoning the country with political propaganda. We have to stop it."

Ghassan said, "But of course Baptist Publications is not involved in politics."

He said, "I know, but you are caught in this law, so you have to obey it." Then he turned to me again, "You have to get two licenses. First, one for your publishing house. Then a license to publish a magazine."

He made it sound simple. I thought I might just as easily flap my wings and fly.

Back in my office, I realized that I had dreaded this day for years and the dread of it had been worse than the event itself. I didn't feel mistreated. On the contrary, I was aware that the General Security officer could have sent men to search our offices instead of trusting me. He could have sent trucks to take everything from our storeroom, which was probably $150,000 worth of stock. The loss would have wiped out our publishing program.

Later it occurred to me that maybe I would be deported. I said this to Wayne, who said first, "Naw. They don't care that much." And then, having almost persuaded me, he said, "We have plenty of other places we can go."

I said, "Sure, I'll just cut out my heart, eat it and go somewhere else."

But when I tried to imagine how much leaving Lebanon would hurt, I couldn't compare it to anything I knew, except maybe the pain of living in Lebanon.

Mary, the Dragon-Slayer

When it was time for action Mary kept her focus. Refraining even from saying, "I told you so," she began to plot. What she planned was the Twentieth Century Crusades, and she did not intend for either of us to be a martyr. Lebanon was a religious country; she would not let a law made to stop political revolutionaries be used to stop religious literature. She would sue whoever it was who so misused the law. She mapped strategies, laying them out in steps. She would block General Security's report; it would never reach The Ministry of Information. If the mission still refused to become a society, we would not worry about them; we would form a commercial company. No need to think about the tax issue now. We would solve it when we came to it. She fired off lists of documents I must bring, but first I had to call a meeting of the Near East Baptist Mission. Everyone had to be there. Everyone. I started to feel that I had made her day.

About that possible penalty which the General Security officer had mentioned, she said, "*Baseeta*, maybe 1000 LL."

"So little?"

"Frances, you haven't committed a crime."

"Are you sure they won't deport me?"

"No way!" she shouted. "Over my dead body!"

She brought to the mission meeting a letter that she had prepared, putting the right words into our mouths. Addressed to the General Security office, the letter said that the mission, not Frances Fuller, was responsible for BP and for everything BP did. Her rationale in front of the mission was: "They might deport one of you, but they won't deport the whole NEBM." She wanted everyone in the mission to sign this letter, and they did.

She scared us a little. She said that there was an apparent anti-evangelical mood in the government. Someone was accusing missionaries of working for the CIA. Our friend Sam Yagnazar, head of the Lebanon Bible Society, was being investigated for some kind of subversive activity. Sam was an Armenian with Iranian citizenship, and his wife was British. All of us knew these people, and we knew that such an accusation was ridiculous.

"Exactly," Mary said. "This is what makes it so scary. If a man can get in trouble when he is innocent, what if he breaks the law?"

To be believed at last by my colleagues was some relief, and to have Mary at work on my problem made me strong. I went on with my projects.

Preparing for the best of all possible solutions, I wrote an article called "How to Write an Article for *Al-Manaa'ir.*" It was designated for the next issue.

The Occupation Army

On the only road between our office in Monsourieh and our home in Beit Meri we drove through a broad intersection where a second road angled off down the hill—to the river in the bottom of the canyon and on to Ras el-Metn and the towns on top of the opposite mountain. Some people just called it the road to Kachuk, which was a small Christian campground not far down the road.

Opposite the road to Kachuk stood a lovely Lebanese house, abandoned for reasons I didn't know, though I suspected that it would not be fun to live there, with a roadblock just outside the gate—sandbags, barbed wire, armed men, traffic jams.

In the several years that we had traveled through this intersection regularly, five different armies had manned this roadblock. First, the Kata'ib—the Phalangist militia, which Wayne always called "the local boys." Then the Syrians. The Lebanese Forces, which was several Christian militias combined who had driven the Syrians from our mountain. The Lebanese Army, which was then calling itself "The United Army of the United Country." And now the Israelis.

Each of these armies had its own personality, and a new one always required the population to make adjustments. I thought sometimes that the entire history of the war could be told by talking about the roadblocks, their locations, the behavior of their occupants, the people who had disappeared or been shot there, the new animosities provoked by roadblocks.

Everybody noticed immediately the super carefulness of the Israelis. They never stood in the middle of the intersection or unprotected by armor. They stood beside the road with a tank behind them. At our intersection there were two tanks, one in the gate of the graceful stone house and another across the road, blocking the way to Kachuk. Rolls of barbed wire obstructed access to the intersection in all three directions.

Tension at the checkpoint was palpable. Going home, tired and hungry, I would come to this roadblock and feel that any wrong move would create shooting, and everybody would die except this nervous army.

One afternoon I arrived there after work, and across the intersection, against the hill, sat a crushed and burned automobile. No part of it was higher than two feet off the ground; the vehicle might have been put through a trash compacter, or squashed by a tank. Quiet prevailed in the intersection, the traffic moving as though on ice.

The Israeli unit assigned to the intersection bivouacked nearby on the road to Kachuk. At sundown every day they retreated to their camp. They even removed the tank and the barbed wire from across the road to Kachuk. This behavior mystified me. Why would they scrutinize and control us so totally during the day, and at night lose all interest in who went up the road?

Another mystery was the gunfire in the middle of the night. At first residents thought the area was under attack, but it turned out that the Israelis were shooting. No one shot back; they shot alone into the trees and rocks of the canyon, in the darkness.

In the morning, sometime after sunrise but not on any schedule, they came back to the roadblock. They came shooting. They had left the intersection, so now they took it again, as though it had been occupied by an enemy during the night. The lovely house they considered a special hazard, apparently. The tank advanced on it, firing. Foot soldiers crawled close and lobbed in grenades. I speak as a witness.

The first time, coming down the road on the way to work, I thought I had driven into a street battle. First, a flurry of gunfire around the curve, and suddenly a tank rumbling across, guns blazing. No one had warned me. I screeched to a halt, and another car nearly hit mine from the rear. In front of me soldiers were advancing across the road on their bellies. I waited, while explosions blew debris out the vaulted windows of the house.

At first all this strange behavior drove the population slightly crazy. Seven years of "events," followed by the thunderous bombardment of the invasion, had made people rather sensitive to loud noises. School buses turned around and took the children home again. People on the way to work detoured and tried to get down the hill by narrow and devious paths through forests and gardens.

People talked it over. Some said, "It is a war game. They practice."

"With live ammunition? On a busy road? And all of us on the way to work?"

"And the kids on the school buses?"

"They don't care."

"Maybe they want to frighten us, terrorize us."

"No, they are the ones afraid."

"But this is Christian Lebanon. They took our men for special training. We have a common enemy."

"Look, they trust no one. They are paranoid."

"We should be careful. They shoot first and look later to see who's dead."

On the mountain a lot of people who welcomed the Israelis in the summer were griping their heads off by Christmas—about the purposeless checkpoint on the Beit Meri road, about their staying so long and acting like they were among enemies, and especially about the constant fighting in the Shouf Mountains and their refusal to disarm the combatants.

Occupying a country, I thought, is like taking someone's house. They always want it back very soon. Already people were saying, "If they don't go soon, we will know that we are another West Bank."

I mentioned to a Lebanese friend that an occupation army can wear out its welcome in a hurry.

"In about three days," she said.

Neighbors

Bishara and his mother were the first visitors in our new home, and from the instant they walked in we felt welcome in The Hara.

A fine-looking young man, with an athletic build and skin both dark and ruddy, Bishara smiled a lot, showing perfect white teeth. His diminutive mother, with limbs like twigs, was a tightly packaged bundle of energy. She moved quickly, spoke rapidly, and her wrinkled little face twinkled and scowled and threatened and flashed friendly messages.

They sat in the cave with us that evening sipping tea, as we all repeatedly welcomed one another and talked about our families. Their eldest, Fouad, lived with his wife and children in the second floor of their house, and Tony and Bishara lived with their parents. While Abu Fouad worked on his land—a lot of it, all covered with vineyards, orchards and vegetable gardens—Fouad went to a factory each day where he was an accountant, and Tony and Bishara were Kata'ib militiamen, Tony a high-ranking officer. They had no other occupation, and the war had already consumed a significant chunk of their lives.

When we showed them what we had done to the house, Um Fouad, who spoke no English, kept saying, "*Afaiki*," meaning "Good for you," and Bishara said, "You have saved a piece of our history."

This was the beginning of a real friendship. Numerous times in the next two years we ate Sunday lunch with Abu and Um Fouad in their home, maybe a hundred and fifty yards from us, at the end of the road and down the slope. Um Fouad made sumptuous meals and Bishara was inclined to invite people without warning her, but it never seemed to matter. There was always a crowd around their table—mostly extended family but sometimes other neighbors.

* * *

Two cute kids came to see us one night, dressed in costumes. It was the *Eid* of Barbarra, a Lebanese version of Halloween. We could have given them a treat at the door, but Wayne insisted that they sit in the cave and talk with us. The teen-aged girl was escorting her cousin, a handsome boy with big dark eyes and thick hair. He must have been seven or eight. The girl said that Abboud had not wanted to come to our house.

The boy looked embarrassed by this and explained to us in Arabic, "She said, let's go to the foreigners' house, and I didn't want to, because I don't speak foreign."

Wayne did everything he could to keep them. He asked questions about their families and about school. When I gave them bags of nuts, he went to the kitchen to get Pepsis.

As soon as Wayne left the room, Abboud looked at his cousin and said, "He's nice, though he's Egyptian."

She corrected him, but the child had trouble believing that Wayne was an American.

* * *

Soon after we moved into the house, Wayne traveled to Jordan on business, so I was alone in the house, reading in bed at well past ten p.m. when I was startled by a pounding on the front door. The sound continued while I put on slippers and a robe and went down the stairs. At the door, I asked in Arabic, "Who's there?" and a woman's voice shouted, "Lulu, your neighbor."

With panic in her face and voice, the woman told me, "My baby is sick. She's burning up, and I don't have a car. Could you take us to a doctor?"

Hurriedly I dressed, and when I stopped the car at the bottom of the long steps up to her house, Lulu was standing there, with the child in a blanket. Maha was a beautiful little girl, less than a-year-old, with fair skin and pale, softly curling hair. Her cheeks were flushed, and she was in fact "burning up."

When I asked Lulu where she wanted to go, she said, "In the middle of the night, I don't know where to find a doctor."

By the time we were up to the Maronite church at the end of our road, I remembered that a young pediatrician—our former landlord's son—lived in the building where we used to live on the top of the hill. So we did not have far to go, and the doctor admitted us to a little office in his home. Then, of course, we had to drive around a while to discover which pharmacy was open, and it was midnight when I fell into bed again, happy that I had been of some use and was getting to know my neighbors.

Lulu and her children, and sometimes her husband George, became frequent visitors in our house, and Lulu liked to boast to others in the community that I loved Maha and would do anything for her. The other two children, Terez and Lubnan (named for the country, "so if Lubnan dies, we still have Lubnan," George told me with his ear-splitting laugh). Both were olive-skinned, totally unlike Maha. Terez had the tightest curls I have ever seen. We had a platform rocker that turned in complete circles, and the kids considered it an amusement apparatus. Lubnan would push the chair until he got momentum and then jump in. Sometimes Terez fought him for possession, and Lulu would threaten bodily harm to make them stop.

The children had a hard time learning to say our name, and Lubnan always called us "the Americans." He would pound on our door and shout, "*Ya*, American!" emphasizing the last syllable, pronouncing it like "can." One day when Wayne and I came home from work, Lubnan and his cousin were sitting on the little step in front of our door, small hands on trousered knees. They said, "We came to visit you, but you weren't home, so we just waited."

We told them, "Welcome, come in," and they sat down and had refreshments with us like two adults. They didn't even play with the rocker.

George's brother Boutros, with Jaqueline (pronounced Jack-leen) and their kids, lived in the apartment under Lulu and George's house. In front of their shabby rooms they had a large patio with a clothesline and a grapevine, a nice place for drinking coffee in the afternoon. Jaqueline looked fifty, maybe because of decaying teeth and a couple of gaping holes in her mouth, but she had a new baby and must have been at least ten years younger. The way her tummy bulged, though she was not pregnant, worried me. In her baggy dresses, always working, carrying the baby on her hip while taking clothes off the line or turning food in the skillet with the other hand, she looked poor and overworked and careless and cheerful. I liked her. She was relaxed in her friendliness. She never complained about anything.

George and Boutros' mother, who had the surprising name Susanna, also lived with Boutros and Jaqueline. She became my favorite neighbor. She was old and plump, with a smooth, sweet face. Her age gave her the right to say what she wanted to say—to anyone, and I found her bluntness both endearing and instructive. Once she followed me up the hill as I came home from work and walked into my kitchen with me, exclaiming in a shocked voice, "You have dirty dishes!" I laughed before defending myself for leaving two breakfast bowls and some cups in the sink. She told me that her son Boutros was lazy; I had thought he just couldn't find a job. "No," she said, "He just doesn't want the jobs he finds." Then she added, "Not George. He will do anything to make a lira."

Once when I was getting into my car, Susanna was strolling on the road and we stopped to talk. She asked me, "Where are you going?"

I happened to be going to see Georgette. I told her, "I am going to visit a dear friend. Come with me. She would love you very much."

She stood there, her hair white in the sun, her face soft and pink. "Where does she live?"

"In Nabay."

"Where is that?"

I explained that it was on the hill above Antelias and told her I would get there through Broummana.

She said, "*Habibti* (my dear), I didn't see all of Beit Meri yet." And she wouldn't go.

One day I saw her squatting in the field across the road. Big guns were banging over in the Shouf, and she seemed to be oblivious, digging in the ground and putting something into a pot. I walked down and squatted beside her.

She said, "*Ahlan, habibti.*" Welcome, dear.

I said, "I came to see what you are doing."

She said, "I'm picking *hindbi* and praying. Between the children and the guns, I would go crazy if I couldn't pick *hindbi* and pray."

"I pray a lot, too," I told her, "but maybe I should learn to pick *hindbi*."

"What do you say when you pray?"

I found this awkward, to repeat words that I say when I pray, but I said a few phrases from the Lord's Prayer and then told her that I pray for my children to be well and for Lebanon.

"*Afaiki,*" she said, "but you don't need to pick *hindbi*. I will pick for you."

I watched her old, skillful hands. The leaves of the wild *hindbi* plants lay flat against the ground, and she ran a little spade underneath them, making scratching noises in the rocky soil, and then lifted them up.

"Go get a pot," she told me, "and I will give you some for your dinner. Look, there's enough here for everybody in Beit Meri." While she worked and I squatted beside her, big booms continued across the canyon. I told her that I had never eaten *hindbi,* but I liked *khubaizi* very much. (*Khubaizi* is mallow in the Arabic-English dictionary, but I have never used this word.)

"*Khubaizi* is everywhere," she told me.

That night I sauteed the *hindbi* leaves with onions. Because they were a bit tough, I simmered them a few minutes. I found that I liked them with lemon juice, but they were too bitter for Wayne.

Not long after that, as I was driving into the village in the afternoon, a woman motioned from a balcony, asking me to stop. Then she ran down to the road carrying a big plastic bag full of *khubaizi*. She told me it was a gift "from all your neighbors."

I was so amazed I couldn't find the right words to say.

She said, "We went together, five of us, to pick, and somebody said, Mrs. Fuller likes *khubaizi* but, *haram,* she has to work all day, so we picked for you. Everybody helped."

I thought, that's a true and wise saying—"the neighbor before the house."

Tours

The Shatila refugee camp was not some separate entity, but a part of Beirut, a city slum, a ghetto with ragged edges—disorderly and damaged and permanent. Because it would bewilder any outsider, Jean drove his car ahead of me, escorting me to the spot where I would be met. At the corner where we turned into the camp, a soldier watched from a high, sandbagged perch, the Italian flag flying beside him. This was the post the Israeli army had occupied when the right-wing militias swarmed through the camp, attacking unarmed civilians. I drove carefully, following Jean through the dusty street, avoiding holes, scattered chunks of concrete and a running child. My landmarks for the way back would be these gaping broken walls and these open spaces where rubble had been cleared away.

Trying to park, we got involved in a traffic crisis, created by our two cars, a horse-drawn cart and an Italian tank.

Um Na'im herself met us in the street, extending her hand and saying, "*Ahlan wa sahlan*" in a strong, cheerful voice. She was a tall woman, as tall as I, and about my age, wearing a limp, flowered dress, down to her ankles. She walked with straight shoulders, her head always erect, and that smooth strong gait which I had learned in Jordan to associate with women who carried water on their heads. Her face was rough and seamed, unacquainted with oils or make-up, and framed by a white scarf tied under her chin. Her hand in mine was strong and dry. As I grasped it, I remembered what Jean had told me about her—that she had borne seven children in refugee camps, after carrying one in her arms into exile.

We had parked in front of a little shop whose owner wanted us to come inside, so we took time to look at his wares—cheap pots and dishes spread out on packing crates, covered with dust. I said to him, "How is business? Prosperous, I hope."

His smile faded slightly as he replied, "Praise God, not bad." He was a young man in a crisp, clean blue shirt. On the sidewalk several children with runny noses stared at me, and an old man, pale and thin, stared at nothing.

After I assured Jean that I could find my way home, he left us, and Um Na'im, watching him drive off, said, "Jean is like my son."

The wonder of this remark hung in the air, as the two of us turned and walked through an alley, picking our way around half-dried mudholes and strewn rubble, toward her house, experiencing some awkwardness on the way, because she felt conflicting needs to lead me and to walk behind me. We entered a door in a wall, which, I noted, had fresh mortar between the concrete blocks, then past huts, all similar to one another, concrete blocks or concrete covered with plaster, both plaster and concrete gouged by flying shrapnel, Arabic scribbles on the damaged walls, corrugated tin roofs, some held down with stones. Um Na'im's one-room house was ready for a gathering, with straight chairs around the walls—probably gathered from several houses. Two crude couches sat at right angles to one another, opposite the door, and a thin mat covered the middle of the concrete floor.

Um Na'im was eager to tell me stories, and I wanted to hear them all. I took out my pen and little notebook as she began, "The day of the massacre..." I stopped her and suggested that we begin at the beginning, so she shifted to 1948 and in quick, forceful sentences, took me to a village "one hour by car from Acco." (Acco was a city on the coast, only about twenty-five miles from the Lebanese city of Tyre.) She had no idea of the population of her community. "A small village. Just peasants, farmers."

"We grew a little wheat. We ground it and kept it in the house for winter. It was so good. We grew lentils, all kinds of vegetables. We had olives and figs and grapes."

Both of us were sitting on one of the couches. It was hard and covered with a worn cloth. As we talked, the room filled up with women and children, young mothers with the wide hips of Palestinian women and old, wrinkled women, wearing black, all looking at me expectantly. I felt suddenly that my visit might be a mistake, that maybe they thought I could make some difference.

"No," she told me, "we didn't farm someone else's land. It was ours. A small farm, but ours."

She kicked off her plastic sandals and pulled her feet up under her skirt, sitting in what we Americans might call "Indian style." I noticed that one of her eyes was smaller than the other and clouded. Beyond her, against the far wall, I could see the family's possessions, bundled and stacked. Like the tents of refugees in the Baqa, when I had visited twenty years earlier, her room was clean and neat. One large crack zigzagged, like a streak of black lightning, down one of the whitewashed walls. Cold came in through two shattered windows, small and high.

"How was your house there different from this house?" It was a small point, but I wanted to visualize. Also I had read that the refugees exaggerated what they had in Palestine, all claiming to have villas with gardens around them.

Not Um Na'im. "It was two rooms," she said, "a rock house with two rooms."

"Was it one level or was it an old Arab house with a place for animals below and a higher level for the people?"

"Yes. Yes." She was delighted that I knew such a house. She said, "You have been to Palestine!"

I explained that I had seen such houses in Jordan, and this led us away from the subject.

A young woman arrived carrying an infant girl and towing a curly-haired toddler, a boy. Her oval, smooth face might have been pretty except for the dark circles under her eyes. Um Na'im told me, "This is my daughter, Al-Moeeny," and mother and children settled near us on the other couch.

Because Al-Moeeny means "the helper," I commented that it must be nice to have a name with such a beautiful meaning.

She turned her baby tummy-down across her knees, looked at me with brown, oddly tilted eyes, and said, "Where is the benefit? How did it help me when my husband was slaughtered in front of me?" When I didn't answer, she went on, "He was holding our son, and they took the child from him and gave him to me and then shot my husband."

Um Na'im stopped her. "We are talking now about Palestine. We will come to all that." And she continued her story, going back to the village of farmers in northern Palestine.

"We heard the Jews were going to kill us. My husband fled. Most of the young men fled, but some stayed. Then the soldiers came. We put up a white flag. They told us to come out of our houses and sat us down under the olive trees. When we were all there, then they told us to get up and go to Lubnan. They began shooting at our feet, saying, "*Yallah*, go. Go to Lubnan."

"Did they shoot some of the people?"

"No. They just shot the ground."

"So it would have been O.K., if your husband had stayed."

"Oh no. They would have killed him already. They killed the young men they found in the houses."

"How many?" I asked, but then I was surprised by her precise answer.

"Seven," she said, holding up seven fingers. "Two of them were brothers. When they realized they were going to die, they embraced one another." She threw her arms around herself to demonstrate. "And when they were shot they fell down together, like this." She tipped sideways, clutching her own shoulders. "Their parents saw the bodies; they were holding each other."

She went on talking, but I missed a couple of sentences, because I was still seeing those two boys fall together, clutching one another in death. My sons, Jim and Dwight, might have done the same.

"We walked," she was saying, as I began scribbling in my notebook again, "from 11:00 in the morning until—I don't know. It was dark."

"What were you thinking, I mean about leaving Palestine and going to Lebanon?"

"We didn't think anything, except that they not kill us."

Al-Moeeny broke in. "Did you tell her about the massacre?"

"Not yet."

The little boy was crying, sitting on the floor. His mother said, "Hush, Ahmad," and he hushed.

"The weather was hot that day, very hot, and we had no food or water. I was carrying my daughter, one year old. I had five piasters. That's all the money we left Palestine with." Spreading the fingers, she held up one hand, a large, hard-working hand. "Five piasters. I bought grapes from a farmer for one piaster and fed my baby."

I had heard so many of these stories when we lived in Jordan, all of them the same, all of them different. We went on, through the reunion with her husband at a Red Cross camp near Tyre, through nights of sleeping on the ground, moving into tents, being shuttled from camp to camp, having babies, gathering them under her skirts like a hen when the rain came through the tent, and finally settling there in Shatila and working for Lebanese Christians in Beirut, "very nice people, good to me. They used to visit us, right here in this house, before the troubles started."

The troubles. War with Israel. War with Lebanon.

"Life got very hard then. We couldn't go out to work. We were hungry. Sometimes we had no water. And we were afraid, always afraid. We would hear the guns and everybody would run helter-skelter to the shelters."

I knew about their underground shelters, little tunnels bored through the rocky ground. In 1976, under the rubble of Tel az-Zaater, I had entered one of these, a dark, smelly, gravelly space like the burrow of an animal, too small even for young children to stand up in, just large enough for adults to crawl into, one person behind the other, and go out in the opposite order. I had become panicky, without any bombs falling, because my back was bent and I was afraid to touch the ground in that intense darkness.

Lebanese had seen the existence of these underground shelters as evidence of wicked intentions. While the Israelis claimed that the Palestinians armed and prepared themselves to fight Israel, the Lebanese, like the Jordanians, felt the eminent danger of this armed and alien presence inside their land. Many of them believed there was a plot, a conspiracy of the big powers, including America—the Palestinians would fight for a share of power in Lebanon, joined by Muslims who didn't like the system; Lebanon would become the new Palestine. This would solve a lot of problems. Only the Lebanese Christians would lose. (Hearing this I remembered that in 1969 or maybe 1970 a Palestinian commander down in the valley, had told me, "The big story is going to be in Lebanon." I knew already that whole guerrilla groups were moving from Jordan to Lebanon and assumed that they were looking only for a place to stand while they fought Israel.) For this reason, the theory went, Israel had destabilized Lebanon, to start the ball moving in this direction, but the plot had not worked. The Christians had been tougher than anybody expected. Boys named George and Samir and Fufu might wear gold bracelets and look like playboys and have an obvious preference for cruising on the mountain roads, but they would fight. They had let the world know that they could be courageous, even brutal.

Knowing all this, I had for a long time wanted to ask, and this was my chance. "When did you build those tunnels?"

"Long ago." Um Na'im said. She sat on the couch, her body twisted toward me. She kept pushing her white scarf down closer to her face, and it kept creeping back, exposing curly graying hair.

"Before the first problems in 1973?"

"Yes, before that."

"Why?"

"Because we were afraid."

"Of whom? Why?"

"Of everybody. Because nothing is ours." She turned more sharply and struck the whitewashed wall with her strong hand, thumping it again and again as she said, "Look. This is my house. We built this house with our hands. We bought the stones we put in it. But the land under this house," she gestured toward the floor with a hacking motion, "the land is not ours. We built our house on someone else's land, because we had no choice, no place to go."

She stared at me, and I stared at her. "We always knew," she said, "someone could come and say go." She made a shooing motion with her hand. "It happened to us in Palestine, where we had a right. For sure it would happen in another country where we had no right."

Without writing this down, I would never forget it. I had often explained this simple principle to Americans when talking about refugees or the homeless—that people take up space, that a place to be is fundamental to life on earth. Without a home, people go crazy; they do self-destructive things; they become everybody's enemy.

Al-Moeeny was walking around the room, patting her baby on the back. It occurred to me that her husband had been dead longer than this baby had lived.

The call to prayer floated in through the open doors and windows. I didn't notice until Um Na'im said, "*Laa illah il allah.*" Then I heard it from the mosque, "*Laa illah il allah,*" and acknowledged her words. "True," I said, "there is no God but God."

We waited through the whining, recorded chant and then I turned to Um Na'im again and said, "What did you do down there in the tunnel, while the bombs were falling?" I had wondered about this when the planes were diving on Shatila and Sabra, remembering the horror of those tunnels.

Without a moment's hesitation, she said, "I prayed. The men were outside, defending us. I could hear the planes attacking; I could hear the guns shooting at them. So, I asked God to keep my son for me and some Jewish mother's son for her."

This is not in my notes. It is written on my brain. This woman could surprise me. She must have surprised Jean. My countrymen would be surprised, if they could spend an hour with her, but they might be uncomfortable with the surprise. She would complicate their opinions.

Al-Moeeny sat down again. She said, "I begged them not to kill him. I put my hands on the soldier's arm and begged him. And then he shot him six or seven times—in the face, the body, his hand."

Her baby started screaming, but she kept talking. "Ali was on the ground, all his blood running in the dust, and my tears just dried up in my eyes. We ran away, and I knew he was dead, and I couldn't weep."

We all sat in silence, in the shadow of her shock. I considered that detail: she had noticed his hand. I wrote it down. I wondered if he was buried in one of the mass graves, but I didn't want to ask. I said, "Where did you go?"

"To Al-Hammand Street. There are Lebanese Muslims there. They kept us and fed us."

Other women started talking about the massacre. Sometimes several of them talked at once. Their accounts were chaotic, like the event itself. Each person had one tiny confusing piece of the story, and these pieces came to me scrambled, like a jigsaw puzzle. No one knew when the militiamen entered Shatila. Women were surprised in the kitchen, at the clothesline. Children were playing in the streets. There was a lot of shooting. People hid. The shooting stopped for a while. People came out and were surprised again. Young men were executed against the walls. Little boys and girls were shot running away, groups of them in the alleys. (I wrote frantically, meaning to sort it out later. Um Na'im seemed to take satisfaction in watching the scribbles grow.) Throats were slit. Bodies were thrown on the garbage heaps. Women were raped before they were killed. Swollen bellies were slit open. Babies, born and unborn were not spared. (Al-Moeeny was lucky.) No one knew when it ended either. People who fled cowered in neighboring streets, not knowing when to come back. They tried, and the smell drove them away again. They vomited, trying to identify corpses.

A woman across the room from us became emotional and kept talking, the same words over and over, drowning out the others. Um Na'im motioned to her and said, "Bring the boy." She led a child about seven years old across the room, stood him in front of me and lifted his shirt. A thick red line of scar tissue, not quite straight and crisscrossed by the marks of stitches, ran down the middle of his chest to his waist, turned a corner raggedly and traveled around the curve of his left side.

"A bayonet," his mother screamed. "They grabbed this child in the street and cut him open."

My breath left me. Questions stuck in my throat. The boy looked cold and embarrassed. He was barefooted.

I told him, *"Al-hamdillah ala salaame, ya sabi,"* which means "Praise God for your health, little boy." His chin trembled, and he said nothing.

"And for your health," his mother said, speaking automatically, her voice cooler.

Finally, after we were exhausted, I looked around the room and said, "What do you want now—from Lebanon? From America?"

Only Um Na'im answered. Quietly, she said, "Nothing. We want to go home."

"Nothing," she said. It should be nothing. People do it every day. The U.N. Declaration of Human Rights states that every person has this right—to leave home and go back.

But when Um Na'im said this, something that I had long suspected hit me like the blow of a fist. They never would. Surely they knew it themselves but could not speak a truth so enormous, so hideous. I shut my eyes, trying to keep tears from coming, to stabilize myself, to breathe calmly, and when I opened them again every woman in the room was weeping.

* * *

Outside the gate I turned in the wrong direction and wandered past the colossal wreck of Cite Sportive, then realized my mistake and made a U turn. At some point I noticed that I was passing a brilliant vegetable stand and thought with some disconnected part of my brain that I should buy something for dinner but kept driving, feeling that my going had been useless because for years already I had known everything, had known that it was hopeless, that this hopelessness condemned everybody—the Palestinians, the Lebanese, the Israelis. I had known even that there were no good guys and bad guys in this war. There were still friends, the people

I loved because I knew them. I hoped none of these people I loved had gone to Shatila with a gun and a bayonet. I supposed that I would never be sure anymore.

Sitting with Um Na'im in her one room had had a disturbing effect on my conscience. People kept coming to visit us, and every visitor wanted a tour of our house. Neighbors who had seen everything and heard the spiel brought relatives on Sunday afternoons. ("My cousins from Jounieh are here; could we show them the house?") Wayne conducted the tours: upstairs bedroom, bathroom-sans-counter-top, closet and office, the downstairs kitchen with doorless cupboards, walk-in pantry, furnace room, toilet. He explained that he had bought wood for cupboard doors in the U.S, where it was cheap, and it was now aboard a ship somewhere on the Atlantic. Describing the process of transforming the house, he used the conspicuous square opening that he had left just above the bottom stair, where the final ceiling tile belonged. Through this opening everyone could see the fiberglass insulation that helped our house retain so efficiently either cool or warm air. He explained that between the insulation and the concrete roof he had left an air space, because air was also an insulator. Hearing it all, accepting compliments, I grew weary, self-conscious, guilty, especially when the door into the camps slammed shut again.

The Syrians decided to get the Palestinians under their control and lay siege to Shatila, using the Shia militia called Amal to do their dirty work. Hearing the booming, day in and day out, I imagined another chapter of misery down there—the women and children in those little burrows without even tea or cookies or stories. Jean comforted me with some positive thinking. He reminded me that Um Na'im's son had found a new and purposeful life and was prepared to help others. "And don't forget there is a whole Christian library in Shatila—Bibles, many books and all those story leaflets you gave us."

I acknowledged this small gain.

He said, "We do what we can do, Mrs. Fuller, and we leave the rest to God."

* * *

In time I realized that, just as the massacre in the camp exposed the raw evil in human beings and threatened to unravel my last scrap of confidence in the people around me, what happened afterwards gave me a glimpse of the amazing possibilities that still existed. I heard Jean say, "I could go and live with the Palestinians," and I heard Um Na'im say, "Jean is like a son to me." Twice there seemed to be hope for the human race, and Jesus sounded sane.

Big Decisions and Narrow Escapes

The Oldest Man

The oldest man in the village was at lunch with us at Abu Fouad's, wearing, as always, his baggy trousers and a red tarboush. He sat at the far end of the table from us, where we hardly noticed him, until about the time we had finished the main course and Um Fouad was bringing out platters of fruit. That's when the old man began to make soft groaning noises, sitting upright against the back of his chair, wiping tears with the back of his hand. Fouad's wife handed him a clean napkin; Abu Fouad asked him what was wrong. He mumbled something about his brothers, and Bishara said, "He is crying for his brothers who all died in the war. He always does this when he drinks *arak*. One glass, and he feels like crying."

"In which war did they die?" I asked.

And he said, "The Big War," which is what the Lebanese call The World War. He checked with his father and then added, "The First Big War. A lot of people died in Lebanon, you know."

I did know. Most of them died of starvation, when the allies set a blockade around Lebanon to starve out the Turkish Army. The Turks simply took the food of the Lebanese. But before that the Turks had assassinated a lot of Lebanese who had opposed them.

I looked at the old man, now blotting his eyes with the napkin. It had been almost sixty-five years since he lost his brothers. I was amazed for only a moment, then became sad thinking that sixty-five years down the road someone would cry because his brother died in the Shouf Mountains in 1983. Maybe the reason would be unknown or nonsensical by then, in the inconceivable year of 2048, or maybe the feud now tearing the Shouf would be more bitter than ever. But, either way, and with or without a glass of *arak*, the old grief might come back.

Later, I noticed this ancient man again and again, sitting stone-faced, always wearing his red tarboush, on a balcony facing the Shouf, where guns were booming. I would drive into the village in the afternoon, see him as I passed his house, and wonder what he thought sitting there, looking permanent and dusty like one of the carved faces at Rushmore. He stared, but not at the road or passersby. One could honk and wave and raise a cloud of dust without making him blink. I don't think he saw the changing moods and colors of the hills. Great booms rolled off their slopes and smoke went up, but he never noticed these events any more than Mt. Sunnin noticed. Then one day I was standing on my roof to look across the canyon, when he came walking up the road with his knobby stick, his back bent and legs bowed. I ran for my camera, but by the time I was ready to click he had passed the house. I got only a picture of his back, leaning over the stick, his old fashioned trousers drooping under his crotch, his stockinged legs like black parentheses. I wished I could talk with him. About the wars he remembered. About his brothers and how they died. About where he was when this happened. What did the people of Beit Meri el-Hara think or feel or remember back then when they looked across the canyon into the Shouf?

Shortly afterwards, without warning or fuss, his heart stopped. I was surprised; he had looked eternal. They buried him the same day in the white shirt and the pantaloons and his black leather slippers and red tarboush. The village mourned him, following his casket up the road toward the church, and I mourned for a piece of Lebanon's history, lost forever. I had nothing but my questions and this snapshot of him hobbling away. In his pantaloons with his tarboush and his crooked stick, he made a picture of the past, disappearing.

Yet, the past was always with us in Lebanon. It pressed on us, explaining prejudices, contributing to the strife. The loss—my loss—was about the chance to understand the pressure.

I lived in a house, part of which had stood for a hundred and fifty years. It was full of voices and stories that I strained to hear and interpret. It occurred to me that someone had lived in it when the old man's brothers were dying. It had stood here long before that, had been facing the Shouf mountains in the 1840s when the Christians and Druze were fighting, as now. I wished I could know who built it and what it meant to the first woman who lived in it. Was she happy there? Did she love the view—blue sky showing under the *snobars* along the top of the mountain, the way shadows came up between the flanks of the hills, defining their shapes? (There would have been no towering electric pole, no crisscross of wires, no satellite dish across the river.) Did she give birth here? Die in one of these rooms, on the dirt floor? Surely she was incapable of imagining an ignorant, twentieth century American or thinking that such a person would ever live in *her* house. But I didn't know much more about her than she knew about me, and I was so busy being me that I had no time for research and imagination. The old man's life had overlapped ours; he had been there down the road from us for months, and all I learned was that he cried for his brothers sixty-five years after they died.

A Missed Appointment

It was Monday morning, April 18. My desk calendar, prepared on Friday afternoon, was open on my desk. I had an appointment at the American Embassy at 1:00 p.m. to take care of some "passport business." (I wasn't telling people what I meant to do. Actually, I was going to ask for a second passport, because I needed to go to Israel. I had needed to go many times before, but always I had resisted and found another way to do my work. I couldn't afford an Israeli stamp in my passport.) Joseph Karam had advised me that at this time of day he could get the job done quickly. The plan I had made was to leave the office about 10:00 a.m. so that I could take care of several errands in West Beirut on the way. The most important of these errands was a chat with Colin Chapman at the InterVarsity office.

At that time Gerritt Kamphuis, a Canadian citizen, had been serving perhaps a year as our sales manager. Having come to Lebanon for another purpose that had not worked out, he had volunteered his services to BP and had worked hard and successfully. At 9:30 that morning Gerritt came into my office and asked if I had time to talk with him about a problem. I looked at my watch and told him, "I have half an hour."

The problem was our salesman—a converted Muslim whom both of us wanted to encourage by giving him a job. We wanted especially to help him grow spiritually and become a part of the Christian community. But his job was not going well. Sales receipts were poor, and someone had accused him of inappropriate behavior at a West Beirut book fair. Though we had already spoken to him about specific problems and he had responded with humility, even contrition, the old patterns had continued.

At 10:00 a.m. we had not begun to figure out what to do. Gerritt wanted to act. I could see this in his bony face, with its bristle of beard on the chin, and in his posture. Even his stringy muscles wanted to move. He paced in front of my desk. He said, "We talked before and nothing happened."

I knew he was right, but I hated firing people and would always try to find a way to make them succeed. Whatever we were going to do, Gerritt wanted to do it immediately. "I've got all these things coming up, and I have to depend on him or get somebody else, and right now I can't depend on him."

I knew I had to stay in the office until we found a solution, so in the back of my mind I began to make alterations in my schedule. Maybe I could postpone some of my errands until another day. Or, it occurred to me, I could turn my schedule around, start out at noon, be at the embassy by 1:00 as planned, and try to do the other work afterwards.

Finally, we made a decision about our salesman. We were not happy, but we were sure we were right. We would have to dismiss him. We planned just how we would do that. I would write the official letter, and Gerritt would give it to him. Then Gerritt would invite him for dinner that night. I too would make a specific effort to assure him of our ongoing friendship. Among other things, I would try to help him find a job that was less public.

Gerritt thanked me for my time and went down the hall to his office. It was 12 o'clock. An electric buzzer sounded, and the seminary students began chattering in the hall downstairs. Abu John's cowbell clanged the signal that lunch was on the tables. The smell of garlic drifted upstairs. There was still time to get to the embassy, but I didn't want to go all the way to West Beirut and not see Colin Chapman. Otherwise I would have to go twice. So I made a phone call to the InterVarsity office. The secretary told me that Colin had just left and would not return in the afternoon.

With Monday's schedule wrecked, I studied the list of work for Tuesday. Maybe I could get most of it done today before I went home; then I could go to the embassy tomorrow. First of all I would write that difficult letter.

While I scribbled it on a yellow pad, I ate my lunch—the apple and peanuts I had expected to munch in the car. Satisfied with my draft, I put paper and carbons into my typewriter, noticing when I glanced out the window that a small rain cloud had appeared over the far edge of Beirut. It cast a shadow over the Ain Mreisseh area, where I should be—at the embassy. For an instant I hated not being there, not getting a new passport today. Another passport would give me so much freedom.

I was typing the letter when an explosion, like thunder with a lightning strike, hit something, hit the city, and a rumble rolled toward us. I jumped up, while turning to face Beirut, and saw a column of smoke already towering over Ain Mreisseh, where the rain had stopped and something terrible had happened. The dark column was already three times taller than the highest skyscraper in Beirut.

Suddenly several staff members were in my office. Gerritt saying, "What in the world?" Waleed declaring, "Something BIG!" Abu Issam holding his little squawking radio to his ear. Even Abu Sleiman sauntered in, calm, but wanting to be with the rest of us. We stood on the balcony to see better.

Gerritt said, "Looks like it's right down there where you meant to go."

Abu Issam turned up the radio. The American Embassy had been hit by something.

Waleed said, "*Haram,*" which he probably would have said whatever the target named.

We kept standing there, watching the smoke and waiting for details. A gigantic explosion, an announcer was saying. Part of the building collapsed. The front wall gone. No one knew the cause yet. No one knew how many people were in the building or anything about casualties.

The announcer's voice went on, but for a while I didn't understand anything. The truth seemed to be coming to me in slow motion, through a fog. The others were looking at me. Should I feel something? Gerritt said, "You were supposed to be there. I messed up your plan."

A reporter was describing the scene, his words rapid, high-pitched, panicky. It all came to us like blowing scraps—fire, smoke and dust, bodies, pieces of bodies everywhere. Shattered glass. The road slippery with blood. The front wall obliterated, office furniture dangling. At a corner of the building, multiple floors folded down on one another, the underpinnings gone. A corpse hanging by the feet. Emergency crews running with bodies on stretchers.

My knees started to wobble, and I stumbled through the door to my chair. The clock on my desk said, "1:06." My desk calendar still said, "embassy, 1:00 p.m."

Without the radio, we could hear sirens.

Waleed towered over the corner of my desk, his arms hairy. "*Nushkar ar-rab* (thank the Lord), Mrs. Fuller. *Nushkar ar-rab.*"

I just sat there, I think, trying to grasp the truth, not really feeling anything. I tried to imagine myself standing across the counter from Joseph Karam, filling out a form. And what happens next? The floor collapses? The roof? The walls fall away? I was in my office. Why was I in my office? I was trembling. I was fine. And Joseph?

Eventually we would know that a truck driven by a suicide bomber had smashed through the entrance of the embassy; 63 people were dead or dying, only 17 of them Americans; dozens of Lebanese lined up for visas had been burned alive and would be brought out in pieces; my friend Joseph Karam lay in the rubble, gravely injured; and I was in my office, as flimsy and senseless as a feather on the wind, unable to comprehend that I had been saved by a blessing which arrived looking like a failure and making me very sad.

Afterwards

The Lebanese kept expressing sympathy for us because of the embassy. A friend I hadn't seen for a long time hailed me on the road and put his head into my car window to say, "I'm sorry." But everybody had lost something—a relative or a friend or a measure of optimism about the future. I didn't want to mention my missed appointment. Even inside myself I didn't know how to exult.

We visited Abu and Um Fouad's son-in-law in his home to say "*Al-hamdillah ala salaame*"—praise God for your safety. A driver for the military attaché, he was in the embassy at the time but got out with a bruised leg. He, too, was not celebrating. He seemed glum, acted like it was unimportant that he had walked away. His wife lit a cigarette, her movements jerky, and exhaled smoke in sudden gusts. The coffee cups rattled in her hands.

I went to a hospital to see Joseph Karam, who was sedated, wrapped in bandages and attached to tubes and monitors. His beautiful wife sat by the bed. We did not know each other.

Outside his window the sun was shining on banana trees. Beirut is like that. Concrete everywhere and then suddenly avocado trees or a banana grove or a stand of tall bamboo, hanging on.

Staring at the frail figure under the sheets, I said, "I'm sorry."

She said, "Thank you for your visit," and waited to know who in the world I was. My identity seemed so complicated and simultaneously insignificant that I couldn't make myself explain it, not with Joseph lying there that ashy gray color—the little I could see of him—one cheek, the back of a hand.

Then I realized that a bandage circled his head and covered one eye. I had brought a book, gift-wrapped. Now I felt it was a silly gift. I placed the package on the bedside table and explained, "I didn't know about his eye."

* * *

A lot of hope had gone, like air through a hole in a balloon. Sandbags reappeared in the streets, sandbags that had disappeared when the Lebanese Army took control of Beirut after the Israelis left the city. And slowly we Americans understood that some people wanted to hurt us so badly that they were willing to kill a lot of Lebanese to accomplish it.

Though I never got another passport, I did go to Israel, flying through Larnaca to Tel Aviv. In four and a half days I made a difficult decision about our distribution system and picked up a lot of information about literature needs. I delivered news about hope for a curriculum project and secured the participation of several Arab leaders in Israel and the West Bank. In between work appointments, I saw the Sea of Galilee up close for the first time, drank tea with a famous old Palestinian leader in a barber shop in Nazareth and worshipped at the Garden Tomb. By vigilance and aggressiveness, I managed, going in and going out, not to get my passport stamped. Of course, I had suspicious evidence—a passport full of stamps from Arab countries, plus a Cypriot entry stamp, then an exit an hour later. And when I left Israel I was asked to name the Palestinians I had talked with, and I left out some deliberately and said truly that they were far too many for me to remember their names. Not satisfied with me, a conscientious young man emptied my suitcase and carried it away, leaving my underwear on public display.

Finally, they let me board the plane back to Cyprus. The clerk in the hotel where I would sleep before flying back to Lebanon, asked me a lot of questions (for the police book, he said) and wrote down where I had come from and why and where I was going. I told the truth, then asked why they wanted to know. He said, "Oh, the Cypriots don't care. I think it's for the Arabs and the Israelis."

"Great," I said. "Just great."

Measure Twice, Cut Once

The sound was unmistakable; something was alive up there in the network of beams that formed the ceiling of our cave, something that slithered and glided. I heard it at night, lying under it, with Wayne asleep. Once I woke him, and he listened, but the sound had stopped. He thought I imagined things.

Everything seemed contrary that spring: the government, the armies, the window screens, my allergy.

Without any apparent reason for it, something was happening to our mail. Letters from our kids were scarce. After a long drought, we got a nice letter from Tim, but the content confirmed our suspicion that there were others that we had not received. I felt robbed. Somebody had written small, dear details, wanting us to know, and we never would.

General Security denied visas to the people we wanted to bring from Egypt and Jordan for a curriculum planning meeting. Forced to meet without these people, we promised to send our work for their consideration and comments. Wayne was the designated traveler this time, because he already needed to go to Jordan to do an inventory of our stock. He set a date, then postponed because battles kept breaking out, and he didn't like leaving me alone in a volatile situation. I can't say I wanted him to leave with shooting in the streets and some secretive creature crawling in the ceiling beams of my shelter.

The Israelis were jittery, too, and they scared me out of my wits yet again one early morning during their battle at the intersection against an enemy who didn't show.

Wayne put up one cupboard in the bathroom but no door. All doors for all cupboards would be made at once sometime in the unknown future. Window screens were more urgent, he pointed out. Mosquitoes would be showing up soon. So he measured all the windows. He had this slogan he always quoted when he was building or renovating. He said, "Measure twice and cut once." So he measured the windows twice, then ordered screening material and went to work on the frames.

The mention of mosquitoes reminded me that allergy season was also on its way. The air was warm and dirty, Beirut obscured by a layer of smog. I was super sensitive to the pine pollen that always fell like yellow snow in the month of May. The previous year Dr. Habash in Monsourieh had given me shots of histaminic gamma globulin, and they had made life much easier. So back to Dr. Habash I went and then to the pharmacy for one dose of gamma globulin and a syringe. Dr. Habash had said that all I needed was a booster shot. The friendly woman in the pharmacy said, "Would you like me to give you the shot?"

I thought that was a great idea, since it saved me the time of waiting in the doctor's office again. I pushed up my sleeve, and she jabbed me with the needle. I left the pharmacy feeling fortunate in every way and wrote to Cynthia about the wonders of gamma globulin.

Getting window screens was also a happy event. Wayne finished them at his shop in the seminary basement and brought them up all at once. They were fine professional looking screens, with their new, clean mesh and painted frames. They also fit perfectly, proving Wayne's motto, except the last to be installed, the one for the dining room window. He set it into its place and looked up to discover a gap at the top. When he said it was six inches short, I thought I had misunderstood or he had said it wrong. Six centimeters, maybe.

"No, six inches," he said. "Look." And there was a space big enough for a coyote to come in.

I laughed. All these years later I still laugh, visualizing that screen in its place with half a foot of sky left naked and remembering Wayne's reaction.

He dug around in various pants pockets, found his original figures, and verified that the screen was exactly the dimensions he had written down. The rest of the evening he muttered and mumbled about how he could have made such a gross mistake. He said, "Puke," under his breath and showed no appreciation for my amusement.

I tried cheering him up with one of his own sly slogans: "It's a place for the flies to get out."

"It's the royal pukes," he said.

I told him, "It's O.K. You're nice, though you're Egyptian."

He ignored this clever joke.

Finally I became sympathetic and said, "Sorry that you have to do that screen all over again."

And he said, "Funny thing is I can't. I cut the screen to make it fit this frame. Now I have nothing but scraps."

"Then I guess you'll just have to order another piece."

"Yeah, except I bought all the guy had, and I don't know where to find more."

* * *

In May Wayne finally went to Egypt and Jordan, dreading it like a beating, and while he was gone the pine pollen fell, sprinkling the fields, the roofs of the village and my car with a golden frosting, a lovely poison. I went back to Dr. Habash with red eyes and a tissue under my nose, headachy and limp. I told him, "I sneeze ten times without stopping." He asked me a few questions and ascertained that my friend in the pharmacy had squirted the fluid into my muscle, when it absolutely had to be given under the skin. "Too late now," he said, so I overdosed on antihistamines and still couldn't hold up my head.

When Wayne was away I didn't sleep well. I read too long before turning off the light. I woke in the night and noticed I was alone. Unidentified anxieties found a way to jump on me. One night I dreamed about Jan. She was a little girl sitting in her playhouse, the one she really had in our backyard in Jordan—an enormous empty packing crate. She had long blond hair and adult teeth in an eight-year-old face. She invited me to come in and sit with her, because "I have a question I need to ask you." Busy, trying to take care of some other urgent matter, I put her off, and when I came back, she was all grown-up, quite sophisticated and poised in that big box. She said, "Thanks, that's O.K. I don't really need you now."

I woke and lay rigid under the weight of this dream, trying to remember moments in which I had failed to be present in my own life. What questions had I ignored? And where was I when my children disappeared? That little girl with the long blond hair—when did I lose her? A square of moonlight slid imperceptibly all the way across the bedroom wall while I pondered the mystery of how children evolve into memories.

A letter came from Dwight. He had entered himself in a motorcycle race, just "for kicks" to see how well he could do. And he had won the second place trophy, so he would now be racing once a week. I told Emmett Barnes how much I abhorred this reckless sport and worried that Dwight would break his neck. He looked at me and said, "Well, you have not exactly set an example of a cautious lifestyle."

One morning I opened my closet door, looking for something to wear to work and shoved aside a few hangars, exposing the end wall and a tarantula as big as my hand. The creature didn't move but clung to the wall with those eight huge, crooked, hairy legs, shocking to the limit my inordinate fear and hatred of spiders. For a while I stood as still as the enemy, unable to imagine solving this problem for myself. But if I went for help... *George? Bishara?*...he would probably be gone when we got back. If I left him in the closet I could not open the door and take out a piece of clothing, not ever, until he was eliminated. Wayne would not be home for another week.

I backed up, keeping my eye on him. I picked up a shoe, Wayne's shoe, from the floor. I advanced with my weapon. *How hard do you have to hit a tarantula to kill it? What if I miss it? What if it jumps out and starts running around the room? What if it runs around the corner onto the back wall of the closet, behind my clothes? I get one swing. An awkward sideways backhanded swing. It has to be perfect. Where are their eyes? Will he see the shoe coming? Quick; you're giving him too much time!*

I swung. I hit the wall and jumped back. The spider's body fell to the floor, a dark lump surrounded by crumpled legs. I hit it again. I was shaking. I had won, but I didn't feel like a winner. My suspicions about this house were proving true. More than a mule had lived here, and some of those sneaky, slimy, revolting residents were staying on and reproducing. I needed all the courage I had left just to sweep the thing into my dustpan.

* * *

The day Wayne came home, finding me stuffy and exhausted, he said, "Next year I'm taking you out of Lebanon for the month of May."

When I told him about the spider, he thought I was brave and self-sufficient, mainly because that was a long-held illusion of his.

The next time the guns drove us into our cave to sleep, I lay down, looking up at the ceiling beams and said, "Uh oh, what's that?"

"What?"

"That little gray sliver. Right there. Between the beams."

Sitting on the edge of our mat, he looked up. "A spider web."

I knew it wasn't a spider web. He stood, still looking up, and said, "A piece of plastic." Then he brought a chair to stand on, reached and pulled down a snakeskin.

Twenty-four Crazy Hours

On a Friday morning in July the Metn was full of zombies, because on Thursday night a big battle between the Kata'ib and Druze militias kept us all awake. A lot of people didn't come to work. Michel and Waleed and Wayne and I dragged around, drinking coffee and forcing ourselves to move. Still, our problem was small compared to that of the high school students who, in this state of sleeplessness and exhaustion, had to take a part of their Baccalaureate I exams. Without passing these government exams no one could get a university degree in Lebanon. Among these students was Najat Abou Khair. She was scheduled for the physics portion of her exam.

Najat was good in the sciences and felt better prepared for the physics than any other part of the test. She had read the previous year's exam and could answer every question, so though the questions would be different and though she had not slept, Najat left home that morning feeling confident. Then it turned out that the questions were all on trivialities.

She came home bawling. I heard her crying down in the parking lot and telling the story to her parents and a couple of friends, so I went down. Her slender face looked horror stricken, as though she had witnessed some bloody disaster. She told us she thought she had scored about three out of forty. She gave examples of some of the questions asked, not questions to test a student's knowledge of basic physics, but details related to obscure specialties.

Someone in the group turned to me and said with anger, "This is a favorite trick in government exams. If there is no space in the universities, they force the students to fail."

With tears falling like rain, Najat said, "I hate this country. I'm going to leave. Wait and see. I'M GOING TO LEAVE AND NEVER COME BACK."

We all stood around, dismayed, helpless. Um John wiped tears.

* * *

Right after that some of us sat down to a planning meeting—Wayne and I, Anne Nicholas, Waleed, Pauline Atiyeh and a couple of other people not on our staff. Intending to work for several hours, we dragged in extra chairs and sat in a circle in my office. We were there because sometimes you just have to do the impossible.

I had made a deal with the Arab Baptists. Together we would create an indigenous church curriculum, the one I had said we could not do. The decision had been made in a historic meeting of leaders in Cairo where we faced all of our options, helped by the expert instruction of Robert Reekie of the David C. Cook Foundation. We imagined an indigenous Arabic curriculum and got excited, we faced the gigantic obstacles and got scared, we asked the hard questions, we struggled, we argued, we prayed, and we decided that we had to try. On that crazy day when Najat unjustly failed the government exam in physics, we already had done months of groundwork and expected to hold our first writer training workshop in no more than two weeks, right there on the campus.

Several big artillery pieces began to fire. These were "friendly" guns located just below us on the other side of the road to Mkalles, but every sharp bang rattled the windows and made all of us jump. We kept working. We were fighting that deadline, the date for the workshop, and everybody present knew how hard it was to get together again. Trying to hurry, knowing that shells might start coming in our direction at any moment, we became inefficient. The more we tried to rush our decisions, the more we noticed that the walls were shaking.

After we had pushed determinedly to the end of one task, Anne asked, "Shall we begin this other thing or leave?"

Everybody said simultaneously, "Let's get out of here." And before we could shuffle our papers together and stand up there were incoming shells, not very near, but obviously coming, not going. We all began to scurry, the visitors leaving immediately, the staff trying to put things away and lock up for the weekend. Then I rushed to the parking lot and bent my key in the ignition of our car. I had no idea how I had done that. The guns were raging, the world shaking, and I sat there in a car as hot as an oven, fumbling with a key that wouldn't work.

Back upstairs to ask Wayne to bring his key, I couldn't see him anywhere. I yelled. He answered from the pressroom, but when I got there he was gone. I heard him calling from down stairs. I yelled back,

"I'm here," and as I went down, he came up. It must have looked like a Laurel and Hardy comedy.

I was in the parking lot alone when a gun fired from over toward Aley. As soon as I heard the muzzle blast there was a whining sound like a small jet diving and then a big explosion just beyond the far end of the campus. The next time I heard the blast and then the whine I ran for cover and found Waleed pacing the floor and muttering aloud. "Where is he? Where is he?"

Seeing me he began to talk like a machine gun, throwing up his big arms in wild gestures. "I'm supposed to ride with Wissam today, but I can't find him. His car isn't here. I don't know if he left me."

Wayne came with the key, and as we walked outside, he said, "Shall I give Waleed the key to our other car?" Just then the gun fired again, and Wayne looked up nonchalantly to see what was making the whining noise.

I shouted, "Incoming..." but the shell crashed down before we could get inside, and we turned and saw the smoke of the explosion. I told Wayne, "Just do what you are going to do quickly."

At the last moment I felt torn between leaving and going to the basement, but as we drove up the hill, we were bombarded only by noise and shock waves. Safely home, I made some iced tea, and, with the Boggle game in his hand, Wayne said, "I think we'd better do something to unwind."

During a lull (a pause at supper time was part of the craziness, I thought), we cooked hamburgers, not even in our kitchen but up on the roof. When the firing started again, Wayne brought our sleeping rolls down to the cave. Fighting was widespread. The Christians were fighting against both Druze villages and Syrian Army positions. Radio announcers began reading the names of dead and wounded. A young man had died in Monsourieh.

Wayne made me nervous standing at the living room window to watch the battle. I kept telling him to come back into the cave. Just after he did, eight rockets slammed down somewhere nearby, so rapidly that I didn't know how I knew there were eight. I wondered if we should have gone to the Bustan with the neighbors (the hotel had rooms, presumably safe, and provided them free-of-charge to those needing shelter), but it was too late. I tried to read a *Monday Morning* magazine, with shells whistling past, each whistle followed by a one-second silence and then an explosion. In spite of it all, we got sleepy, with the help of that deficit from the night before.

The next morning, concerned already about how I would hold a conference at the seminary, I got a cable from Larry Brook and Georges Houssney, the two men who were coming from America to lead our workshop. They said they were scared and asked if I planned to go ahead with it.

Finding a Way

Sayyadat al-Bir, a small hotel/conference center run by nuns, was situated on the seaward side of the mountain, above Antelias. Following the directions I had been given, I found the turn-off and followed a small road that wound through tall trees, spaced out, with grass under them, until I saw the church and one large building across the parking lot. The forest wrapped around the back of the building, enveloping the center in a calm and shady atmosphere.

A short, middle-aged nun, showed me around. She had a colorless but sweet face and spoke a minimum of words, flinging open doors and letting me notice whatever I noticed. Most of the rooms contained one narrow bed, one desk, a single chair, and a crucifix on the wall. Perfect, I thought, for either a convent or a writing conference. The meeting room was well-designed and equipped for the functions we needed, and its long western windows framed a view of the sea.

Though the center was a popular spot, used by numerous Christian groups, the date we needed was open. I signed a commitment and left immensely pleased and grateful that I had found a quieter, safer location for our workshop. From the Broummana post office I sent Larry and Georges a telex: "The workshop is still on."

So was the battle.

As soon as our guests arrived the airport closed.

Guns boomed. Our guests got scared. They did their jobs anyway.

Twenty participants, thinking together, worked out the shape that all the lessons in our curriculum would take. Then we learned step by step how to select biblical material for a specific age group, how to move from the scripture passage to an appropriate lesson objective, how to write the objective and plan a lesson that would achieve it. Everyone wrote at least one lesson. One young woman wrote three.

On the last day we had product demonstrations. One writer on each age level taught his lesson to the others who acted like children could be expected to act. We laughed and applauded and said, "Sure we can. We can write curriculum."

We had written curriculum with shells falling far and near.

The writers all accepted assignments and agreed to follow-up sessions with me in September. September was my vacation month, but I didn't care.

As soon as our foreign guests finished their work, the airport opened again.

Our Sunday School material, later given a name—The Faith and Life Curriculum—had been born. Never mind that it had come into a risky, uncertain world.

Houses on Battlefields

From My Seat in the Front Row

What woke us was not the battle raging across the canyon or even the artillery thundering all around us, but an unusual sound—the drone of an airplane, circling. Then we saw the flares, five gorgeous lights, hanging like stars loose from their orbits, above the cities along the Damascus highway. Suddenly we knew that the Israelis were withdrawing. What we had feared and waited for all summer was finally happening on Sunday, September 4, 1983. Our clock said 1:30 a.m.

For fifteen months Israeli troops had occupied the mountain across the canyon and the area beyond, called the Shouf. During that time an armed struggle had begun between the Druze and Christian militias within the area. Now in the wake of the Israeli withdrawal, both would try to get the upper hand. We had expected this. We even knew that the Syrians would rush back in. What we had not predicted was that the Lebanese Army would be neither informed of the timing nor allowed to take the Israeli positions as they withdrew. The Israelis were exiting by the only road the Army could use to go up, stopping them cold at Suq al-Gharb. Meanwhile the other end of the road was wide open for the Syrians.

The other thing we had not anticipated was that our little house would be caught in a war zone. Because Kata'ib forces across the wadi were fighting the Druze, the Syrians and all their allies, the Army and Kata'ib positions on our side of the canyon fired in their support, and shells were going over us in both directions, with some falling on Beit Meri. It was a man-made storm, with continuous thunder and a raging wind—the sound of all those shells rushing through the air. The towns across the canyon disappeared under smoke and dust. The sun became dingy and dim and at moments went suddenly dark. My curtains lifted and billowed from blasts four or five miles away on the opposite hill, and the smell of gunpowder and battle dust drifted through our windows. This continued for two days, three days, six days.

Wayne went up on the roof to check our water supply and came back saying, "Look what I found on the roof." He held in his hands several vicious pieces of shrapnel, with edges like razors. Um Fouad, passing on her way to buy bread, picked up a heavy chunk in the road under our living room window.

This was supposed to be our vacation. We could have gone to the coast or to Cyprus, but we had wanted just to spend some time at home. Wayne wanted to putter in the house, doing small neglected jobs. I meant to concoct great salads, eat watermelon and read books.

I tried to read, lying in the cave with my head toward the light. A friend had lent me a novel, recommending it highly. On about page fifty something scary happened—imagine that with guns booming everywhere I have to read about a murder—and I threw the book against the stone wall. Instantly I was shocked that I had thrown it, shocked to see the borrowed book lying on my floor with its pages bent, but when I picked it up, I knew I would not read it—not during the battle or afterwards. And that was the last time I ever tried to read a scary book. Life is scary enough for me.

Wayne constantly listened to the news, searched the Arabic dictionary and then tried to teach me something. Once he informed me that *kateeba* is a motorized squadron. I thought, *now there's a word I need.*

The Syrians and Palestinians captured Bhamdoun. The BBC told us. Apparently there was a great loss of life. The Red Cross began calling for a ceasefire, at least one hour, so they could evacuate the wounded. Also shells fell on the airport and the adjacent base of American Marines, who were part of a multi-national peacekeeping force. Two Marines were killed that day, and another day several Marines died but they did not fire back.

Then the whole mountain in front of us fell under the control of a Druze-Syrian-Palestinian-Libyan alliance. The Lebanese Army still could not advance, in fact could barely hang on to what it had.

All the time I prayed. What else to do? We had no electricity. The weather was insufferably hot. We drank the last ice cubes in our refrigerator. My watermelon soured. The salad greens ran out. I made a soup from our last vegetables, and cut the mold from an old piece of cornbread. It didn't matter. Our stomachs were very small.

In less than a week, 56,000 missiles fell on our side of the canyon, some as far as Beirut, killing 518 people, injuring 1200 and causing 150,000 to flee.

I got so tired. One morning a newscaster mentioned Sofar, and I thought, *Sofar, Sofar. Where is Sofar? Oh yes,* and then I remembered how we always slowed up when driving through Sofar because it was so pretty with those big trees lining the road, the old stone houses with pale red roofs, the crates of apples for sale, the view from there of all the towns on our side of the canyon. In 1976 Syrian soldiers threw snowballs at me as I drove through Sofar. Now they were throwing fireballs. Literally! Phosphorous bombs.

Exhausted, I slept nine hours through the noise. The earth was shaking under the floor of our cave; I could feel the vibrations all along my body, through my mat. The guns near us fired and kept firing. I felt the towns across from us being pulverized. Though I knew everything, I slept as though drugged, struggling through nightmares that I forgot in the morning except for some vague memory of blood in the bowl of the bathroom sink.

Scary Saturday

The fighting got worse on Saturday, the seventh day. Druze forces had surrounded Deir al-Qamar, a Christian town, out of sight, deep in the mountains. It was a town of 5,000 to which 30,000 or 40,000 refugees had fled. Red Cross vehicles kept trying to enter the town to give aid, but the soldiers prevented them. Christians feared a massacre if the Druze took the city, though Kamal Jumblatt, the Druze leader, promised that nothing like that would happen. French and American reconnaissance planes circled repeatedly.

With flurries of shells falling on Beit Meri, getting hit seemed so possible that I took my children's art work off the walls of the living room and dining area and stashed those dear pictures in the most sheltered corner of the cave. Wayne went to the stove and turned off the gas. We couldn't get a chance to get any supper or even a drink, because the firing was so continuous and fearful.

We listened to the news. Israel said that 2000 Israeli Druze were asking to leave in order to fight alongside the Druze in Lebanon. The Voice of Lebanon said that a vicious plot was being carried out against the Christian community of Lebanon under the umbrella of the western powers, who were supposed to be protecting Lebanon and instead were "parading through the skies."

Terms of a ceasefire were almost agreed upon, but Syria toughened its stand at the last minute and rejected the agreement. *Why,* I wondered, *has Israel delivered Lebanon into the hands of the Syrians?*

I went to bed in my clothes again, as I had every night for a week, fearing the possibility that I would need to flee with no time to dress. Wayne lighted a little lantern for me so I could read in bed. He was already asleep when a shell came screaming in and crashed near us. I had the impression it just missed the corner of the house and landed in the field on the other side of the road. I tried telling myself that explosions always sound closer than they really are. In half a minute another came in the same place, and I was convinced that I could have read its serial numbers from the front window. Terrified, I turned off the lantern. A third shell exploded on top of the rubble of the other two.

I woke Wayne. He lifted his head in surprise, then let it drop again.

I said, "They're shelling us."

He listened to the firing for a moment and then mumbled, "Whadaya want me to do about it?"

At the time I was not amused by his practicality. I said, "Stay awake with me. I'm scared."

He threw a heavy arm across me and slept again.

The rest of the night missiles flew in all directions. A new artillery piece joined the action, so close I could hear the recoil after each firing. I finally slept a little, but even then I was aware of noise and fear and the discomfort of my underclothes and long skirt.

A Prayer for Sodom

Sunday again. The battle had slacked off. I found Wayne standing in the kitchen. He hugged me and said, "I hoped you would sleep longer."

"The quiet woke me up."

He said, "Yeah. Some of the gunners are having breakfast."

When the coffee water was hot, I could hardly lift the kettle. I thought I needed about ten cups to make me feel alive.

At 9:26 we suddenly decided to go to church, which began at 10:30, twenty minutes away in Monsourieh. We bathed and dressed and ran down the path to the car. Guns were banging again somewhere. A big chunk of shrapnel sat on the hood of my car, inches from the windshield.

As he backed the car into the road Wayne said, "We're crazy to go down there."

I felt compelled to go, like my life depended on it.

He stopped at Chaanine's store and went in, leaving me in the car. I knew he was looking for some other human encouragement for going or not. When he came back he said, "Those three shells that scared you so bad..."

"Yeah?"

"They struck the steps down to Abdu's house."

That was maybe twenty yards farther away than I had thought. I was not comforted.

Before we went into the church we talked with Abu and Um John in the parking lot behind the building. They looked frazzled. She was sweeping small pieces of glass into a pile, and he was scooping it up and pouring it into a box.

To our routine "*Keefcom*?" meaning "How are you?" they gave a routine reply, "*Al-hamdulilah*."

Then he said, "Believe me, it was the worst night of our lives."

And she said, "I never expected to live through such a night."

About thirty mortar shells had landed on or near the campus, breaking windows in the classroom building, the church, the Barnes' house. The closest neighbors had gotten two direct hits on their house.

Having told us all this, Abu John then looked up at us and exploded a bomb himself. "Did you hear the news from Ras el-Metn?"

"What news?"

"There's been a massacre of Christians. Thirty members of the Freiha family are dead."

We just stood there looking at his face, an exhausted face with intense blue eyes. Visions of the Freiha home flashed through my head—and Mr. Freiha at the blackboard in our classroom explaining a difficult verb to me. Explosions were rocking the world up beyond the Damascus highway, and unbelievable things were being said. I couldn't absorb them.

Um John was saying, "We are going backwards. It happened like this in the old days. We hear stories from our history, and we think, Nobody respected life then. We think it's different now. But it's not." Her voice was toneless, flat. She pushed glass into Abu John's dustpan and said, "We're going back to the old ways."

He straightened again and said, "I want all my kids to go to America. I don't want them to live in a place like this."

Twelve people came to church. Twelve sleep-deprived, broken-hearted people. Normally about sixty attended on a Sunday morning. The men moved pews so we could face one another, and we prayed, with the assault on Suq al-Gharb thundering in the background. That particular battle was much louder down there in Monsourieh, and I jumped sometimes when one boom seemed closer than others.

In his prayer George Bassous said something that I knew I would never forget. George was someone we had known for eighteen years. He was a calm, unemotional man, who held a high position in the British Bank of the Middle East. He said, "Lord, you were willing to save Sodom if you could find ten good men in it. There are more than ten in Lebanon."

I wept then and could say nothing when my turn came to pray, but he had lighted a candle in my heart. Or maybe a torch. Silently I was saying,

"YES! That's it. You were willing to bargain with Abraham for Sodom. Now we've come to bargain for Lebanon. And we've come strong."

(Actually, I have never believed in a God with whom I could bargain, but I will say crazy things, even to God, especially to God, when I am desperate. Later I reread the story of Sodom and noticed that before Abraham spoke, God had said that he was checking out Sodom to see if there were any reason to save it. Abraham then discussed this with God. How many good men would there have to be in order to save Sodom? God agreed with continually decreasing suggestions down to ten, and finding only one, God saved the one. But not Sodom.)

That dreadful Sunday I just named good Lebanese men... George himself, the eight or ten others there in our circle (I think I was the only woman there)... And other men—Abu John, and Mr. Feghali, the printer, "an EXCELLENT man, God, honest and responsible and trustworthy." I thought of Waleed and his eagerness for every good work; Abu Sleiman, our chief editor, a gentle Palestinian, the humblest of men; Mustapha, the honest Druze grocer in Musaitbeh; Abu Fouad in the village, hard-working, generous; Joseph Karam, efficient in his duties, caring and patient; our friend Elie, who was in the Shouf defending some village, though he hated fighting. "And the good women," I told God, "I know they count just as much." But I didn't name any; I was so impressed with how many good men there were and how much I loved them all.

George Atiyeh spoke for a few minutes quietly, about praising God in hard situations, and then we stood up and sang "Count Your Blessings." Every Christian should get to do that at least once—to sing "Count your blessings," with a broken heart and guns booming. By then I was thinking again about our Arabic teacher, Selim Freiha from Ras el-Metn. The last we knew about Mr. Freiha—the most encouraging of teachers, the soul of patience—he was sitting in his daughter's backyard in Texas weeping from homesickness. I thought that his elderly sister had never left Ras el-Metn. We had a lovely lunch there in their home one day in 1965. The house was high-ceilinged and cool in summer, with bare tile floors, and a grapevine on the roof. The old sister made us *fatayir,* the best I had ever eaten, and climbed the stairs and brought down a pan of grapes. Lately it had not been advisable to go over there. People had died trying.

In the afternoon we heard the news ourselves. Among those murdered was a one hundred-year-old woman.

War and Words

Words flew as thick as bullets, and people listened to them, though often the words contradicted one another or disagreed with the bullets. While we were wondering why the Marines didn't defend themselves, the Russians told the Middle East countries that the U.S. was getting ready to launch a war in their part of the world. The U.S. planned, they said, to seize Lebanon and then "make military provocations" against Syria. And while Israel was saying that she would not permit Palestinians who had been driven from Lebanon to return and take the places vacated by the Israeli Army, the Voice of Lebanon claimed that 8,500 had already arrived and were fighting with the Druze against the Army.

Usually we didn't know what to believe. Still we listened, sifting the reports to find nuggets of truth, often very ugly but necessary nuggets. For obscure human reasons, we needed to hear the improbable news that six people had died of hunger in Deir al-Qamar. The bakeries there had to quit working because of lack of fuel, but that didn't explain to me why no one could intervene to help that stricken city.

And the news that a woman had escaped from Ma'asar es-Shouf, a Christian village, and told a horrifying story—that report rang true and seemed to be read for my benefit. Several months earlier I had received a letter from someone in the U.S. asking me to investigate the safety of one Mary Haddad in this village. Her family in the States had not heard from her for a year. I tried but failed to learn anything and because of fighting had found it impossible to go there. The escapee told how Druze militiamen entered the village and began shooting people. She saw her own daughter shot and thought that as many as eighty people may have died. But, of course, I still didn't know what happened to Mary Haddad.

The Druze were killing people house to house in Bhamdoun. For all I knew, the Kata'ib could be doing the same in some other town. Why? Distrust. Fear. The stuff that keeps rocks from melting. And memory. It happened 140 years ago, so it is happening again. I should be informed about these things. Otherwise, now that a southwest wind had blown away the haze, I might sit there looking at the minarets and red roofs of Bhamdoun on the rocky bluff, among the trees, and think only that Lebanon is a beautiful place.

Coming after a few quieter days and all that silly talk and bad news, the sound of guns filled me with dismay. There were muzzle blasts that made a hollow boom and others that sounded like a bowling ball dropped on a wooden floor. Smoke billowed up all over the hills. Briefly I was so heartsick I thought I would cry. Syria had rejected another ceasefire offer.

Filled with words and cynicism, my attitude not changed by the arrival of electricity, I sat at my electric typewriter—an old instrument that limped and creaked and decapitated whole sentences—and worked on a story I eventually called "Human Battles." I always think that any horror can be redeemed a little, if someone can make a story out of it. In my fiction, human battles were bad, but not nearly so bad as the reality. I would have gotten that draft done all the way to the end, but the electricity went off again in the middle of a word.

Patience

We spent an evening visiting neighbors.

First we walked the length of our terraces to the home of Abu and Um Edward. Their house was a work in progress and had a raw, unfinished look. The walls of the stairwell were unpainted concrete. Bare light bulbs hung from the ceiling.

Um Edward, a pretty woman with a soft kind of femininity, always dressed prettily, wearing lacy collars and nice shoes with heels. She seemed more sophisticated than her husband who was a shepherd and went out every day with his herd of goats and a staff. He talked to the goats in whistles and grunts that they obviously understood. Once when I was coming along the road through the village, I drove upon his flock, as they were crossing the road just beyond a curve. Quicker than I could hit my brake, Abu Edward tossed his staff into the air and it came down among the black goats, who scattered swiftly, with a clattering of small hooves.

Um Edward made coffee, of course, and while we sat drinking it, guns were banging, making all of us jittery. One shell came in quite near, shaking the walls, and our host and hostess looked at one another. I wondered if they would be sitting somewhere else if we were not there.

Abu Edward smoked and seemed ill. "He is nervous," she whispered to me. "He can't endure times like this." This revelation clashed with my image of shepherds. All over the Middle East shepherds walked, sometimes on nearly barren hills, leading their flocks to food and water. I saw them from a distance, assuming their health and vigor and imagining that the simplicity of their lives made them the calmest of people. I looked at Abu Edward. A small man already, he shrank into his upholstered chair, pale and anxious.

We didn't find much to talk about. When we tried gently to mention The Good Shepherd walking us through the valley of death the nervous shepherd did not respond. Um Edward had been hit in the leg by a small piece of shrapnel a few months earlier, while hanging clothes on the line, so I inquired about the wound, and she said it had healed completely. I said, "*Al-hamdillah ala salaame.*" Their only son was in the army; they weren't sure where. Abu Edward let her do the talking. We said, "May God keep him for you."

Behind her on the otherwise bare wall was a small plaque, one word, written in Arabic calligraphy—patience. In Arabic this word has a graceful shape, a wholeness in three letters. In the mouth it has a toughness, like the skin protecting a soft fruit. Hanging on the wall in a house that shook, it seemed to mean much more than it said.

No one answered the door at Haroun's house. We found him and his family at Abu and Um Fouad's, sitting on the covered back patio that had a wonderful view of the mountains and was the coolest place we had been all summer. Um Fouad was making supper and absolutely insisted that we eat with them. Fouad was there and Um Fouad's brother. The men were drinking *arak,* a liquor flavored with anise.

Tony came in with a five or six-day beard, surprising everyone. His mother kissed him the way mothers kiss their sons when they are afraid that something will snatch them away. He held her for a moment and then sat down wearily, leaning his gun against the balcony railing. She raced off to the kitchen, re-energized.

For a while we all sat in a row facing the Shouf. A big star appeared out of the darkening sky. No lights came on in the villages.

An incoming shell whistled and then a sharp explosion made most of us jump to our feet. Fouad laughed, then the rest of us. A tower of smoke went up, half a kilometer away, below the road to Broummana. Tony didn't react, except to tell us that it would be just chance if a shell hit anyone's house.

I asked Tony if he knew a way to learn anything about someone in Ma'asar as-Shouf. He said that if any inhabitants had survived they were probably in Deir al-Qamar.

Um Fouad set the table outside, refusing my help. There was no electricity, so she brought candles and lighted them. We ate *fattoush*—a salad with toasted bread among the greens and a sprinkle of sumac, chicken wings cooked black over charcoal, fried potatoes, a dip made of squash, and finally heaps of white grapes. Fouad and his uncle got a little tipsy. Fouad kept joking in a cynical way. He said there would not be any ceasefire soon. America would come and take the Shouf first; then there would be a ceasefire.

One of the men mentioned that several days before in Aleppo eighteen Syrians had been arrested and jailed in connection with a demonstration protesting Syria's role in the war in Lebanon. Some of the demonstrators had carried signs that said, "If you want to fight Israel, it is not in Suq al-Gharb." Everyone on the balcony enjoyed knowing that even in Syria there were people who recognized the irony that Israel and all her enemies had chosen to fight one another in Lebanon and then just to fight Lebanon. "What did Lebanon do wrong?" someone asked, and the group identified two "sins"—she had always received refugees, and she existed there on Israel's northern border.

The battle started again, and I suspected that we were all crazy to be sitting there. Even so, I enjoyed the breeze and the candlelight and the food and being with people who bore so well the dangers and the bitter ironies of their lives.

Reality Check

Somewhere beyond the thunder and smoke, an alternative world was waiting, the world in which we set goals and worked toward them. Now and then I remembered the existence of this other world and wondered how I would deal with it when the nightmare ended and dumped me back into my life at the wrong point.

All this time my staff had not been to the office. I was worried about the *MasterLife,* a church leadership training program that we were translating. Churches all over the Middle East were depending on us to produce a test version, which would be used in a conference in mid-November. Completing it on time was now going to be tough.

Thinking all of this on a relatively quiet day, I went to my office and brought home two of the English books, the two in which Abu Sleiman was still working. The next morning I drove to his house in Musaitbeh.

Abu Sleiman was alone. His wife had died in the summer, and I knew he was acutely lonely without her. He made tea for me—strong and sweet. He was glad to receive the books and told me not to worry, he would get the job done.

Nightmares and Ceasefires

I often dreamed about Jan. In my dreams I thought she had gone to the battle with her friends. She called me on the phone, her voice nearly inaudible. I thought she said, "Mom, I need an aspirin."

"Jan, are you hurt?"

"Yes, it hurts," and her voice faded away. I screamed into the phone and waited, but I heard only static.

In another dream gunfire crackled outside the house, and one of my children was out there somewhere, exposed to flying bullets. When I opened my mouth to call him, nothing but agony came out. I tried to go to him, my limbs heavy and slow. I heard him scream and then cry a little. It was Dwight. Struggling toward him, I realized that I was wearing only my slip. What bothered me was that the slip was white; in the twilight, I was an excellent target.

Barely able to drag my feet in the direction of his voice, I found him, lying in tall dead grass, with a dark wound in his leg. He was a young child, wearing short pants, a helpless distress in his face—that delicate, slender face that Dwight had when he was a little boy. Just as I stooped to pick him up, a soldier appeared, not arriving but standing, as though he had already been there behind the wire fence.

I said, "Don't let anyone shoot us. Please."

The soldier stared at me in silence, holding a rifle across his body. His face contained neither malice nor sympathy. Whatever he was supposed to do he would do.

I lifted Dwight and stood up; he was small and light. He whimpered and let his eyelids fall. I looked back at the soldier whose expression had not changed. "Please help me; don't shoot us." I tried to run. When I turned my back on the soldier, my fear became so unbearable that it woke me.

I was lying in bed in my stone house, choking and sweaty. My children were all safe in America.

At 2:20 in the afternoon the Voice of Lebanon reported that the Christian leader, Camille Chamoun, had come out of a "religious" meeting and announced a ceasefire. The announcer was Magda, who often added her own entertaining thoughts to the news. I had loved Magda ever since the night in 1976 when for fifteen minutes she read a litany of gun battles and roadblocks and sniping and murders and kidnappings and then concluded, "In other words, ladies and gentlemen, everything is perfectly normal."

The ceasefire, Chamoun said, would begin after two hours, and Magda added, "He didn't say after which two hours."

The fighting lasted until 4:00 the next morning. In the middle of the night I sat up and turned on a flashlight to write in my diary, "With ceasefires like this, who needs war?" Then, having said my piece, I went to sleep.

On September 26, 1983, ceasefire number 179, counting since the first battle of the civil war in 1975, was holding, with only a few infractions.

The only thing that was over for sure was my vacation.

Losses

Morning devotions were very long on our first day back at work. The whole staff sat in my office, tired, somber. Everyone seemed diminished, like after a death, and I felt that if we didn't talk enough at the beginning, we might be distracted all day.

Waleed had been in the South and told us how terrified people were down there. Rumors about Israel's intentions were rampant.

Abu Issam delivered the sad news that the Khairallahs, members of the Ras Beirut Baptist Church, were missing, along with three of their young sons. This couple lived in Bhamdoun but always drove down to West Beirut for church. Wayne and I had witnessed their baptism, because Waleed was baptized in the same service. Nadim Khairallah, a tailor, was a large, slightly crippled man, with a lot of energy in his dipping and rising gait; his blond Polish wife, Maria, drove him everywhere.

Because of the bloody fighting and the house-to-house killing in Bhamdoun the man's relatives were very concerned and searching for them. Their names had been read on the radio without response. They had not turned up among the refugees in Deir al-Qamar, so the church was conducting its own search, led by their youthful pastor, Charles Costa.

The Khairallahs' nine-year-old son had been on a school trip outside the battle area when the fighting in the Shouf began. His name had been found on a list of children who were taken to a monastery for safe-keeping.

We talked about the results of American involvement in the war; the facts were unclear. Reports out of the Shouf claimed that the New Jersey's powerful shells hit only civilian targets and empty hillsides. Christian Lebanese, even without believing this, were disappointed. Once the ships began shooting they had expected the Marines to do much more. Now they were quoting one of their proverbs: "The camel went into profound labor and delivered a mouse."

Finally we talked about our work, reviewing our project and task lists, lest we had forgotten what we were supposed to be doing. Right away we realized how far behind we were on all our schedules. Both dates for follow-up meetings with the curriculum writers had come and gone. Rescheduling these conferences required calling or intercepting somewhere twenty people, one by one, not easy when phones so often didn't work. The task of producing sixty test copies of the *MasterLife* material by the deadline now loomed as a major challenge. When we started to feel overwhelmed, we prayed and finally knuckled down.

With the battle for the Shouf barely over, Najat Abou Khair confided that she had a friend who lived down in Beirut. Seeing him was difficult, and she would really like to give him a birthday party in our house. We were thrilled to do that little thing for Najat.

We scheduled the party for Sunday night after church, but it was spoiled for Najat by an unexpected development. The guest of honor could not come. Just before he was to leave home, armed men attacked the Army in Ain ar-Rommaneh and Tayyuni. They brought bulldozers and shoved dirt across roads to seal off an area and give themselves barriers to fight behind. The birthday boy's mother was too frightened to let him leave home.

Poor Najat. She had baked a cake and chocolate chip cookies. In fact she had searched the whole area for those chocolate chips and then baked the cookies at our house so she could serve them hot.

Except for the absence of the guest of honor, it was an excellent party. We played all sorts of table games in the living room, let the music Najat chose burst out of the speakers, engaged in cozy talks by the stove in the cave, went up to the roof to see the waning moon, ate hot cookies in the kitchen, but we couldn't find any way to pull Najat out of the doldrums. She didn't cry, but neither did she fake any smiles or try to say "*Ma'leish* (Never mind)." Quieter than the day she was robbed of her baccalaureate but more certain than before, Najat said, "Wait and see, I'm going to leave this country and not come back."

She kept her word, and Lebanon was the loser.

* * *

The search for the Khairallahs went on. When the Kata'ib released 200 Druze women and children held since the fighting, that encouraged me. Maybe the Khairallahs were still safe somewhere. Though it seemed cruel to hope that they were prisoners, this was now the best we could imagine. Day after day Abu Issam brought us the news that there was no news, except that the nine-year-old was with an uncle and crying for his family. After both sides claimed that every hostage had been released, all reasonable hope was gone. Eventually a relative was able to go to their house where he found the bodies of Nadim and Maria. The fate of three little boys—ages two, five and six—remained a dreadful mystery.

John and Elena

I have a snapshot of John and Elena taken the day we went to the Marine base. I need to describe this picture, something I should be able to do with my eyes closed now.

John is in his work clothes—camouflage, rolled-up sleeves, an olive green undershirt showing under the open collar. Elena wears his vest over a white blouse with sleeves to her elbows. His helmet sits toward the back of her head, with dark, silky hair spilling out on both sides of her forehead and framing her oval face. I can see the indentation, the almost dimple in her chin. With John's left arm behind her, she seems to be leaning only a little into the hollow of his shoulder. His head tilts, also only a little, toward Elena. The glare of the sun bleaches the right side of his fair head, making his clipped hair white, hair that is a bit misshapen as though he has just taken off the helmet. They are both looking into the camera. His smile is easy, honest, hers coy, close-lipped, hopeful. The background of the picture is spotted like the camouflage clothes, a mass of leaves in sun and shadow.

When Elena received this picture from John in the mail, she brought it to my office, her face a confusion of pain and frightened hope. "Could it be? Do you think maybe..." Months later she gave it to me. I have kept it in my files for seventeen years. For many weeks while preparing to write this story, I have seen it every day, propped up beside my computer, because only by looking at it can I get beyond all the other emotions and remember the happiness of that afternoon, the three-hours-at-a-time kind of happiness, the ceasefire-in-the-middle-of-war kind, tentative, irrational, a warm liquid sloshing in a bowl. Only by looking at the snapshot can I recall that Elena was once so young and beautiful and innocent.

I never meant to be involved in any of this. I never even wanted the Marines to be in Lebanon. Neither the Syrians nor the Israelis could do anything right in the streets of this country. What did the Marines know about it? But that wasn't the reason, when the University Baptist Church had a party for fifty-five or sixty Marines and invited all of us missionaries to come, bringing homemade cookies, that Wayne and I didn't go. It was a matter of priorities. Before the war thousands of Americans lived in Beirut, and except to be courteous to our children's friends, we spent no time with them. The Marines might be lonely and need homemade cookies, but this was not why we came to Lebanon. We heard that the Marines had issued an open invitation to friends to visit them on their ships, that they flew their guests out on helicopters. Wayne really wanted to go but never found the opportunity. Even when the Marine chaplain and his assistant spoke at our seminary chapel, I stayed in my office and worked. I did not routinely attend this chapel service and saw no need to make an exception because the speakers happened to be visiting Americans. Neither did I go down to the dining room for lunch that day but ate my fruit and peanuts between sentences of whatever document I had in my typewriter.

That's why I didn't know that the chaplain's assistant, a blue-eyed blond with a captivating smile, and Elena Makhoul, Michel's sister, Pete Dunn's secretary, had gravitated to one another in the back of the chapel, had—engrossed in conversation—strolled down to the dining room together and told the stories of their lives over lunch. All of this happened in the spring, back before the Shouf Mountain War, and it came to my attention only afterwards when Elena walked into my office to ask a favor. She had a box in her hand that she had addressed to Cpl. John Olson at the Marine base. She wondered if I might deliver it there for her.

"You didn't know?" she said. Her smile turned shy, but her brown eyes locked onto mine. "I like him. A lot. I made him a scarf with his initials."

I delivered the package, handing it over to the guard at the gate and asking him to pass it on. The boy was cheerful. "Sure," he said, "glad to." And in a few days Elena reported back that she had heard from John. He had received the package; he loved his scarf. I am surprised now that we could so easily send a package into a military barracks surrounded by enemies.

The Shouf Mountain War had changed the rules for the Marines. No longer could they come up to the mountain to visit. With our area now off-limits John had no way of seeing Elena unless she could come to the base. "He is inviting me," she said, "but, of course, I can't go. My parents would never let me."

John kept inviting. He said, "Maybe if your brother came, too..." The Makhouls compromised. They said she could go, provided that Michel went, and the Fullers. So, we agreed to visit the Marines on their own turf, Sunday noon, October 16, and to bring a picnic for several men. For Elena I was willing to do this, but I expected to feel awkward with military men and jittery about being on their base. Besides that, I was stressed about time. We had to stop on the way there and buy food, because I had been unable to prepare anything except cookies. And afterwards, we had another event. The mission was hosting a small party in honor of Mabel Summers just before evening church. Honoring Mabel was difficult, because she ran away from the spotlight, so we couldn't miss this rare occasion.

Later every detail of that afternoon became important, what we remembered and what we didn't—the arrangement of the camp, the things we talked about, the Marines filling sandbags, Pedro's sadness, Terry's horror that we drank Beirut's water. We strained to bring it all back and ached for another chance. I know that John met us at the gate, with a rifle slung from his shoulder by a strap. He was not very big; I thought Marines were supposed to be bigger. He had a clean, fresh look about him and my dermatologist would have judged him too fair to be in the Middle East at all.

A guard swung the front gate open for us, and we were permitted to bring the car inside and park it in an open space beyond the central part of the base. It was a short walk back to the picnic table that Terry and Pedro were holding for us, to the right of the gate, in view of the busy airport road. The picnic tables (there were two) surprised me. They looked like the tables in any American park, and I had never before seen one in Lebanon. Mostly the camp was makeshift and included various types of facilities, built for other purposes and co-opted for barracks and mess hall and other military functions. The long warehouse kind of structures might have had something to do with the airport once, since the road through the base led right to the airport employees' parking lot on the south side. I know that an iron gate closed this road, separating the base from the airport, though I don't remember seeing this second gate. Barbed wire surrounded the base, broken only by the two gates.

Wayne and I tore open bags of broasted chicken and French fries, pizza, canned drinks and the cookies I had made. John suggested that we pray, and we circled the table—three Marines, two Lebanese young people, and two missionaries—while he asked God's blessings on our gathering. The food was hot and greasy, the drinks still cold.

I wish I could remember more about John's friends, like the color of Terry's eyes and that fine, appreciative thing he said about his family, which moved me so much. He was a Southerner; his speech told me that. I vaguely remember a slender face and slender hands. Terry's specialty was preventive medicine, and he was particularly concerned that the Marines not consume impure water or food. He asked me if we drank the Beirut water and then if we boiled or treated it in any way. I told him that a few of the missionaries boiled their drinking water but most of us did not. He said, "You should be dead." We laughed, but he didn't. He said, "I actually don't understand how the whole city isn't dying." He elaborated—tests the Marines had made found the water full of typhoid, bubonic plague, polio and millions of nasty amoebas. He showed us big containers, black with white markings, which he said held the only water the men were allowed to drink. It was all brought to them by American ships. I am still amazed, imagining the logistics of keeping those tanks supplied.

(This conversation piqued my interest so that later I labored through a scientific paper from which I learned that the Lebanese, especially those who grew up in Beirut, are immune to numerous horrible diseases, because they have ingested the bacteria in small amounts from infancy.)

I remember a lot of activity. Other uniformed men strolled by, called greetings and got invited to join us. Some came over and shook hands. One or two sat down for a while. Somewhere out of sight men were shouting and laughing, while nearby, a group of fellows were filling sandbags, their shovels making soft scraping sounds.

At some point the men told us about the big party planned for the base on Saturday. There would be guests from outside and live music and probably lots of food. Their anticipation of this break in the routine was obvious.

John, Terry and Pedro all lived, they told us, in the huge concrete building maybe a hundred yards from us, also just inside the gate but on the left side. We who sat with our backs to it turned and looked. It was an ugly, hulking structure, with a raw, cold look. Because it was an unfinished building, the bottom level had not been closed in, revealing the local system of supporting buildings with pillars, so that no walls were bearing walls, except for the elevator shaft. I admit I didn't check it out closely, so later when I wanted to remember it, I couldn't.

The sun shone on our picnic, on the world. Every leaf and pine needle, every stone, every roof, every floating cloud, every horizon shimmered. The sandy earth under us was bright, and the smiles around the table. John looked at Elena who held his eyes a moment, then glanced away, with the corners of her mouth quivering. I took off my jacket. The fellows rolled up their sleeves. From the camp the mountain where we lived looked like a park, like Eden with towns scattered through it. Michel, Elena, Wayne and I all pointed out landmarks, beginning with the Bustan Hotel and told them how to take that as a starting point and know where the Makhouls lived and the Fullers and where our offices were.

The Marines in turn pointed at places they knew. "Right there, see that big rock; there's a big gun behind it. It shoots at us."

Wayne said, "Where do we hide if it shoots today?"

"Right here," Pedro said, pointing, "just jump in." Only then did we notice the trench, a few yards from our table, a clean-cut, straight foxhole, eight feet long and several feet deep.

I visualized squatting in it to get my head down and said, "I'm going to hate getting that red mud on my skirt."

We all laughed, even Pedro who had just returned from Puerto Rico, because he had escorted home the body of his best friend. When John told us that, everyone got very quiet. Finally, one of us asked, "How did he die?"

"We took some big shells." Pedro said. "Several men died."

Now we knew that one of those reports we had heard about casualties was about Pedro's friend, maybe a boy with square shoulders and warm eyes like Pedro, a Spanish rhythm in his speech.

"I'm sorry," we all said.

They told us then that John and Terry both had duty on "the line," the perimeter around their area, where they were vulnerable to snipers and where most of their casualties occurred. Terry said, "It takes ten years off my life every time I go out there."

"Casualties have made us humble," John said. "The chaplain's congregation has really picked up."

Now we had a chance to ask what we had wondered so many times. "Why do we always hear that you have been fired on and didn't return the fire?"

"That's our orders," John said. "You see us walk around with our guns, but they are empty. We need special orders to load our rifles."

And Pedro said, "The standing order is, If your buddy falls beside you, pick him up and bring him in."

Michel looked astonished. "You can't defend yourself?"

"What you can do is get on the radio," John said, "and ask for permission to fire back. Anybody who fires without permission is subject to court martial and prison."

"You can die before you get permission," Pedro said. He didn't sound bitter, just sad.

And Terry added, "The enemy has our radio signal and hears when we get the order to fire back, so the snipers usually disappear immediately."

Knowing what I knew about the other armed factions running around Lebanon, I admired such discipline, but the policy seemed ridiculous to me. I had to tell them that no one, friend or enemy, was impressed with their "show of force," since it became apparent that they lost men and didn't retaliate.

They said they knew this, but reminded us that they had proven they would shoot under some circumstances. With considerable pride they related the story about their participation in the fighting for Suq al-Gharb.

The Lebanese Army had been close to losing Suq al-Gharb, they said, and had begged the Marines for help. In September when that powerful attack, combining Druze and foreign forces, had been sweeping down the road toward Suq al-Gharb, with massacres in its wake, the Marines had held their fire. But if the Lebanese Army lost Suq al-Gharb, the enemy would break into the suburbs of Beirut. There would be chaos and more massacres. Maybe the whole Lebanese government would fall. Finally, the enemy launched a tremendous tank attack, and the Army officers did not think they could hold out against it. Hearing this, the Marine commanders ordered their men to stop the tanks without hitting one, and they had laid down a wall of fire in front of the attack. Though no tank had been hit, all of them turned back, and the battle ended.

The story sounded to me like something written by Marine brass for press consumption, and I noted that an effort had been made to help the men believe in what they were doing. But in fact, their version fit with what we had seen and heard, and it agreed with what had been reported by the BBC.

We took a walk, passing a game of horseshoes, enjoying the ringing and thudding sounds as metal struck metal and iron flopped into the sand pit, and then we came upon a group of men playing touch football. A big fellow with bulging muscles, wearing a T shirt and ragged cut-off pants, held the ball instead of snapping it and shouted, "Hey, we got visitors. We got girls."

The line of men crouching in front of him lifted their heads.

"Who's winning?" Wayne said.

"We're all winning. Come play with us."

"Wish I could."

"Come on. We're celebrating the Navy's birthday. We got steaks on the grill."

I could smell the meat. I said, "Too bad we ate so much chicken and pizza."

The football game resumed.

The base was like a village, like Beit Meri—busy, hospitable, happy, under siege—except it was an alien, lonely village. I became infected with happiness against my will, catching it like a shivery disease, feeling its nearness to love and loss and fear, fighting miserable symptoms such as regret that we had never come before.

John and Elena took a stroll alone, asking permission to leave us. We reminded them of the exact time that we must depart for Monsourieh, and they looked at their watches, promised to meet us at the car and disappeared, holding hands.

Terry and Pedro played host to the rest of us. Michel remembers that they showed us an amphibious vehicle, and Wayne recalls seeing the infrared glasses that gave them night vision. I guess I was not impressed with this kind of thing. What I remember is the way Terry talked about his family. He missed them all—his wife, his parents and a whole circle of loving and faithful people—and he was so grateful for them. Their loyalty and support kept him going, he said, gave him comfort and courage. Pedro was quieter but, in some way I can't identify now, he was a warm presence, and sometimes made us smile. It was Pedro I mentioned a few days later to my kids, telling them only that "I liked him so much."

At the car, shaking hands, our mountain home hovering so near but so essentially far, Terry said, "It sure is good to talk to somebody besides Marines."

And Pedro said, "I hope I get to see you again before I leave."

John and Elena were late, and I began to feel anxious about getting up the hill to Mabel's party. Michel, Wayne and I milled around at the car, looking at our watches, not blaming them for wanting to be alone but getting irritated because they had overstayed, and when we saw them coming, we signaled our hurry by piling into the car. Consequently, we said goodbye to John through the car windows. As we drove away he was bending over to see our faces, lifting a hand and saying, "Thank you for coming." Because he looked like a little boy being left at summer camp, I wanted to reach out and touch him, but the car was moving, and I had rolled up the window.

All the way through Chiyah and Sin el-Fil we were silent, our happiness having spilled out along the airport road, as the brilliant afternoon spilled out over the edge of the sea. I knew that we had been rude, or at least cold. It was my fault. I had been the one so anxious to leave. He was a kid far from home; I should have hugged him. I could have done it for his mother. I should have taken his hand at least and said that I would pray for him, but I had missed my chance. On the stretch of road up to Monsourieh, we tried to pick ourselves up again, agreeing that the visit had been wonderful and promising one another that we would go again. I didn't know how to tell the others about this image of John, bending to wave goodbye, the memory that was following me home.

That's why I need this snapshot. So long as I stare, it replaces the other one in my head.

Getting to Know John

Elena came to my office to talk about John.

"I think I love him."

"And how does John feel?"

"I know he likes me a lot. He says that if anything happens, like he gets orders to leave suddenly—and he thinks he's leaving in November anyway—he wants to come back and see me. He wants a chance for us to know each other."

I hoped John and Elena would have plenty of time, because I could see that he would be good for her, but their opportunities were shrinking. Already, our peaceful sun-drenched Sunday looked like a small opening in the clouds. The storm had resumed. On Tuesday the Marines had been shelled. We were having this talk on Wednesday, after hearing booming off and on all day. Lebanon's National Reconciliation Committee was supposed to meet on Thursday, but the parties were still in dispute about where. Some factions didn't want the meeting to happen at all, so they shelled all proposed spots, plus the Army in Suq al-Gharb and the Marines at the airport.

My hopes conflicted with one another, because more than ever since our visit with the Marines, I wanted America to get them out of this dirty war before any more of them died. In my head I composed letters to Ronald Reagan telling him there was no way the Marines were going to make peace out of this chaos. Sometimes my imaginary letters became tirades telling him that this was a wicked place and a dangerous place, a war zone, a snakepit, and not a place for idealistic boys with no bullets in their guns. But the letters never left my head. The people who made American policy in the Middle East, I told myself, had never showed an interest in the opinions of Americans who had lived there for many years. They probably assumed we were prejudiced; and they were probably right. A letter from me would make no difference, I said, to excuse myself. I didn't even know that it was already too late.

Are You Lonesome Tonight?

While we were dressing for church on Sunday morning we heard the news on the radio. An explosion at the Marine base. Two Marines had died, the announcer said. Wayne and I looked at one another and said, "*Haram*! More casualties," and went on buttoning shirts and wiping shoes.

A few minutes later we knew that the French paratroopers had also been attacked. The two explosions were only twenty seconds apart. That was odd. And interesting. No, that was ominous.

More announcements. Five Marines dead. Then eleven. By the time we left for church, the numbers were above twenty. A truck had crashed into a barracks building and exploded.

In the vestibule of the church we saw Elena, looking out of touch, confused. She said, "I don't feel anything."

"We're the same," I told her. "We don't know what to feel."

I reminded her that hundreds of Marines lived on the base, and we knew only three. There must be other barracks, too, besides the one in which John and Terry and Pedro slept.

She said, "That's right. Maybe he's O.K."

She told me that she had sent a letter to John on Saturday. Michel had delivered it to his building, but he didn't see John.

All day the numbers mounted. By evening we knew that the big concrete building just inside the gate had been attacked, the one I had turned to look at over my shoulder, when one of the fellows said, "That's our barracks." It was the headquarters building as well as a barracks. The suicide bomber had crashed through the south gate and driven past the horseshoe pits and the picnic table and the main gate, where we knew that the sentry stood helpless.

I don't remember when we knew the final toll of Marines killed: 241.

On Monday I called the embassy. No one would tell me anything. I called again, a different office. They said they were not ready to disclose information about individual casualties.

I got a number for the Marine base, told whoever answered the phone that I was a friend of Cpl. John Olson and needed to know if he had survived. They referred me to the Commandant's Office in Washington! I was furious.

Elena and I got into my car and drove to the base. Traffic on the airport road was outrageous. Streams of cars were cruising past the base while their drivers stared at the destroyed building. First they passed on the far side of the road, going toward the airport, then they made a U-turn and came back, getting a closer look on their way back to the city. Young Marines with dazed expressions on their faces stood in the street just outside the gate, directing this traffic. It seemed absurd that they should be there, facilitating drive-by tours of their own humiliation. I wondered if they now had bullets in their guns.

The bombed building was nothing but a heap of broken concrete. Three cement floors had pancaked down and great slabs of concrete lay on top of one another. When I saw it, I felt hopeless.

Like all the other drivers, I turned around, but what I wanted to do was more complicated. I had to talk to someone. First, signaling my intentions to one of the boys in the street, I pulled out of the traffic. Uncertainty showed on his face. He seemed to be looking for a way to protect himself if I were not trustworthy, and at the same time he was trying to be nice to this woman who didn't fit his idea of an enemy.

I told him that we were desperate for news about John Olson. He said he didn't know anything.

"He lived on the second floor."

He glanced toward the building, as though it might tell him something. He said, "I don't think anybody survived on that floor."

I asked then about Terry, not remembering at the moment the rest of his name. The soldier said he knew a Terry who died, but maybe there was more than one Terry.

We were parked in front of the closed gate of the compound, and I could see that this gentlemanly and disciplined boy needed to get rid of us. He kept looking toward the guard in the little sentry box by the gate, maybe expecting him to say something.

I felt I couldn't just drive away. Elena had an idea. She said, "Will you pass a message for me?" She wrote, as quickly as she could, a note to the disc jockey of the Marine radio station and asked him to send us a signal. In case John was alive the jockey should play the Elvis Presley song "Are You Lonesome Tonight?" on Tuesday—the next day. It was a song that John had once requested for Elena. If John was dead, she said, then the jockey must not play that record on Tuesday.

The boy promised that he would pass the note to the disc jockey and we thanked him. Finally I asked him if he would be at his position other times. He didn't know. I told him that I wanted to come back again to ask about John. "If you aren't going to be here, please tell the one who is, so he can tell me what happened to John." I knew it was a lot to ask, but I felt that these young men on duty in the street were our only hope of getting past the bureaucracy.

He said, "I don't know if I can. I will try."

All day on Tuesday Elena listened to the Marine station. She said that the jockey's voice sounded so sad. He kept saying to his fellow Marines, "Please take care of yourselves." All day he never played "Are You Lonesome Tonight?"

Elena came to see me on Wednesday morning. The skin trembled on her cheek as she said, "I am losing hope." We talked and decided that we still didn't know. Maybe the disc jockey didn't even get the note. Maybe he got the note but didn't know about John.

My office was a madhouse of activity. Abu Sleiman was putting the final touches on his translation of the *MasterLife* books, and I had organized the rest of the staff, everybody but the sales people, to finish the production in time for the conference in Cyprus. Everybody, regardless of his job description, was typing, printing, collating, stacking, punching, binding or boxing—sixty sets of three huge books. This rush was part of the cost of five weeks lost during the fighting.

I deserted the job and my staff and drove to the base again—down the hill, through the clutter of Chiyah to the airport circle, where the traffic seemed less than two days earlier—thinking all the way that not everybody in that barracks had died. If there were three survivors, they could be John and Terry and Pedro.

The soldier near the gate was not the same one. I could see he felt threatened by my pulling out of the traffic and stopping and opening the car door. This made me feel sad, and I held up my empty hands as I approached. When I told him that I had come before to ask about John Olson and hoped he might have a message for me, he glanced away, as though looking for support, first to his left at the gate, then to his right at his comrade who was waving on other cars.

Without quite looking at me, he said, "Yes, John Olson is missing."

"Missing. What does that mean exactly?"

"It means that they don't have a body they can identify."

That brought unspeakable images into my head. It also left me too suddenly with nothing more to ask. Behind the soldier were those slabs of broken concrete, the collapsed floors of the barracks, making the unspeakable simply logical. I couldn't think of a reason to keep standing there; neither could I decide what else to do.

I said, "Thank you," and turned toward my car. When I did, I faced the closed gate and the picnic table behind the barbed wire. It had been only ten days since we all sat there telling stories, since we drove away in a hurry, with John lifting his hand in farewell, leaning in toward the car window, with some brave uncertainty in his face.

With my hand on the car door, I couldn't decide to open it, but turned and went back to the guard, noticing then how he held his rifle with both hands at an angle across his body. He must have been twenty years old. His eyes looked very tired.

I said, "Is there... maybe...something we can do for you guys?"

I was very close to crying, probably because John was crushed under those tons of concrete, but at the moment I thought it might be because some mother's twenty-year-old was obliged to stand in the middle of this nightmare with a rifle.

Slowly he said, "Thank you. I guess we have everything we need." And then he looked at my eyes for the first time and added, "People have been kind," as though to comfort me.

When I got back to my office Elena came in. I left my desk and sat beside her on the little plastic sofa against the wall. And I told her.

She cried immediately. She twisted her hands and groaned. She raged. "It's not fair. It's not fair. We had no time." Her tears ran like a flash flood. I gave her a tissue from my pocket, then got up to bring a whole box. I was standing up, holding the box toward her when she opened her right hand and said, "He held this hand." Wringing it in pain she said, "He held my hand, and he told me that after things are better in Lebanon he wanted to come back and see me so we would have a chance to know if we wanted to be together."

I cried with her. Someone opened the door and found us sobbing and left again.

After she became calmer, she began to wonder about small practical things, like the scarf she had knitted for John. I told her that I knew they sent personal effects to families, but it seemed doubtful that a scarf would be pulled out of the rubble of that building. That reminded us that somewhere in Minnesota a family named Olson was devastated.

She did not have his home address and neither did I. I wondered how we could have lived in this situation for so long and still let things like that happen.

I offered to call Pete Dunn, her boss, and tell him that Elena needed the rest of the afternoon off, but she decided that it would be easier to go back to the office and work than to go home with nothing to do.

I went to the bathroom to wash my eyes, and then I joined my staff at the collating table.

Mastering Life

All that week Wayne and I stayed at the office and worked into the evening, and the following week we never ate supper at home, except once when

Maxine King sent over food and we took it home. We had to let the staff go at the end of the work day, but Wayne had figured out exactly how much we had to accomplish every twenty-four hours in order to travel with those books on Saturday, November 5. His calculations told us there was no way, unless somebody worked in the evenings. So at suppertime one of us would go out for a rotisserie chicken or sandwiches, and we would eat and keep on working. He ran the copy machine and the punching gadget in the big workroom at the end of the hall. The collating tables extended out of that room and down the middle of the hall, so I walked, down one side of it and up the other, gathering the pages, hundreds per volume. Each volume had to be placed into a three-ring binder. And each finished book had to be packed into an appropriate box.

I wrote my kids a letter dated October 30, saying that I was going with the Lebanon group to the conference, "that is, if my new ID card comes from the Amin al-Am, and if there isn't new fighting serious enough to close the airport. Yesterday someone observed a part of my frantic effort to finish the material and told me, 'Never mind, the airport will be closed by that time, and you won't have to go.'" Not going was not even an option. People were coming from Jordan, Egypt and Israel for the study. If the planes didn't fly I would have to swim with the books on my back.

The sound of shelling made me move faster around the table. Life felt so precarious. Anything could happen and leave me with my work unfinished. The hallway in which I was working had our offices on one side of it and on the other a long row of windows opening into the parking lot. I would get scared sometimes and jump into one of the offices for a few moments. One evening shells fell so close that shrapnel showered down in the parking lot—jagged metal, cracking against the walls, ricocheting, pinging against somebody's car, gouging holes in the asphalt. The seminary students all ran toward the basement, yelling at us to come. Wayne told me to go, so I did, but when he didn't come, I ran back up the stairs to see what had happened to him. He said, "I've got this machine going really well now, and I can't stop it." So I went back to the collating table.

All the while the tragedy at the Marine base was never far from anyone's mind. Our Christian friends wanted to comfort us but were almost too embarrassed to talk about it. This terrible thing had happened in their country, to their friend. Lebanese honor had been soiled. What it said about their country was untrue but would be believed everywhere for as long as this event was remembered. And the disaster had another side—America, the ally they had counted on, looked now like an inept giant. This was a setback they had not expected. Life was totally confusing.

My own mind was on the other men with whom we had picnicked. From somewhere I got the idea that a few injured Marines had been taken to the American University Hospital, and when I called I learned about Pedro. A talkative Lebanese nurse told me he had been there and was in good shape when they transferred him out to a ship.

I was so encouraged that I asked if there had been anyone named Terry. There was, she thought; she didn't know the rest of his name, because apparently he didn't know. His eardrums were so damaged that he couldn't hear. Sometimes he said he was married, but he couldn't remember his wife's name.

We finished the books. My ID came, and the airport stayed open. The conference was work, too, but I had stopped rushing and, since there was no gunfire, I slept better there in Cyprus than I did in Lebanon. We sat in meetings most of the day and then did homework in our rooms at night. In addition to what everyone else was doing I had to organize some method of getting an adaptation of the material as soon as possible.

Jewish as well as Arab Christians from Israel attended the conference. For most of us this was our first chance to meet Jewish believers. I didn't have much time to get acquainted with them. They were at a big table for English speakers, and I was at a table with Arab women. But in places like the dining room I witnessed some honest discussions between the Jews and the Lebanese. The most memorable involved Charlie Costa, who vented his strong resentment over Israeli leaflets dropped on Beirut during the invasion, advising the population to flee, giving them a map of the routes they should take out of the city.

The Israelis did not understand his attitude. They said, "That was for your protection. They gave you a chance."

Charlie raised his powerful voice and beat on his chest, as he said, "Beirut is mine! I was born there. I was raised there. My school is there.

My house is there. My church is there. My friends are there. No one has a right to tell me that I must flee if I want to live."

At the end, because of plane schedules, the Lebanese group was the first to leave the conference hotel. The Jewish believers stood on the front steps to tell us goodbye, and I watched Jewish and Lebanese Christians hugging one another. That was an item for my diary of peace.

Only Spectators

We discovered that there were SAM missiles a few miles from our door, just across the canyon. The only reason this seemed important was that we had heard so much about SAM missiles, a Soviet anti-aircraft weapon. I could not claim to know any specifics about the nature and capabilities of this weapon.

We had seen activity and known for a while about the presence of something significant at that spot, without wondering much what it was. Of course the Israelis knew exactly. When their planes appeared we heard the pop and whoosh of the missiles and watched their fiery progress through the air, but shiny silver balloons suddenly billowed out behind the attacking planes and none of them were hit.

This happened on November 20. For about ten minutes the situation looked and sounded like World War III. Syrian jets went up and circled—away from the action, over the Biqaa. In the other direction American planes scrambled to circle our ships, while a dozen Israeli aircraft dived and dropped bombs just in front of us. The whole village came out to watch. Israeli planes were frequent visitors in our skies, but we did not often see them drop bombs, and war is such a fascinating spectacle when we feel safe in the grandstands.

Two weeks later, on December 4, we left our soup on the dining table, when we heard warplanes again, and this time we witnessed two U.S. Navy fighter planes being shot down over this same missile site. Some Western press agencies reported that this happened in the Biqaa. I have to differ. The Biqaa was beyond a mountain range and not visible from our house. This happened more or less under Jabal Kanisa, up-canyon from our house and just across, in a part of the Metn that had been occupied by the Syrians for a long time. We stood in our front door and watched and didn't realize yet that the planes were American.

They came in quite close to the ground, slowly enough that we could easily find them and follow their flight. They were not our best fighter planes, I decided. Streaks of flame went up, out of the woods. One jet erupted into a ball of fire—a sudden red blossom with black-edged petals. Burning debris fell out of the fire, and almost immediately we saw a parachute floating down with a person hanging from its lines. The other plane tumbled wing over wing, trailing smoke, and disappeared toward the north. We went back to the table and finished our soup.

Later we heard on the news that this second plane struck a house in Jounieh and killed an occupant as well as the crewman. The pilot we saw parachuting down was taken prisoner by the Syrians. The battleship New Jersey began shelling the Shouf Mountains.

Jesse Jackson came to Lebanon and negotiated the release of the captured pilot.

It was all very confusing and depressing. We wondered what America might be trying to do in Lebanon, and what it would take to make her regret it. I don't think I even considered what it could do to us.

Two Ways of Thinking

The time has come to explain my theory about what I call the small-country mentality and its corollary, the big-country mentality—two opposite ways of thinking which get assigned to people's heads by fate, along with their place of birth.

This understanding is of importance to me, because I lived for so long in a very small and weak country, while being a citizen of a very big and powerful country. Only because I lived in this small country do I truly understand the big one. Only because I stayed in Lebanon for years at a time and then came back to America and then went again, did I manage to compare and to figure out what bigness and smallness have done to our heads—why I was disgusted in Lebanon and angry in America—why the

Lebanese blamed everything on somebody else and Americans were so complacent. Below are some of my observations.

> The big country cannot find the little country on a globe. The little country knows the cost of airfare to the big country and has memorized its states and capitals.
>
> The big country does not know what language is spoken in the little country. The little country studies the language of the big country in school and looks for people to speak it with.
>
> The big country hears mostly news about itself. The little country hears every day broadcasts from its own cities and from all its neighbors, as well as propaganda beamed in from the other side of the world.
>
> The big country believes its news. The little country does not believe much of what it hears.
>
> The big country considers the little country an interesting place to take a vacation, if there is no trouble and the exchange rate is favorable. The little country thinks of the big country as an option in case of famine or persecution.
>
> The big country thinks of the little country as one they ought to help when it is in trouble. The small country thinks it is entitled to this help.
>
> The big country thinks its responsibilities include policing the affairs of the small country. The small country deduces from this behavior that the big country is responsible, along with God, for everything that happens in the world.
>
> The big country enjoys throwing its weight around. The little country enjoys seeing the big guy get knocked down once in a while.

> The big country is afraid of losing its power. The little country understands fear perfectly and knows well the peril of being less powerful.
>
> The big country admires people who stand up against injustice. The little country knows that sometimes it must bend before the wind and stand up only after the wind has passed.
>
> The big country maintains a spy network, runs a propaganda program, and works secretly to get its way all over the world. The small country believes that its own misfortunes are part of a plot created by this network.

* * *

When 241 Marines died in their barracks, the Beirut newspapers claimed they were all sleeping off hangovers from the party they had the night before. I guessed they thought Americans wouldn't be vulnerable when sober.

When two of our planes were shot out of the sky, and the rest of the Marines left, the Syrians became larger in the Lebanese mind. Now we heard people say, "Whatever Syria wants is what will happen. We will wait and see." The Syrians were bigger and stronger than the Lebanese and perhaps more patient than America. America had come and gone, and the Syrian Army still occupied Lebanon.

Lebanon was a small, small country and disappeared, our children told us, from the evening news in America.

Letters

I helped Elena write a letter to the Olsons, though she still had no address. She planned to mail it to the Marine base and hoped that they would send it on.

While I was in Cyprus she had received a letter from John, written on Friday and mailed on Saturday, before he died on Sunday morning. The letter contained the snapshot taken on his camera the afternoon of our visit. I stared at the picture, at their youth and hope, seeing the intention of closeness expressed by posture, the sunshine that fell on them and the absence of warning. I thought that it could be the last picture ever taken of him.

She said, "Do I need to send it to them?" And when I didn't answer, she said, "It's the only picture I have of him."

I, who had no authority, gave her permission to keep it. I said, "Maybe John sent them a copy."

She said, "Oh, yes, maybe he did."

Reading and rereading John's letter, looking at the snapshot, she found it harder to believe that he was gone. She said, "Could he be in a hospital somewhere?" She wrote the Olsons that she needed to hear the truth from them. Helping her write this, I again felt puzzled and angry that, while in America the information we needed was in the newspapers, in Lebanon it remained unattainable. We saw pictures and news articles, but names of individual Marines were naturally less newsworthy, and both the embassy and the Marine base still refused to give out lists or answer questions about who had died.

Wayne and I received frightened letters from our children. They worried about us, and that made us worry about them. Jan was so stressed that she had arranged sessions with a counselor. Remembering that in 1976 she had come unglued over a package of pictures I sent her, black and white snapshots I had taken along the Green Line, I felt that her distress was even bigger than concern for us. It was about the disintegration of Lebanon, a home she had lost.

I wrote the kids a long letter, made five copies, and in the late afternoon delivered them to a Beit Meri man who was leaving the next day for the States. I loved thinking that in a few days they would have news from us. When I got to the man's house the guns in Beit Meri and Broummana were banging, and I was anxious to get off the streets, but then I had to stop at Chaanine's store for some badly needed groceries.

Coming out of the store into all that booming, I stepped into the unexpected splendor of sunset. My car was parked on a small cliff in front of the store, near an old *snobar* tree. From the knoll one could see the whole city of Beirut, even its wandering streets and tall buildings when the air was clean and the light was right, but that late afternoon, the city was a blue blur under the spreading limbs of the great tree, and the tree, with its twisted branches and million needles, now backlighted by the setting sun, had become a piece of black lace against the orange sky. I stopped, with plastic bags of groceries pulling my arms to my sides, awestruck, because the sun created art while the guns spoke of death, each oblivious to the other. Shoppers dashed to their cars and fled, while I stood transfixed by the sense that something invisible had taken shape in front of my eyes, but then it was gone and there was only artillery and sunset.

When I turned toward home, there was Jabal Sunnin, its snow as orange as the western sky, and by the time I trudged up the path to my house, flinching from another great bang, I was thinking that the light kept on shining into our darkness, though the darkness never understood.

A Tough Question

Our son Jim was getting married in West Monroe, Louisiana, on December 26. We planned a reunion with my family, Christmas with everybody there, the wedding, and a whirlwind trip across the country. We would go and return between December 14 and January 14.

We flew Royal Jordanian to Amman and New York, then went on to Chicago for a day of rest, before business consultations at the David C. Cook Company. On our rest day I went to a city library and asked for the Minneapolis newspapers between October 23 and the end of the month. For the first time I read the stories and saw the pictures that people in America had seen about what happened to the Marines. I found the name "Cpl. John Arnie Olson" on the list of casualties from Minnesota. Then I found an article about John's family, with enough information that I was able to get their telephone number from the information operator.

I talked with both his mother and father. They already knew my name, because they had received a letter from John telling about our Sunday afternoon visit. He had given them Elena's address and asked them to write to her. Though they had gotten the letter after they knew that John was dead, Mr. Olson had written to her. I told them some things about our visit with John and his friends—that they were happy that day, and calm and brave when they talked about the war. I said that John was a fine boy and they should be proud of what he had become. They said it was good to talk with someone who had seen him more recently than they.

To my surprise they mentioned the scarf that Elena had made for John. They wondered if maybe there was a way they could get it. I learned from them that Terry had survived.

The Olsons had some questions that I couldn't answer. Especially they wanted to know what John's death had accomplished. Understanding their need to find some meaning in their loss, I promised to write to them about that. I dreaded it.

Strategies and Damages

Dinner Music

In January, 1984, on the first day that Wayne and I were back at work after our son's wedding, the Druze unloaded five thousand shells on Christian areas from Jounieh to Khalde, and Pat Dunn and I planned a dinner party. Five thousand shells create ten thousand booms—a suitable introduction to the coming weeks. Attacks and counter-attacks continued, Malcolm Kerr, president of the American University of Beirut and indisputably a friend of Lebanon, was shot dead in the hall outside his office, and every day brought us new excuses not to plan anything.

On the very day of the party everybody was bleary-eyed and clumsy, having spent the night listening to noise, and the morning headlines warned of a decisive battle coming. Nobody called off the party—a modest progressive dinner, only two steps. The main course would be at the Dunns', and then everyone would drive up to Beit Meri for dessert and coffee at our house.

That afternoon another "party" started and was too loud to ignore. I sat in my office, trying to concentrate on the business letter in my typewriter, aware that nothing else in life seemed even partially controllable.

The phone rang. It was Pat. "Frances, I don't think it's going to work."

"Yeah, you're right," I conceded, but Pat didn't intend to give up—just to compromise.

"I've been talking to some of our guests. They want to go home early anyway, so come to dinner, O.K.? but I'll do dessert here. That way we don't all have to be on the road, and people can get home earlier, too."

By dinner time shells were falling everywhere, from Jounieh to towns on the mountain, but Pat's dining table sparkled with china and her best glasses and silver, and the house smelled of roast beef and coffee. We sat down to one of Pat's perfect meals. We ate, we talked, we laughed, everything we did punctuated with emphatic explosions. I noted with one corner of my brain, while following the conversation, that maybe Beit Meri was being hit.

Bill Trimble told jokes, as always, often giving credit for his funny stories to someone else, like Dr. Manoogian. Pete, who traveled frequently in his work, sometimes to Monaco and frequently to North Africa, told travel stories. He talked about unusual foods he had discovered in little restaurants in places like Casablanca, and about losing his wallet to a pickpocket, whom he followed until he got his money back. Of course, everyone wanted from us the details about Jim's wedding and the Louisiana ice storm that had stranded our whole family and some of the guests afterwards.

Occasionally a shell landed nearby, and the explosion would be an ear-splitting crash, and the house would vibrate. One of these close ones put the lights out, and for a while we sat in the dark, going on with the chatter and the laughter, until someone in the neighborhood got the community generator going. We heard it sputter and roar into action a few seconds before the lights flared on again, glinting off the rim of a china platter and Pete's bald head and Bill's glasses.

Sometimes we talked about the battle noises. When a series of rockets passed over our heads, various people at the table tried to describe their sounds. Pat, walking around with the coffee pot, said they made her think that someone was moving the furniture upstairs. I added my idea that the furniture must be on wheels; I had always imagined, hearing such rockets, that they were rolling across a concrete sky on skateboards. The analogies made us laugh.

I felt disturbed by the explosions up the hill toward Beit Meri and a little worried about how we would get home, but thinking about either seemed useless. The food was delicious, the coffee hot, and the company perfect. We enjoyed all of it; with determination we enjoyed it.

Maybe the others would find, as I did, that when they tried to write home about this party they noticed a bizarre quality in the experience. They would become aware of questions hard to answer. Perhaps they would tear up their paper and start over and never be satisfied with the way they told it. Even now, I feel defensive and think I should explain that we went on with this social occasion, not because we had no fear or because we didn't care what was happening, but because having dinner with our friends was important and sitting there was as good as any of our options.

About 8:30 p.m., Bill made a phone call and confirmed that nothing was falling right then in the direction of his house, so the Trimbles and others dashed out. Though I wanted badly to go home, driving up the hill to Beit Meri seemed risky, so we accepted the Dunns' invitation to sleep at their house. As we were going to bed in their daughter's room, a big fire glowed down in the suburbs of Beirut. Bright flashes from new explosions lighted the city, and red tracers drew slow arcs through the air. Wayne closed the shutters and his ears and began to snore. I slept lightly and knew that the noise continued all night, slacking off toward daylight.

Writing Day

Thursday, loveliest day of the week—my writing day, but all I wanted was to verify the safety of our house. Wayne went to the office, riding with Pete. As I got into my car to go home, I saw that smoke hovered over the Beirut suburbs, not just yesterday's smoke, because it thickened seconds before the sound of another explosion reached my ears.

The village seemed to be intact—*snobars* sheltering the winding road, water bubbling out of the pipe at the spring, the simple houses facing the winter sun—until I got to the little store, where the road was littered with glass, dirt and stones. In front of me our house stood on the hill, accidental and ancient and dear as always, but when I got out of the car I looked over my shoulder at the stair-step apartments of Boutros and Jaqueline, George and Lulu, and saw that the cement block wall that was supposed to surround the patio of the lower apartment had disappeared, leaving a broken, jagged edge. Running back, I saw that the front wall of Jaqueline's apartment had also vanished, exposing the inner walls and ceiling which were now scarred by shrapnel. Rubble covered the steps up to their house. Dreading to go up, I spoke with a man who was pacing back and forth in front of the store, and he told me that the family was "safe, praise God."

If a high-speed train had passed through the house, the effect might have been the same. Their meager possessions had been shattered, crushed, blown away, along with the front wall. A great pile of debris on the front side of the patio—chunks and crumbs of concrete blocks, splintered wood, glass which used to be plates and cups, a few fragments of cloth—expressed a part of their loss and indicated that they had already worked to clean up the mess. On the edge of the heap lay two bent pieces of the shell that hit them.

Against the back wall of the sitting room, little Boulos sat on what remained of their couch, cheap and frayed before, its cushions now gouged by ragged pieces of shrapnel or concrete. Sprigs of cotton and coiled metal springs protruded from the holes. The child, who normally called out to me from a distance, "*Ya* American!" did not even brighten or speak to me but kept staring at his dusty toes.

Jaqueline, in her long, baggy dress, pushed at the rubble with a broom. I told her, "*Al-hamdilla ala salaame,*" and when she looked up, she extended both hands in a helpless gesture, letting the broom handle fall loose between them, as she said, "Where were you when I needed you?" My heart sank without knowing how I had failed.

Then I saw Susanna and the two men through the doorway of the back room. The old woman waddled toward me, her gray hair awry, put her arms around me and wept. Tough Susanna weeping in my arms was a shock, like cheerful Jaqueline complaining, and I began to moan with her, to ask if everyone was all right, and to repeat again and again, "Praise God for your safety." She asked me to come in and see the room where they had been when the shell hit, a tiny cluttered room. Sitting there had put one more wall between them and the incoming shells. All of them talked at once, explaining it to me. It had happened early, around 6 p.m. (about the time we arrived at the Dunns'). The way they described the noise and the dust and the crumbling of their house, the event could have lasted an hour instead of an instant. Afterwards, they explained, they were shaking and the children were crying, so they ran down to our house seeking shelter and found our door locked. I apologized over and over, filled with a groundless guilt for this absence. I told them we had been with friends who persuaded us to spend the night. I wanted them never to know that we had eaten and chatted through the worst of the battle.

"*Yarait,*" Susanna kept saying. "If only."

Later the questions in me found words—Why did providence, or grace, or the kind God often move me to safer places, when I had not even asked for this favor? Why did the shell hit Boutros and Jaqueline's house and not mine? And did I have any right to be grateful? But at that moment these questions were formless and disturbing shadows moving in the back of my mind.

I asked about Lulu and her children. They had gone earlier in the morning to her sister's home higher up the hill. George tried to make a place for me to sit, as though I had come to visit. In the middle of the chaos of their day Jaqueline and Susanna offered to make coffee, and I had to insist on the need to go home. I did ask them what I could do for them, but they said there was nothing.

On the road I met Bishara, unshaven, walking with heavy feet. He said his family was O.K. and told me that some houses had burned at the top of the hill, near where we lived before we moved to The Hara.

In my kitchen I found a little pile of fiberglass insulation and dust on the floor under the fluorescent light. Chunks of plaster and slivers of paint were scattered over the dining table, and I could see spaces where the putty had been blown out from around the window frame. Without getting a direct hit, our rock house had suffered a jolt.

I went on an inspection tour. Upstairs I spotted a little hole in one of the concrete blocks that edged the roof, but later Wayne would discover the perforation in the thick iron door of a tiny room that housed our generator. Having cut through a layer of iron, a little piece of flying metal still had power to punch its way through the air space at the end of the generator battery and damage the wall beyond. I didn't like to visualize what it could have done to a human body.

Instead of writing, I cleaned up the dust and debris and cooked a chicken with some vegetables. At 11:30 I went over to tell Jaqueline that I was bringing lunch for all of them, but I found only Susanna. The others had gone to one of those complimentary rooms at the Bustan. Susanna was leaving shortly for her sister's house. "Another time," she said, and I went home feeling useless.

My writing day was mostly a loss. Sitting with my notebook and pen, I kept hearing battle sounds and hoping Wayne was not staying away to give me privacy. Battles usually started getting worse toward night.

I decided to go upstairs and take a bath. Sitting in the tub with shells going in both directions over me, bathing in warm water and stereophonic sound, I remembered my Mother telling me to wear clean underwear in case "something happened" and I had to go to the hospital.

At bedtime Magda told us that once again Lebanon was on the brink of total war. She gave us a lot of details, but the big picture was totally missing. I had no idea what was really happening to Lebanon.

Things That Had to Be Said

Eleven days after our return to Lebanon, I wrote to the Olsons. I told them that Elena deeply appreciated the fact that Mr. Olson had written to her, though she had not received the letter. Since it had not come back to them, we still hoped that it was in some stack of undelivered mail in the Beirut post office. She waited for it daily,

Elena, I said, was making for them a scarf exactly like the one she gave John and would be sending it to the States with a friend in about a week.

The rest was much harder.

I told them first that I hated war and never liked admitting that anything good was achieved by it in the long run. And I said, "I love Lebanon a lot, having lived here since 1970, but I felt from the beginning that America should not get involved in this war and would come out with our faces black if we did. However, there are facts which I have to admit."

Then I told them the story that John and the others told us about their response to save the Lebanese Army. Perhaps the Olsons had heard this from John himself, but I added, "We knew that the Marines had fired, and we were aware that they had somehow turned the tide. Since then several Lebanese, more informed than we are, have told us that Lebanon was within two days of annihilation, and the Marines saved the country."

What I did not point out to them was that, though the enemy the Marines stopped included foreign troops—Syrians, Palestinians—this was still a Lebanese war. Once the Marines fired, they had taken sides in a civil war, and the Lebanese Druze and their local sympathizers, as well as their foreign allies, saw them as an enemy. I did not say that America was already the enemy in some quarters, or mention the natural attitude toward occupation armies, foreigners on Lebanese soil.

I only dropped a hint about the relevance of history: "I believe that when the Marines began shooting there was nothing else they could do. But years ago our country looked the other way while the seeds of war were sown in the Middle East. That was our mistake. The injustice is that it was not John's mistake. He was innocent and brave, with no animosity toward anyone. He was a victim of evil... but he had peace with God and did not lose his soul... I hope that you can find comfort in this."

Even while I wrote this letter, I remembered the sentry with no bullet in his gun and Pedro's words, "You can die before you get permission." I saw the ignorance and uncertainty behind America's policy in Lebanon, but I did not have the heart to speak my mind to the Olson's. I could not say what I really thought: "We threw those boys away."

Another thing that made the letter so complicated for me was that the battle was not over, the tide was not turned forever. It never is in Lebanon.

In March both Elena and I received letters from Bertha Olson, full of newspaper clippings, news about a flagpole memorial to John, even a copy of the program from his funeral. She responded to that message I had struggled over: "Thank you so much for your comforting letter." She told me, "My husband was in the battle on Okinawa in WW II...Our oldest son was a Marine in Vietnam. We just figured since those two made it home, John would too. We just hadn't thought about how there are people in this world who don't value human life, not even their own."

I understood how she felt, to the extent of marveling that she could keep her words so mild and gentle. I could excuse a grieving mother for anything she said. But I was baffled by the way Americans differentiated between acts of violence that were all the same to people who have lived through war in their own streets. Americans seemed to think it natural for soldiers to die in a tank assault or an artillery battle, while they felt that a suicide bomber in a truck had broken the rules of war. In Lebanon we heard that 20,000 people died in the Israeli invasion, a majority of them civilians who happened to be in the way. Could Americans know that and still believe that war had rules? Had they never noticed that it was people with causes but no planes and no tanks who resorted to ordinary vehicles, loaded with explosives and delivered by a human being? And what about the possibility that car bombs and artillery shells were morally equivalent?

Later—a long time later—I realized that I had not actually addressed the question of what John's death had accomplished. I had spoken only to the question: What did the Marines accomplish by their presence in Lebanon? Maybe that was the question the Olsons meant to ask. And what could I have said? Rarely does death accomplish anything. That is the role of life.

If I should die in Lebanon, probably no one would be stronger or smarter or happier because of it. The meaning to be found would have to be in why I was there and what I had done before that moment of death. So... if I didn't believe that what I meant to accomplish was worth the risk, I should scram out of there.

The thought made me concentrate hard on accomplishing something with my life.

The Highest Price

Going out of the village, on our way to the office, we stopped to talk with Susanna who was sweeping debris off the long steps up to their house.

She said, "See, we thought we paid a lot, but now our neighbors paid more."

"Who?"

Her face squinched up as though to survive a screeching noise, and her voice pitched into a higher than usual register. "Beit Abu Jbreil. Their son was killed yesterday. *Haram*! A *shab* of 20 years old."

"Where?" I asked her.

"He was with the Army at the Green Line. They're bringing him now to the hotel."

We expressed regrets feebly and told her again that we were ready to help them in any way we could.

She said, "May God bless your ancestors and your children," and kept sweeping.

We knew by then that their house was one of a thousand hit by shells, and as we drove up the road, I was thinking about how right Susanna was. A house was nothing; a son was everything. And this boy, a neighbor we didn't know, was one of twenty-two soldiers killed already in the battle. One hundred and seventy-nine had been injured. I imagined the unspeakable grief of looking down on the face of a dead son, the torn body laid in a box and brought to the fancy hotel, in a country splintering and lost. The Abu Jbreils would ask, like the Olsons—for what good purpose did we sacrifice him?

We should have stayed in the village and tried to minister to our neighbors, but in our plans this was a crucial day at BP. Mary and Waleed were supposed to go to a government office together to work on the registration of our second publishing name—Dar Manhal al-Hayat. ("House of the Source of Life" was the name we put on materials for the general public, because it had no sectarian implications.) And I had several appointments.

I had barely opened the door of my office when I heard a series of heavy explosions up toward Beit Meri. I couldn't afford to think about it.

Nobody came from West Beirut, but the really bad news was that Waleed didn't come. He was probably stuck in the South, maybe standing at some roadblock. I called Mary. She sounded cheerful, saying, "I expect the worst part to be over in a few days." I knew that the president's cabinet had resigned, but Mary told a story of the kind I have never heard in my life except in Lebanon—about Muslim cabinet members getting letters, threatening death unless they resigned. She said, "Now all the top Muslim leaders are getting such messages. Syria is sending them," she said.

"What can the president do?"

She said, "The president will have to form a new government."

"But if people refuse to serve...?"

In her emphatic and precise English, Mary said, "If the president cannot form a government in the normal way, he will have to form a military government. Meanwhile, Frances, the enemy will shell us to upset us more while we are under the psychological shock caused by the resignation of the government." Her stress of the word "shock" seemed to say that she had been shocked. Still she was not worried.

When I asked if our license was in any way jeopardized by the situation, she said, "Oh, no. I believe such things are out of the realm of politics." Then she told me, "Be careful and be calm. They want us to be upset, so the best thing is to defeat them by being calm."

I told her that I would go on with my work by keeping an appointment at LESG, the Lebanese Evangelical School for Girls. I don't remember now the purpose of this appointment, but I know that Mary screamed at me, "No, no, Frances. Don't go to West Beirut. Don't go anywhere, especially to West Beirut."

I began working on my Sunday School lesson. Like everybody who had taken the training in August, I had assignments to complete. Michel came in, and we traded depressing stories. I told him about the death of our neighbor. He told me about a little boy in Ain Saadeh. The child, an eleven-year-old, was with his family in a ground floor apartment that faced Beirut. He moved past the apartment's metal door at the instant a shell exploded in the street. A piece of shrapnel pierced the door and killed him. I knew this door well, because I drove past it twice every day.

Michel said, "People are tired. We are ready to accept a dictatorship if it will give us peace."

As he was leaving my office, I asked Michel to design a rubber stamp for us, something we needed for legalizing official documents, like contracts.

He said, "How can I design something with all of this happening?"

I said, "You can. It's the best way to spend the time. It will make you feel great afterwards."

He looked skeptical.

I said, "I'm going to write a Sunday School lesson. You show me a stamp tomorrow, and I'll show you my lesson."

"O.K." he said, "you are right," and left.

I asked Wayne to take my typewriter downstairs, and I finally got settled at Abu Issam's worktable in the storeroom, surrounded by shelves covered with wrapped packages of books. Feeling safe, I could ignore the sounds and tremors of battle, and I made some progress on my lesson.

Toward noon the guns on the mountain got quieter and we ate lunch in the dining room. I could hear the generator—a distinctive sputtering kind of roar—and a radio. Um John told me in her soft, never alarming, voice that Beit Meri had been hit hard. I told her, "I thought so."

The news reports were full of ominous details. The Army was under attack everywhere, not by invaders but by Lebanese militias, and a few soldiers had refused to fight the attackers. Armed men tried to take over the Channel Seven TV station in Musaitbeh.

"The news is all bad," she told me. "Now Jumblatt demands that the president resign and the Marines withdraw."

"I hope the Marines withdraw," I said.

She looked frightened and said, "But what will become of us if they do?"

Finally she told me, "Don't come tomorrow. Nobody knows what will happen."

Shortly after I went back to work, Abu John came to tell me that he needed to turn off the electricity in the building, so he could run the water pump. The generator couldn't power everything at once. I picked up my papers in preparation for going home. He told me, "Be careful, Mrs. Fuller. The situation is very dangerous."

Wayne and I discussed our predicament. Being on the road was risky, but if we didn't go soon, we might be stuck for days. We decided to do something that we had never done before and would rarely do again. We would go home in separate cars, not for reasons of schedule or logistics but to reduce the risk that we would both die at once and leave our children orphans.

I went first, and Wayne followed about five minutes later. "Don't get delayed," I told him, "because I won't know what happened to you." I kept my courage up by praying all the way—for my own safety and Wayne's; for all our colleagues; for our friends Dave and Diane and the orphan boys as I drove past the Home of Onesiphorous; for the other drivers I met, and a militiaman I knew who waved at me; for the family behind the green metal door with the shrapnel hole; for a little group of boys who were playing with a miniature ball and a paddle in Ain Saadeh; for several Egyptian workers walking with one suitcase; for the inhabitants of two cars at the gas station and the attendant pumping gas. Once I got to The Hara, I saw only one person. The village seemed dead. I started breathing again after Wayne's arrival a few minutes later.

Dense Fog

When morning came I felt uncommonly grateful—for daisies blowing on the terrace, for our cozy house with doors and windows still intact against this rainy, wintry day, for Wayne who did so much to make me comfortable and to encourage me, for people praying for us in America—a thousand things. I decided that if we were going to be stuck at home, I would enjoy it and afterwards have something to show for it—a finished Sunday School lesson, a new story, some personal growth.

The news, however, did not inspire rejoicing. Amal fighters were attacking the Army all along the Green Line, at every crossing point. Their seizing only one crossing would be a very dangerous development for East Beirut. By afternoon we knew that the Shia and Druze militias were in control of West Beirut, but that wasn't even the bad part. This takeover had been possible, because whole units of the Army had deserted or defected to the other side when Muslim soldiers refused to fight Muslim militiamen and Druze would not fight Druze.

Loyalty to tribe was stronger than loyalty to country; there was no cohesive core. In America I had often described Lebanon in this way to explain the chaos, the warlords, the militias. But I had been optimistic. The Army had been the one cause for hope, and now it was collapsing. Nothing worse than this could happen.

The implications of the militia takeover were also truly grave for the Marines. Now they, with the French, Italian and British forces were all sitting—at the invitation of the Lebanese government—inside that part of the capital that the government had lost. They had been no help in keeping it. What would they do now? And the Voice of Israel informed us that the State Department had several alternative plans for evacuating American citizens if the Gemayel government should collapse. I didn't like it—that little messages like this came to us through Tel Aviv.

That day a fog as dense as a rain cloud walked silently into The Hara and sat down. This happened now and then. The canyon and the hills beyond disappeared. The woods became spooky, creepy, beautiful, the *snobar* trees rising vague as shadows out of the white vapor. Going in and out by car we would squint into the glare of our own headlights and creep around curves, aided by memory. On such days a mist would collect on my windshield. It was not raining, but everything was wet, every blade of grass strung with round drops of water, bright and still like ice. Once I saw a spider web, in a corner between two rocks, and it appeared to be a small net filled with tiny crystal marbles. I loved the fog then, the way it wrapped my little house—a warm haven, a shelter.

But the day after the army began to collapse, when I sat at the dining table and could not see across the road, a comparable fog filled my head. I did not know how to think about the world.

Wayne went down to Abu Fouad's house to use their phone and get in touch with our colleagues. I watched him disappear into the mist. He came back with lots of news. Four missionary kids—Paul and Julie Sacco and Ashleigh Dunn and Jeannie King—were stuck at the American Community School. Friends who were teaching and living on campus had taken them in, trying to keep them happy and safe, but shells had demolished one faculty apartment and hit the library and the science lab. One hundred refugees were sheltering in the Beirut Baptist School. The American Embassy had evacuated their dependents to the ships offshore.

Clinging to the Deck

For two months I kept a diary that sounds like it was written by an idiot. I left out words; I didn't finish sentences; I wrote nonsense. The nonsense was, I think, mostly true.

After the Army began to fall apart and Reagan announced that he was "redeploying the Marines to ships offshore," the British troops traveled overland to Jounieh to leave by sea, and the Italians said they were pulling out. I thought briefly that somebody's goal had been achieved and the storm would subside. But it had barely started.

West Beirut was in chaos. Two Muslim groups had turned their guns on one another, and one of them declared, "West Beirut has become the prison of the foreigners." I hoped they meant only the alien armies, not any of my personal friends. But, after that, an American, Frank Regier, a professor at the American University of Beirut, was kidnapped.

Some days the Voice of Lebanon gave us martial music all day, as though it would stir up our courage while we hid from the gunfire, but they interrupted the marches over and over to give us breaking news. Sousa would fade, giving way to bursts of the jumpy tune that signaled a "flash." Composed to imitate excitement, this few seconds of rapid notes taught us to fear. Years later I think my blood would freeze if I heard it. We heard it the afternoon the embassy blew up and the morning the Marines died. We heard it when Lebanese Army soldiers began deserting, and when children died on their school playground. It became a brittle, brace-yourself prelude to bad news. After the tune grabbed us, Magda would astonish us by finding new vocabularies to express increased horrors. Indirectly she told us who needed prayer.

"Hadath," she would say, and we would remember the Haddads and meals we had eaten in their home, and Elie Eid, a reluctant and secretive militiaman, who signed notes to us, "your son." "Ashrafieh," Magda would name, and we would visualize the streets and think of Antoine Feghali and know he was worried about his children and had a headache. Mention of "The Nebaa" would make our hearts sink, because of Daniel and Soureya and their little girl.

In one week, during an announced ceasefire, 128 people died and 124 were injured. Our friend Hanni Khalaf lost her brother. He was killed when he left the basement of the Badaro Baptist Church to find food. Members of our church in Hadath, man and wife, were injured in their home and hospitalized. In Monsourieh a woman died lying in bed beside her husband, who was not hurt.

Our neighbors in the large house across the road, just below the store, got a mortar through their roof. Wayne had gone to the living room window to look out. Nobody should do that. Nothing but a few yards of air and a pane of glass separated him from the fountain of fire and sparks that spewed upward. From the inner room, I saw the flash of red light fill my dining room windows. I screamed at him, he ducked, stood up to look again, and dashed for cover. A barrage of shells crashed down while we both sat on the floor with our backs to the stone wall. My legs trembled, and I couldn't make them stop. The Abu Jbreils lost all the glass from their store and their house. The next morning it was in the road. I thought, *It's nothing to them; they already lost their son.*

Needing to reinforce our shelter, we tried in vain to buy sandbags. The manufacturers, we were told, could not keep up with the demand. Instead, we stacked shelves, one set on top of another, and filled them with books to block the entrance to our cave, destroying the beauty of the arch. We left space on the side to wiggle in; I had to pass our supper trays over the top. All this was only to stop shrapnel in case a shell hit the living room; we feared that if one hit the upstairs bedroom, a few tons of stone would come down into our shelter.

We tried hard to go on with our lives. At home I read Thomas Merton's diaries and poetry by Czeslaw Milosz. I worked on a story, trying to write in ten-minute snatches, interrupted by five-minute newscasts. I don't recommend this method. Stories whirled around in my head, got tangled with one another, and I couldn't focus on any strand to separate it from the others or fasten it to paper.

The church youth group was scheduled to meet in our home on a Saturday night. I was the program. They had asked me to lead them in a study of "War and Morality," and it had pleased me very much that they wanted to grapple with this issue. During these years of war one distinctive characteristic of the evangelicals had become a cause for criticism from other Christian groups: they did not fight. I never actually heard sermons in which the pastors exhorted their people not to participate in the war, but they obviously did not want to be a part of it. Even more amazing, again and again it happened that a young militiaman would hear the gospel and respond, and immediately he would try to escape the military, as though he knew intuitively that Jesus would disapprove of it. I knew that they were like the earliest Christians in this way.

Their critics accused them of benefiting from the sacrifices of other Christians, without paying the price themselves. And once a Baptist man, greatly respected in the churches, describing a battle that had taken place in his neighborhood, told me, "We are grateful for the Kata'ib. They saved us from the beasts."

Knowing that the young people were feeling some discrepancy between their need to be defended and their unwillingness to kill, I knew that I had to read again my books on non-violence and especially to study my Bible. But the irony of those days is that instead of preparing, I watched battles, and the meeting never happened. Instead, a force of three thousand Druze attacked the Army's fourth brigade, which splintered and collapsed. And now I have to admit that intellectually I never untangled all the contradictions of war and morality—all those perceived necessities that make people fight; the discrepancy between the commandment not to kill and the orders quoted in Old Testament stories; the presumed duties that conflict with humane and civilized impulses, as well as the teachings of the New Testament; the example of the early Christians and the compromises of "just war" philosophies; the selfless courage and the bestiality; parades and flags and blood coagulating in the street; the fear that drives all of it.

The clarity I had then and the clarity I have now is this: I hate war, and in my Christian gut I know this hatred is right. Living in a world so wicked that it tries to solve its problems by killing people, I recognize my participation and guilt, and I speak up now and then for peace. I pray for peace. I vote for peace.

In reaction to the spreading chaos of 1984, world leaders issued warnings that what was happening in Lebanon could provoke global war. I didn't think I could get out of bed lifting any share of responsibility for that.

Sometimes I asked friends what they thought about the situation—Abu John, Chaanine at the store, our neighbor George. Every one of them looked up helplessly and said, "I don't know what to think. Nobody does."

I had begun to see Lebanon as a sinking ship, twisted by conflicting winds, wallowing in powerful waves, the engines dead, the lights out, the crew murdering one another, mutineers trying to wrestle the commander overboard, the passengers struggling with lifeboats, clinging to the tilting deck or hiding in their cabins to pray. These thoughts were new and shocking to my own head. Until then it had never occurred to me that Lebanon might not survive.

Rescuers arrived with lifeboats of various kinds and took some willing people off the crippled ship. Boatloads of Lebanese fled, and some of our colleagues. Russ Futrell went with Ashleigh Dunn to an evacuation point announced by the embassy, accepting a helicopter ride to the U.S. S. Something-or-Other. They wound up in Cyprus. I was relieved to know that his blond head and southern speech were gone from West Beirut. The Sacco family went all the way to the States. Pat Dunn and Diane Williams left together for Jounieh and went to Cyprus on a commercial ferry. The Foxes went, too. Pete was packing. The Nicholases felt the need to go out for some rest, so I suggested that when they felt like working they should go over to Amman where Anne might accomplish something for the Sunday School project and Ed could work with Fowaz Ameish on songs for the hymnal. We wrote hurried letters and sent them with travelers to be mailed outside.

Once I got to talk to Cynthia, who called us at the Dunns' phone by arrangement. She had been promoted to lead engineer and sounded happy. Then she was obviously disappointed when I said that we were staying. I explained it to her. "We feel really good and think we can deal with the tension, because we just had a great month in America." Cynthia didn't seem to think that was the point. I assured her that we could be at the Jounieh port in an hour if something really terrible happened.

On less chaotic days we went to the office. Abu Sleiman came, crossing a volatile Green Line on foot. He stayed two hours and left, taking his work home with him. Mary called and caught me in the office. She said she had gone to the court "with shells over my head" to keep an appointment concerning our work, and she found the building locked and the premises deserted, except for a young guard at the door. She complained to him about not being able to work, and he had said to her,

"If I can help you I will. Consider me a judge. State your case, and I will make a decision."

"Wasn't that funny?" she said to me. But she seemed discouraged. She said, "I don't know where this country is going."

I made phone calls, trying to inspire our curriculum writers to use time at home during the fighting. One of the best told me, "Writing this lesson needs a brain, and I don't have one."

I got worried about the Barnes. Some of the spark had faded from Emmett's blue eyes and LaNell kept letting out long breaths and saying things like, "I wonder what's going to happen next." They had heard both horror stories and rumors.

I met Um John in the hall, and she wanted to tell me about the decision she had made. "I want to leave. This is the first time I want to go to America, because I am afraid—not to die, Mrs. Fuller—but afraid something will happen to me before I see my children again."

Um John had three sons who had been in the States for several years. Now Naji, the fourth, had gone, and Najat was planning to go. I knew how much she had missed her boys. Once I had been sitting with her on the patio of their house when I noticed a small footprint in the concrete. I said, "Who stepped in the wet cement?"

She smiled and said, "Boulos."

Boulos was a burly kid, the fairest of their children, the only one of the boys who was pink-faced and blue-eyed like Abu John. I could remember when he was a tow-headed toddler. There were people who considered ways to steal him.

I said, "Um John, too bad we didn't think of it. We could have called all the children and let them put in one foot. We could have had a row of footprints—John and Tim and Boulos and Jan and Nabeel and..."

Before I could finish she was wiping tears off her cheeks.

Now I was on my way to the basement, carrying a pack of typing paper. Um John was brushing her long hair, while we talked. It was streaked with gray and had those tight little waves made by plaiting. She seemed cheerful. She said, "I couldn't sleep. So many nights I didn't sleep, trying to decide what to do. Now *khalas* (finish), I'm going."

"Abu John, too?"

"No. He doesn't want to go anywhere. He'll stay and work. Nadia will be here, and Aoun."

Um John coiled her hair around her head and pinned it, and I went to the basement and worked on my Sunday School lesson. My diary claims that I finished it and later says more than once that I was working on it. Probably this is all true. I tend to finish things and then keep hammering at them.

I noticed that my writing and the war had striking similarities. I wrote things, gloated over my success, and then went back to them, rearranged a sentence, killed off a word, moved a comma. The armies fought battles, declared victory but kept shooting, adjusted their lines a few meters here or there and erased a few more people.

Elie Eid called me at the office. He told me that he had succeeded in opening his new shoe store and had a little business. I was surprised, in light of the population exodus from Hadath.

He said, "I called to ask you why you don't leave."

I laughed, since the statement implied some kind of foreknowledge that we had not left.

He said, "Well, I know you that you don't leave, but I don't know why."

At a momentary loss for any explanation, I dodged. I said that Wayne and I would like to come and see his store.

He said, "Don't come here; it's too dangerous."

The line was cut before I could ask any questions.

One afternoon an officer of the Lebanese Army visited Emmett Barnes in his office to explain some digging and scraping his men were doing nearby. He said, "We are preparing a place to put a big gun here beside your building. Until now we are not putting the gun, you understand? We are only preparing the place, to be ready when we need it. But I am responsible to tell you that when we fire this gun, all your windows will break." Emmett then came upstairs to tell me.

On my way home a group of women drinking coffee on a balcony, called me to come up. There were seven of them, all dressed in black. I felt like the undeserving elite because no one in my family had died. Once Wayne had said to me, "When I die, don't wear black." And I asked him,

"What am I supposed to wear to your funeral? My red silk?" "Why not?" But if he died in Lebanon, I would wear black. For a year maybe.

The hostess brought another chair for me, and gave me a cup of coffee, then someone pointed out to her that she had not offered me the cigarettes.

Another said, "She doesn't smoke."

Simultaneously, the hostess touched her head and said, "I don't know what I'm doing anymore. I don't have my mind."

We talked about the war. It didn't seem possible for people to be together and not talk about it. Um Fou'ad said, "We have to pray for the Army at Suq al-Garb. If they lose, we will all be massacred."

I thought, *Weren't we in this same situation last September? Didn't the Marines save us?* And it seemed that nothing had changed—not the position of the armies or their power over one another or the places where smoke went up. The Marines had fired or not fired. The New Jersey had shaken the world or not. John Olson had died and the Jbreil's son, and Hanni's brother, and the little boy in Ain Saadeh. The Marines left, and the Army held. In West Beirut, too, Amal and Ishtiraqiya had gained control, according to the news, but their battle with the Army went on. People's lives changed, but never this infernal war.

The almond trees blossomed anyway. So did the red poppies, all over our terraces and in the field across the road. One morning we studied the opposite mountain with binoculars, because shells had fallen, and we wanted to know what had been hit. I saw flames under the trees near Ras el-Metn and the woods filling up with smoke, and then I got distracted by a blob of color at the bottom edge of my view. Between us and Ras el-Metn, on the rim of a green terrace, stood a rooster, huge and red, his feathers shining, his bearing regal. He jerked his small head—his comb like a red crown, his wattle like a dashing cravat—right, then left, as though surveying the canyon; he strutted and showed me his flared tail, ignoring the continuing bombardment. More than the fire in the forest, I remember that gutsy, stupid rooster. I liked him.

When I got to the office that day LaNell called and told me that she and Emmett felt better.

I said, "What happened?"

"Oh… the sun came up," she said.

I understood. The night before I had packed a suitcase, and now I was at work.

Akram Delivers the Swing

We bought a porch swing. I know it seems like a strange thing to do while clinging to a sinking ship, with suitcases packed. Maybe we had already promised to buy it before we knew how grim things would get.

Akram was leaving. The words still make my heart a little sick. We knew in Lebanon a few totally lovable people, and Akram was one of them. A few years earlier, when he was a bundle of awkward charm and brown muscles and needs and fragile faith and funny expressions, he had spent a lot of time in our home. He had been fascinated with Cynthia, and probably would always love her a little, a love she returned in all of its ambiguity. Akram had married and started building a house, low on the canyon wall, on the far edge of Broummana. They were deserting it now to live in England and saying they would never come back.

Akram arrived one afternoon to deliver the swing. For us, it became a roof swing. After Akram and Wayne carried it up and placed it against the stone wall of our bedroom facing the Shouf, I sat in it, for the second time. We had tried it once, at their house where it was a yard swing. It was all metal, except for the cushions and the awning over the top, with smooth movement and armrests big enough for a glass of tea or a plate of food. A little metal table came with it.

"Leave it in rain, snow, everything," Akram said. "But you must paint it every year." His wife had recently made new covers for the cushions. Nice pastel colors. It was a fine piece of furniture.

As I sat there swinging, Akram yanked something out of a pocket and handed me a small sheep bell. He told me, "I bring this for you. You sit here in the sunshine. You need anything—a sandwich, a cup of coffee—you ring the bell and Mr. Wayne will come for your order."

We all laughed, especially Wayne and Akram. I said, "Is that what your wife does? She rings the bell when she wants coffee?"

He closed his mouth tightly, fluttered his long eyelashes, and then said, "I will not tell."

We went down to the cave to drink a cup of tea together. It was not a good time in our lives to sit on the roof, and I wondered when we would have another.

He wanted all of our children's addresses and talked about how much he missed the three he knew, Cynthia and Jim and Dwight, and would like to visit them. I thought he imagined that he would be a lot closer to them when he got to England, and in a way he would. At least the mail would work. Later I realized he might be thinking that he would be farther away, because he would have to write; he couldn't come to us and ask for news. I brought out my photo album with the new snaps from Christmas and a big picture of Cynthia, holding the combustion device that functioned like the starter of the space shuttle. Wayne explained that she had some responsibility for this piece of hardware. Akram jumped to his feet, stiffened and saluted. Then he sat down again, took the album in his lap, and said, "*Ya,* Cynthia, *keefik*?" making no effort to conceal the longing in his voice.

Looking up from the picture he said, "Really, she has everything, you know; she has wonderful personality. She is strong, she is clever, and she can laugh at the world."

I sat there thinking that he would be an alien soon and jobless. He would get lost in London, feel incompetent, be homesick for the air over the mountains of Lebanon. But he was in a good mood, ready for something new.

As he was leaving, he promised to come another time to say goodbye, but one day we realized that the date of their scheduled departure had passed in the midst of a general turmoil. After that Lebanon was a little lonelier.

We have had a few letters but have never seen Akram again. Telling this, I feel angry against all the evils that caused so many of the best people to leave Lebanon and separated us from our friends. I have no idea what happened to that swing.

Leaders Leading

Solving Lebanon's problems through diplomacy seemed to be more difficult than solving them on the battlefield. It required leaders of the various factions to agree on something, while being pushed and pulled and encouraged and criticized and threatened and coerced by Israel, Syria, Saudi, other Arab countries, the U.S., Russia, France, Iran and probably some powers I have forgotten. This diplomatic work happened on another layer of life, its intricacies unknown to most of us, but when politicians were not working they talked (or maybe that's all they did when they worked), and the talk depressed or outraged or confused the population, partly because it seemed to make no immediate difference whatever in the places where ordinary people lived. Along with the Lebanese, we followed the details through media reports and tried to understand. Straining to find some sense in it all, I started writing down the craziness.

President Gemayel lived under extreme pressure, internal as well as external, to abrogate the agreement with Israel, known as the May 17 Accord. The Accord was supposed to normalize relationships between Lebanon (the occupied) and Israel (the occupier). The average Lebanese had only a vague idea of what it said, but most Arab states as well as Muslim segments of Lebanese society were opposed to it, and some were apoplectic on the subject. On the other side of the argument stood the power that the Israeli Army held over Lebanon and the influence of the American government. Secretary of State Schultz was reluctant to see the scrapping of something he had worked so hard to achieve.

The Saudi government then presented a peace plan, which Gemayel agonized over and finally accepted. The plan had eight points, beginning with tearing up the May 17 Accord, and including the departure of all troops of the Multi-National Force. Gemayel, of course, could do nothing without the agreement of Assad, who had 30,000 men inside his borders and uncounted artillery pieces aimed at the heart of Lebanon.

Strange inconsistencies drove the population crazy. The general understanding on the ground was that Jumblatt and the Shia leader Nabih Berri were in favor of the Saudi plan, but while Gemayel waited for word from Damascus, those two were demanding his resignation. Washington spoke up to say that the plan had no chance of succeeding; it was one sheet of paper with two sentences on each point, entirely too vague to sell to Israel. Instead of backing this up, Israel volunteered that abrogation of The Accord was a slap in the face of Washington but made no practical difference to Israel, and the Voice of Lebanon stated the obvious—that Washington had not proposed any better idea.

The answer came from Syria: "No." They claimed that the plan did not abrogate the May 17 Accord at all, because it required that the Israeli and Syrian armies leave Lebanon simultaneously and that Israel's northern border be protected. These were major points of the Accord.

The Lebanese Forces (a misleading name for the Phalangist militia, the Kata'ib) responded by again calling on people to defend East Beirut and the mountain, otherwise the Lebanese Christians would become like the Armenians, massacred and homeless. This warning felt rather personal since we lived on the threatened mountain.

The Lebanese leaders met in Switzerland to try to form a government of national unity. In Switzerland, I thought, they could take their time, because they would not hear any gunfire. Many of them lived in Europe anyway, where they were keeping safe during all this messy fighting. While they checked into their fine hotels and figured out how to sit at the table, war continued in Lebanon, and from the safety of a distant city Jumblatt warned that there would be ten more years of bloodshed if they did not reach an agreement.

Christian parties, we heard, would recommend a canton system of government for Lebanon, with each part ruling itself, leaving defense and economy in the hands of the central government. The Druze had said they were in favor of such a system. Israel agreed and even worked out for the Lebanese how many cantons they needed—fourteen. Berri threatened to launch a full-scale war if such a system were adopted.

The conference appointed a national security committee to take care of things in Lebanon. The Kata'ib complained that they were already part of a security committee and no one in Lausanne had the authority to appoint someone to represent them. Then the committee had trouble meeting, because the members couldn't agree on a place.

The meeting in Lausanne grew rowdy. Delegates pounded on the table and shouted. Franjieh, a pro-Syrian Christian from north Lebanon, called President Gemayel "an Israeli" and Gemayel called Franjieh "a traitor and a dog." Franjieh left the meeting and went to his room; the president went up and talked to him and brought him back. The meeting then adjourned for a day to commemorate the seventh anniversary of the assassination of Kamal Jumblatt. While I listened to a description of all this on the radio, big fires were burning in Ras el-Metn and Aley, and the English-language *Daily Star* published pictures of dead children.

On the same day, King Hussein of Jordan, one of the best friends America had in the Arab world, said that Washington had lost all credibility as a mediator in the Middle East. According to the BBC man in Beirut, Hussein had asked the U.S. to stop Israel from building new settlements in disputed territories of the West Bank while peace negotiations were going on, and Washington had refused.

On March 20 the Lausanne conference broke up in disarray, unable to reach a compromise. Jumblatt announced it had been a failure, predicting that thousands more people would die. The delegates stayed on another day to write something they could claim as "accomplishments." In conclusion they announced the "consolidation of the ceasefire" and the appointment of a thirty-two man committee to consider constitutional changes. Apparently these considerations were to be individual, since the committee was not scheduled to meet until six months later. In that time the thousands Jumblatt had predicted could die. In the previous three days, during the above-mentioned ceasefire, 252 had been killed or gravely injured.

Between my scribbles about the name-calling and the gunfire is this long-forgotten memo: "This afternoon the most brilliant and complete rainbow I have ever seen planted one foot in Broummana and one in the canyon and stood there for ten minutes, a gift to the righteous and the wicked."

Lots of Refrigerators

If I had known what would happen I wouldn't have gone home ahead of Wayne, but then, we never knew, and he wanted to help Idil cut a tree. At the end of a normal day in the office I was always so drained I could hardly stagger downstairs to my car, but Wayne had energy to spare, and Idil, another workaholic, loved him for that. He always boasted that Wayne would work just for the fun of it, any kind of work; it didn't matter.

The instant I closed the door, before I could get a drink of water or go to the bathroom (two things that were on my mind), a shell arrived, crash landing with no warning just beyond the kitchen wall. The explosion scared me silly and left me standing in the middle of the living room, still holding my briefcase, with my ears ringing. That first shell must have been plugging somebody's gun, because behind it a stream of shells spewed into the village, whistling and banging down—along the road I had just driven, in the forest below us, up the hill among the houses. I hid in our shelter, behind the stone wall, and shivered.

Between explosions I heard another sound. Like a groan. A heavy, hoarse groan, maybe an animal sound, like the complaining of the camel I rode up the slope of Sinai. Unnnhhhh, hunh. I thought it came from my kitchen. It gargled and sputtered, too. Ghghxxx, xxunh. Not quite animal. Maybe an engine, rolling over and falling kerplunk. Something electric, sparking, straining, failing. My refrigerator! My refrigerator was clicking on and groaning and whimpering and gurgling, then giving up—tick, unnnhhhhh, gghghgh, thump. My refrigerator was dying. Again. The new motor that did not exist in Lebanon and had taken us months to obtain.

I knew I should go in there and pull the plug, but fear immobilized me. What if the next shell came through my kitchen wall? A wall basically like Jaqueline's that she swept away with a push broom. I pictured myself spattered around in the rubble and picked up in a shovel.

The room was growing dark. The loaded bookcase we had used to barricade the archway, in lieu of sandbags, cast a huge, black shadow. Scared already, I started to feel creepy about the dark and imagined that I could think better in the light. Near me on the floor was the small lamp that I used when reading, while lying on my mat. I groped for it, got my hand under the shade and pushed the little switch. The result was like a gunshot in my face—an explosion of light, a flash with a loud pop, and darkness again. I sagged against the wall like a punctured balloon, waiting for my breath to come back. When I could think again I knew that something must be wrong with the electricity.

The refrigerator kept trying, but its sounds grew more and more feeble. The focus of the shelling moved a bit farther away, maybe down to Ain Saade, so, gathering all my courage (considerably less impressive than "the whole armor of God"), I raced to the kitchen and started grabbing for the plug. It was too far behind the appliance. On my knees with my face smashed against the wall, all I could reach were spider webs, and I couldn't move the big refrigerator. Neither did I know how much time I could afford to struggle with it. Then I had the bright idea that I could turn it off from inside (*of course*!), so I jerked the door open. The light exploded in my face (*Surprise, Dummy*!) and, before I could recover, another shell came whistling in.

The absolute limit for the number of close-up bangs I could endure in one half hour was drawing near. I retreated to my hideout, even darker now, where I listened with sorrow to the final death rattle of my refrigerator.

Since the last time this happened—the previous summer while we were away—we had spruced up that faithful appliance. Wayne had found a spare sealing rim for the door, having had the foresight to buy it long ago, and Michel had used spray paint to cover the nicks and scratches on its brown face. Because the paint didn't quite match, we boasted about having a rare species—a polka-dotted refrigerator.

Several years before that we had bought a replacement for it, a more sophisticated model, with a cold water faucet on the front, but its crate was dropped in some port, and it arrived with its motor out of position and a couple of broken seams. Wayne puttered with it for weeks, but it never quite got cold again. Anyway, we didn't need a bigger, more clever refrigerator after we sent the kids away, so I had been satisfied with the old brown dappled monster. Now I imagined the cheese molding and the ice cubes losing their edges, on the way to becoming one leaky hunk.

Then I started to visualize Wayne, holding a buzzing, sputtering chain saw, felling a tree, shouting back and forth with Idil, hearing nothing but the noises they made, then getting into his car and coming up the road, blasé, listening to the radio or the merry hum of his tires. I knew him;

he would drive right into the village, suspecting nothing. One quiet day and he forgot he was living in a war. Knowing there was no way to stop him, I felt terrified, then suddenly and unreasonably peeved that he had helped Idil instead of coming home with me. As though we were living in... any place, in some sane world. Besides that my bladder was bursting, and I couldn't give that jerk with the cannon a chance to catch me on the way to the bathroom. As I obsessed about it, the inconvenience became humiliation. I thought I was a rat, hiding from a cat, waiting out the enemy's hunger in my dark little hole.

The cat was close to winning by the time I heard a key scratching in the lock and the front door swing on its hinges. *Thank God.*

Wayne called me. "Pies?"

Already I felt less sorry for myself. "In here."

After the small scraping sounds of his shoes on the hard floor, a rattle of keys and the door clicking shut, he said, "Did we lose any windows?"

"I don't know." I hadn't even thought of that. "Come let me tell you what did happen."

He put his head through the narrow opening beside the bookcase. I could see vaguely the unruly bush of his hair.

I said, "The refrigerator died. I heard it, but I was too scared to go in there." I didn't even want to tell the details, but I added, "Don't turn on any lights."

He didn't move. I could feel him more than I could see him. He said, "Oh," and stood there a few more seconds. Then he said, "That's O.K.; we've got lots of refrigerators."

As long as I had lived with Wayne, I had to think twice to understand this upside down way of saying that there was only one me and I had done the right thing. He slid into the room past the bookshelf, sat on the floor beside me and admitted that he really did drive into the village knowing nothing. "Just after I came around the curve a couple of Kata'ib boys with guns jumped in front of me, yelling, 'Douse your lights!'"

They were pretty unhappy with him, he said. That seemed to relieve me of the responsibility.

After he had turned off his headlights and crept down the road into the village, he thought he saw a shell hole in the asphalt, limped through it and then came to another one, too messy to drive over. He parked then and walked, finding a hole and scattered debris just below our kitchen window, "pieces of metal, hunks of asphalt." And a severed electric wire had fallen, dangling across another, the one into our house. That meant, he explained, that we now had 220 volts instead of 110.

As simple as that: 110 plus 110. In the middle of all this craziness, some phenomena still adhered to the laws of cause and effect. The knowledge brought comfort to my mind and promoted sanity. I jumped up and ran to the bathroom.

20 Rules for Surviving Civil War

(Derived from the effort)

1. Don't drive down a street if no other cars are going that way.
2. While driving, don't talk, sing or play the radio. Pay attention.
3. Turn back if you come to a small propped-up hand-written sign that says, Beware of sniper.
4. Turn back if you come to a small propped-up hand-written sign and you can't read it.
5. Don't go anywhere without telling someone where you're going and the route you plan to take.
6. If you are a woman, don't take a man with you anywhere. He will be a liability.
7. If you are a man, don't go. Send a woman.
8. Don't pass a military guard post just because the soldier is asleep. He may wake in time to shoot you.
9. Make up jokes about your enemies; laugh at yourself, too.
10. Separate your fear from danger; know which one is in the driver's seat.
11. Stay away from the windows during artillery battles.
12. Confine chaos to the street: clean up your house.
13. If you have a silly premonition of danger, consider it a message from God.

14. Don't let a battle start when your cupboard is empty.
15. Don't read scary books or watch scary movies, including the evening news.
16. Get your job done, to keep the guys with the guns from winning.
17. Use any excuse to throw a party.
18. In the event of deportation from earth, have another place to go.
19. Talk to God. Express gratitude, make desperate requests.
20. Play a lot of games.

Playing Games

Without any consciousness that this was a survival tactic, Wayne and I played games. In the middle of a bombardment, he would grab the Boggle set, hand me paper and pencil and start shaking up the letters. Unwinding at the end of a tense day, we played backgammon, game after game. Trapped during long sieges, we chose Scrabble, which required more commitment, like a whole hour. That was a lot for Wayne.

Once when I was chatting over a cup of coffee with Antoine Feghali at Heidelberg Press, we began to compare the games we played. He and his wife played backgammon, of course—it's really a Middle Eastern game—but he didn't know any of our word games.

Mr. Feghali had a big head and no neck. I can still see him sitting behind his desk with that big head set low between his shoulders, smiling at me as he said, "And I suppose you always win."

I said, "Wayne claims I do."

"I'm sure you do. Women always win. Do you know why women always beat men in games?"

"No."

"Ad-dinya haik," he said. Translation: The world is like that.

Mary Mathias, our company lawyer, one of the busiest women I ever knew, played games. She invited me to lunch on Friday, March 23, and taught me a new game. By then the fighting had become more complicated and even harder to interpret, so it was a perfect day for games, though not such a good day to drive to Ashrafieh. I went by way of Jisr al-Waty (The Low Bridge), through a small stretch of farmland, and crossed the Corniche only a couple of blocks from the museum. This was the shortest route but probably not the safest on that day, since there was shooting at the Green Line. When I reached the parking lot behind Mary's building—noting the scarcity of other cars in the street—there was some booming. It sounded very close, but Mary's place was only about four blocks from the line. I remember that I was hurrying, trying to reach the protection of the east side of the building, when a sharp explosion slapped the air and black smoke billowed just a few blocks away.

In the dim vestibule I touched the elevator button and when nothing happened, I realized with dismay that the electricity was off. Mary's apartment was on the fifth floor, the sixth really, because in Lebanon the bottom level was the ground floor and the next level was number one. The worst part of climbing up to Mary's house was doing it in the dark. After I reached the second floor there was no light at all on those stairs or at the landings, not even enough to distinguish the wall beside me.

Mounting in the blackness, I concentrated on not stumbling, took care not to mistake the landing between floors for the next level, and I counted, starting with my fists closed and opening a finger when I said to myself "one" and another when I reached "two." I did not want to knock on the wrong door and ask for Mrs. Mathias, at least not the same door on which I had knocked once before in the dark.

I told myself, *I have to learn to carry a flashlight in my purse.* I wondered how weird it would be to meet someone coming down and decided it might be worse to be overtaken by someone, not knowing who it was.

By the time I got there my legs were hurting. I groped to find the doorjambs. I knocked, heard a shuffling sound, and the door opened slowly, a crack first, then wider. Mr. Mathias looked like an anxious ghost. He said, "I worried about you."

Mary beamed. She was wearing bright red lipstick. "Frances, darling, you are just on time. I am glad to see you."

She had set three places at the end of her rather long dining table and was bringing platters of food and little dishes of olives and nuts and *hommus*. Giant-sized books and scattered papers occupied the other end of the table. The wall at that end was covered with shelves and stacks of files. Her Baptist Publications folder was in there somewhere; she knew where, miraculously.

I remember somewhere in that room a snapshot of Mary when she was young and slender and pretty, sophisticated in a formal dress, her eyes wide, a stemmed glass in her hand. I used to see it from the chair where I sat while she worked behind the typewriter, struggling, because of the nerve problem that made her eyes shut. I once suggested that she hire a typist, and she declared that I was right, she should do that, but she never did.

Fortunately the dining room was open to the living room, which had windows on the far end to give us more light. She asked me to sit down until she was ready, and I did, on the couch, under the little shrapnel scar on the wall. Mr. Mathias shuffled in and joined me. This was before he had a heart attack and became bedridden. Because of the events (the fighting, I mean—I have caught myself speaking like the Lebanese, who always called the war "the events"), he could not work. Today he was wearing bedroom slippers and an elegant robe over trousers and a shirt and tie. In his quavery voice, he asked about my husband and about conditions on the mountain.

Mary ran back and forth between her little kitchen and the table, saying something each time she returned to the dining room. "It's just a simple meal, Frances. Just a little lunch for three. Do you like water or Pepsi with your food? Are you sure?"

When she called us to the table, she announced in a firm voice that this was a social occasion only. We were two hard-working women who needed to relax. We would eat. There would be no conversation about business or politics. "Frances, what do you want first? Take whatever pleases you."

I sat opposite Nicholas, who was wedged in against the buffet. Mary supervised from the end of the table, while eating heartily. I was happy not to talk about politics, though I had intended to use the opportunity to ask her some questions about legalities. I refrained, but Nicholas could not control his worries or the impulse to express them. He raised questions. "Who is shooting? At whom are they shooting?"

Mary told him that she didn't know but was not worried about it, because obviously Ashrafieh was not being shelled.

He wondered aloud how she could tell. I wondered silently. (All their exchanges were in Arabic, and I kept out of them.) He flinched with every big boom. He said, "Why would the Druze attack the Mourabitoun? A month ago they were fighting together, on the same side." Then he wondered who else the Druze meant to attack. "Is this part of some grand design?"

She spoke to him sharply. "We don't want to discuss politics."

"Mary," he said, "I am not talking about politics. I am talking about life and death." His voice shook.

"But we cannot change anything by talking. We can only upset ourselves." And again she said, "Frances and I are two hard-working women. We have met to eat and to play games." Then turning to me, she said, "Frances, I am so glad you like to play Scrabble. I am going to teach you a new Scrabble game, a more challenging game for superior minds."

I feared I was in trouble.

Privately, after Nicholas had gone to the bedroom for his afternoon nap, she admitted that the present fighting was very confusing, and she did not understand it. I had noticed before that Mary was devoted to Nicholas and protected him. Maybe she already suspected that he was sick. Once she had told me, "I don't know how I could survive without Nicholas."

We set up the Scrabble board on the dining table, after clearing away the dishes. She also made coffee for us. Mary was the only person who ever served me Arabic coffee in a standard coffee cup—full. That's a scary dose of caffeine even for a coffee lover like me. Having brought the two giant cups, she sat down and said, "Now...Frances..." and explained the rules for Double Scrabble, played with one board and two sets of letters. It was indeed more challenging, with many rules unlike regular Scrabble. We used a dictionary, an enormous dictionary, the kind you find in libraries. Mary used it more than I, because she understood better what she was trying to do. She took the great book on her lap, moved her head a foot this way and a foot that way, propping an eye open with her fingers, and found the words she needed to beat me. I suspected, after a while, that Mary made up this game, but I was fascinated with it.

Fascination, however, did not prevent my noticing that the fighting escalated and seemed to draw ever closer. The booms became louder and more frequent, and the intervals between them were filled with small arms fire. Uncomfortable but unwilling to spoil Mary's plans to relax, I kept playing, sometimes doing the obvious thing rather than taking time to find a better word or a winning strategy.

Finally, with the outcome of the game clear, I said that maybe I should call my office and try to determine if the way back was safe.

Normal courtesy would demand that she protest, insisting that it was too early to leave, but immediately Mary said, "Yes, Frances, I am feeling anxious about your getting there safely."

What I learned from my phone call was that I should take the longer way and come quickly. So I said goodbye, not having asked Mary any of my questions about business, and went out into the blackness of that stairwell.

(Later, on a nice day when nothing but sunshine was falling on the mountains, I went up to Broummana and bought another Scrabble set, so I could teach Wayne to play Double Scrabble during the next siege. Of course, he didn't like it. While I was reading the dictionary he wandered off.)

When I got back to the office from Mary's house, Wayne said, "We're invited to Nadia and Moussa's tonight, for supper and Rook."

Indispensable Friends

In no Lebanese home were we more comfortable than in Nadia and Moussa's. There were several reasons for this.

The Moussas were totally informal and unpretentious. They had a small, simple apartment and a relaxed attitude toward what they had and what they didn't. They didn't worry about the protocol of entertaining. Moussa would take off his shoes and wear his bedroom slippers when we were there or even peel down to his undershirt when the weather was hot. Nadia would let me come into the kitchen and help.

They didn't invite us for dinner a week ahead and make a big thing out of it. All the customs about gifts and reciprocation were irrelevant. Often they just caught us after church and said, "Come home with us." Some people would say things like that and then I would wonder if they were just trying to act hospitable. Maybe if we went we would discover that they weren't quite expecting us to accept. But one never had to wonder about Nadia and Moussa. They were only what they claimed to be.

Nadia was Abu and Um John's eldest daughter. She had dark hair and blue eyes, not bright blue like her dad's, just a soft blue that looked natural with her fair skin. She was neither thin nor fat, nor concerned about it. She wore comfortable clothes and a casual hair style. She smiled a lot but only when she wanted to smile.

If you wanted Nadia to do something you had to motivate her. She wouldn't do anything from guilt or pride.

Both of her parents were great cooks. Abu John could produce a roasted sheep fit for a king's banquet. He did it for us when our Dwight and their Nabeel graduated from high school. Nadia never felt the need to do what they did.

She was the only Lebanese woman I knew who had no reverence at all for Lebanese recipes. Since I had long believed that Lebanese food was invented by a man with four wives, I admired her for this. She could violate sacred processes without any twinge of conscience, sometimes scandalizing her friends by using a processor to chop parsley for *tabouli* (mangling it, most people would say) or using a pressure cooker to prepare in half an hour a dish (an imitation according to the food police) that was supposed to be done in four steps over two days. Nadia would even invite us for supper and order sandwiches from the shop down the street. Knowing that, we felt comfortable about accepting unplanned invitations. So many times we have eaten bought chicken sandwiches—with lots of garlic and salty pickles—and fried potatoes and Pepsis at their table and then played Rook. Often we ate it off the paper from the shop and them wadded it into the wastebaskets and started dealing the cards.

They were the only Lebanese people we knew who played Rook.

Moussa Moussa was his name. I laughed the first time I heard it. In its context there was nothing strange about this repetition, but the English version—Moses Moses—was definitely funny, I thought. Moussa had dark hair and dark eyes and Middle Eastern skin—ruddy like King David's—and was also very comfortable in himself and easy to be with.

At Rook Moussa and I were always partners against Nadia and Wayne, a devastating pair of players. Occasionally, when the cards really fell our way or Moussa outsmarted Nadia, dealing himself the bird, we would beat them, but our skills were no match for theirs. Rook involves a lot of memory, third grade mathematics and some psychology. Our problems were related to psychology. We never understood one another. If Moussa led green and I played red, he would take that as a signal that he should play red, while actually it never occurred to me to send a signal. I was merely throwing away a card I thought was useless.

Also he was a reckless bidder, and I was cautious. First we wouldn't get the bid because I wasn't aggressive enough, and then we would go set because Moussa overbid. So Nadia and Wayne won, unless Moussa and I got really lucky.

Moussa liked to talk about politics. For every international puzzle he had an opinion, for every insane battle an explanation—often an elaborate, surprising explanation. That night in March we could hear the fighting down in Beirut, and concern caused us to take a break from our game and listen to the news. The Sunni Muslim militia group called Mourabitoun, we heard, had taken back from the Druze the positions they had lost the day before. The Druze had, after negotiations, released one hundred and fifty captives seized the day before, and the Mourabitoun had tricked them and put the one hundred and fifty men back into the battle immediately. They had taken back the Abdin Nasr Mosque, where they had their headquarters and a radio station, from which they regularly broadcast tirades against the Christians.

Moussa, with his usual feeling that whatever was happening was final, said "*Khalas.* The tables are turned. They will push the Druze out of West Beirut."

I said, "You're serious?"

"Of course. This is part of a plot. Israel and America have agreed. It's a step toward dividing Lebanon into cantons."

Nadia said, "Moussa!"

That's how they disagreed. "Moussa!" "Nadia!" The tone of voice said everything.

We went back to the Rook game. Wayne and Nadia trounced us. As always they boasted, "That's the way to play the game!"

At the door, Moussa told me, "They were just lucky. We will get them next time." We always said that.

The whole ritual was part of the game, and the game was part of living through a long war.

Nine Years

Daily life became somewhat like a game—a tense, serious game. The goal was simply to accomplish some work on our lists by overcoming the obstacles thrown in our path.

When the Green Line was open and Abu Sleiman came to work, Abu Issam did not. His fear paralyzed him and BP. Unless Wayne had time to do part of the stock keeper's job, book orders piled up. More than once I sent his salary to his home, though he had not worked, because he was a dear and faithful Christian brother, and I didn't want him to go hungry. Besides that I sympathized. Fear was not unreasonable, and I had known Abu Issam for a long time. He was loyal to the core and incapable of deliberately taking advantage.

In 1976, Abu Issam was walking on the street in West Beirut when shells began exploding everywhere. Rushing toward home, he saw a woman pounding on a doorway, trying to gain admittance to a stranger's house in order to get off the street. Seeing her panic and thinking she had a good idea, he stopped to help. Together they knocked and screamed, until the moment that a shell exploded behind them, and the woman fell forward, with the back of her skull smashed. A bloody chunk of shrapnel lay beside her body. It took Abu Issam a minute to realize that he, too, had been hit.

A doctor removed an uncounted number of metal fragments from his back. Later when he was well, after half the world was traipsing across the Green Line twice a day, a rumor would keep Abu Issam at home. That time I had ignored his absence and paid him anyway for months, but sympathy did not help BP or our customers, and finally I sent a message that I would have to use the money to hire someone else to do the work. He came to work then, and on his first day back, I saw him flinch, grow pale and break into a sweat, because a door banged shut in the wind.

Such things made my job agonizingly difficult. Why should I pay one employee to cross the Green Line and come to work, and pay another who did not come? And how could I get the work done, within our budget, if I could not be tough about how we used our money? But what if my toughness caused someone to die? I struggled and prayed and considered all my alternatives before again giving Abu Issam a deadline for returning to work.

This time his son Issam came to see me. He said that he was worried about his dad and did not want him to cross the Green Line. He asked if I could arrange a place for Abu Issam to live for a while on the campus. The result of this consultation was that Abu Issam brought whatever he needed to live and slept for many weeks in one of the vacant dormitory rooms.

Waleed was gradually slipping away from us. On weekends he worked in a church in the South, and commuting from Beirut was becoming so difficult that he clearly had to choose. Israel cut off the entire South for days at a time, letting a select list of people cross the borders they had drawn.

Many fruits and vegetables disappeared from the Beirut market. The wonderful strawberries we normally enjoyed in the spring must have rotted in the South or been taken to Israel. We never tasted one. Lebanon protested to the United Nations about this violation of its territory, but nothing changed, and Waleed finally resigned. When I received his final decision in writing, I sat still at my desk for many minutes, feeling devastated. His presence, which had been refreshing and hopeful, was a loss, as well as my investment in him. I wrote a long letter to God about how tough it was.

Keeping the curriculum project moving required constant personal contacts, now made nearly impossible by the lack of movement and communication in the country. Our phones worked one hour and not the next. Unable to call even East Beirut from my office, I would go up to the Broummana or Beit Meri post office, and the telephone operator would work half an hour to "catch the line." It was easier to call the U.S. than to call West Beirut. The necessity of using the telephone gave people stomachaches.

I often had stomachaches myself, usually soon after eating. And even more often I lost sleep because of cramps in my feet and ankles. I had to jump out of bed and walk around, then sometimes the cramp would come back again when I lay down. The worst ones, though, were in my calves. I would wake groaning or screaming and find that the muscle in my calf had become a tiny knot or a mere string clinging to the bone. The pain was so intense that I would lose my head and do all the wrong things. Afterwards the leg would be sore for a couple of days.

The Lebanese government added handicaps. Mary informed me that I now had to take every book to a government office for approval before it could be produced, and this office was in Telat al-Khayat in West Beirut.

Unable to call in advance, I had gone to the lawyer's house to ask those questions I never asked over lunch.

I said, "Mary, you mean we have censorship now?"

"We do, Frances. Of course, they are not going to read every word. They will take a look at the subject, maybe try to get the direction of it."

"What are they looking for?"

"Anything divisive, or inflammatory—political or religious. Be careful about anything they could see as an attack on another religion."

"We don't attack other religions."

"I know, Frances, but be careful. It's about perceptions."

I had a large book order from Egypt, and every title had to be approved before it could be shipped. I also had materials being readied for the press, including *Joni*, by Joni Earickson, a story I felt would have great meaning for multitudes of handicapped people in Lebanon.

Mary wanted to take the books to Telat al-Khayat herself. "I don't want you there alone, in case they raise silly arguments," she said. She needed me to come back to Ashrafieh and bring her a printed list and two copies of every title. Each book would be stamped when approved; one copy would go in the government files and one would come back to me, as proof of approval whenever I needed it.

"You and I will talk about the books first," Mary said, "so I can get everything in mind before I go."

Then Mary knocked the props from under me. She said, "I'm giving the situation until Easter to get better. If things stay like this until then, I am giving all of my clients their files and leaving the country."

"Leaving? Mary, how can you do that?"

"Why not, if I can't work?"

"But you're working right now."

"Frances, I need the courts to function."

"You'll come back?"

"If the courts open."

It was like the Army falling apart. Who would save me from the wolves if Mary left? And what did her decision mean about the future?

Letting me out at her front door, she said, "Be careful, Frances. Keep your eyes and ears open. And let Wayne stay close to home. It's a jungle out there."

The day I was to deliver the materials to her, both sides of the Green Line were shelled in the early morning. No one came to work from either West or East Beirut. I got Mary on the phone. She said a lot of shells had fallen around her building and in Karm az-Zeitoun. We postponed our meeting one more day. The second day was only a little better, but I went anyway.

Shells fell around the Palace of Justice while Mary was there, but she called me, triumphant, to say that she got everything past the censorship office with ease. Later she told me, "The officer was quite pleased with some of your books. I suspect he will snitch that Picture Bible from the files and take it to his children, so hang on to your stamped copy."

I visited two presses the day I gave *Joni* to a printer. Both of them were as quiet as sick rooms—the equipment idle, the workers sitting in dim offices drinking coffee and smoking. Edgar at Heidelberg told me that licensing, censorship, exportation restrictions, taxes, the bad economy, even fear had impacted printers. "For a while power cuts were a problem, but now we have so little work, we don't need electricity often."

He beamed at the manuscript of *Joni*, as though it were a prize, and said he could finish it in record time, because it had no competition on his schedule.

In West Beirut, a Lebanese man disappeared, and in the morning his body showed up, thrown out in a field near the Soviet Embassy. Jeremy Levin, an American journalist, disappeared.

It was like waves washing over the deck of the ship, while the tenacious ones and people with no options clung to anything they could grasp, trying not to fall overboard. Actually, these two kinds of people encouraged one another. The tenacious looked at the trapped and said, "If they can take it, we can." The trapped looked at the tenacious and said, "If they are here, the situation must not be hopeless." And in Lebanon there was always something to hold on to. Schools opened. The Post Office distributed mail. Churches of all kinds filled up with people anytime the doors opened. The sun kept coming up in the mornings.

The Lebanese continued to find humor in their own helplessness. The joke circulating at the time was about a bargain available in Beirut. When Reagan wanted to talk to the devil his phone call from Washington to Hades cost $400, but Gemayel could make the call for 25 piasters from Beirut, since it was a local call.

Early one morning, as I wrote "April 8" in my diary I realized that it was John Olson's birthday. He should have been 21 years old. This reminded me that for some people sorrow was the biggest daily obstacle. This thought cut my problems down to size.

One evening when sudden shelling created panic in Beit Meri, a lot of our neighbors jumped into cars and fled. Lulu and her children ran to our house. We all sat in the cave until bedtime, then Wayne and I made extra pallets and gave our guests the inside space. We slept behind the loaded bookcases, where it occurred to me that a strong concussion from the front side would knock them over on us.

The next day was April 13, and the newspapers reminded us of an anniversary that no one was celebrating. Nine years ago that day the civil war had started. All day people talked about it. People who didn't mind expressing their cynicism called it "the first day of the tenth year."

The Fullers' house in The Hara, Beit Meri, after remodeling

Abu Sleiman, chief editor of Baptist Publications, 1975-1985

A display of new Arabic books in 1979: Arabic version of *The Picture Bible for All Ages* by David C. Cook, and *The Greek-Arabic Concordance to the New Testament,* compiled by Ghassan Khalaf

Frances and Georgette at Georgette's house in Nabay

Fullers' neighbor children: Lubnan, Maha
and Terez. In The Hara, Beit Meri

Maria Daoud, physical therapist

Michel Makhoul, BP staff artist, the day he left
for university in the U.S.

The Fullers' inner room ("the cave") protected by sandbags

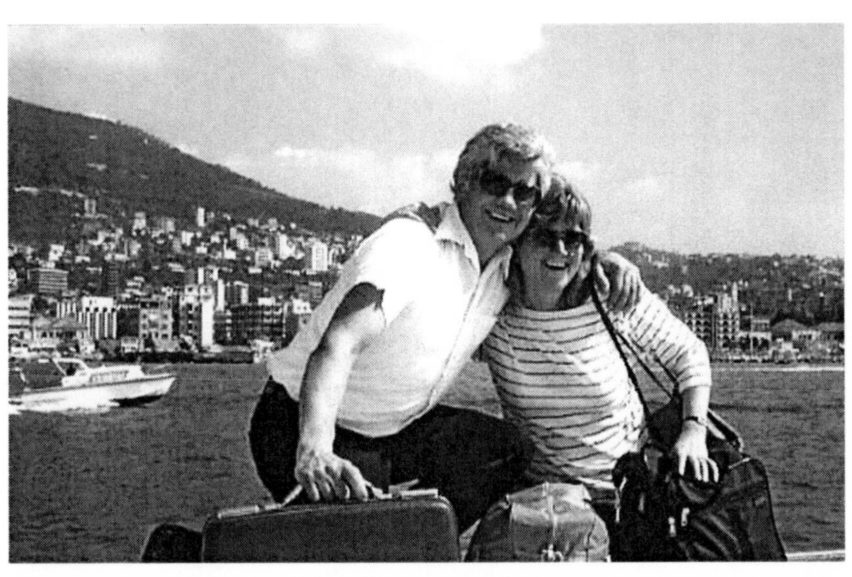

Wayne and daughter Jan at the Jounieh port

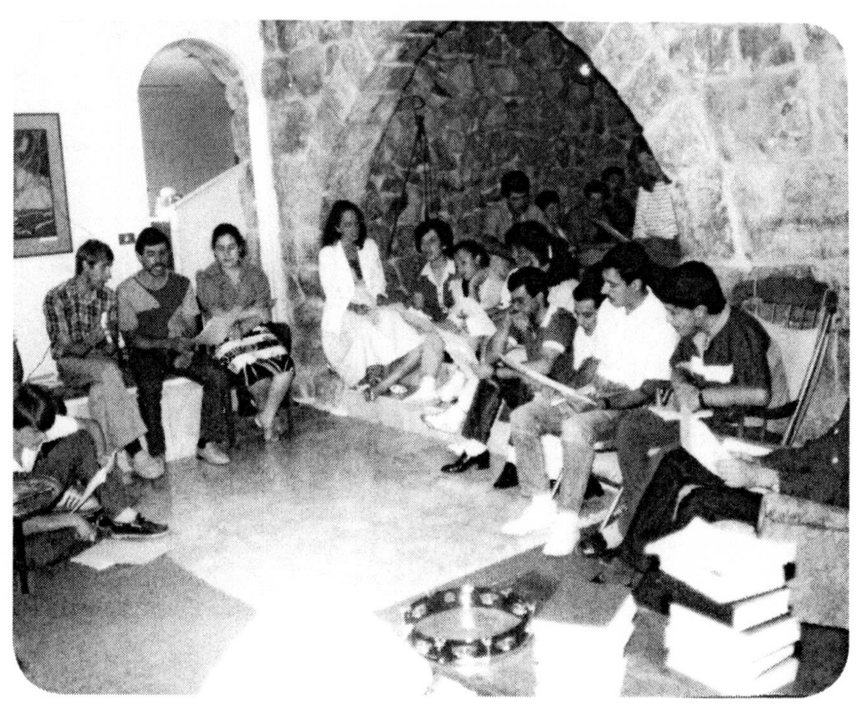

Youth meeting in the Fullers' house

Publishing staff, 1985. Seated: Atiyeh Haddad (Abu Issam), Frances. Standing: Siham Haddad, Saeed Baz, Andre Haddad, Nazih Khater, Naji AbouKhair, Michel Abbas, Charles Costa, Fadia Atiyeh

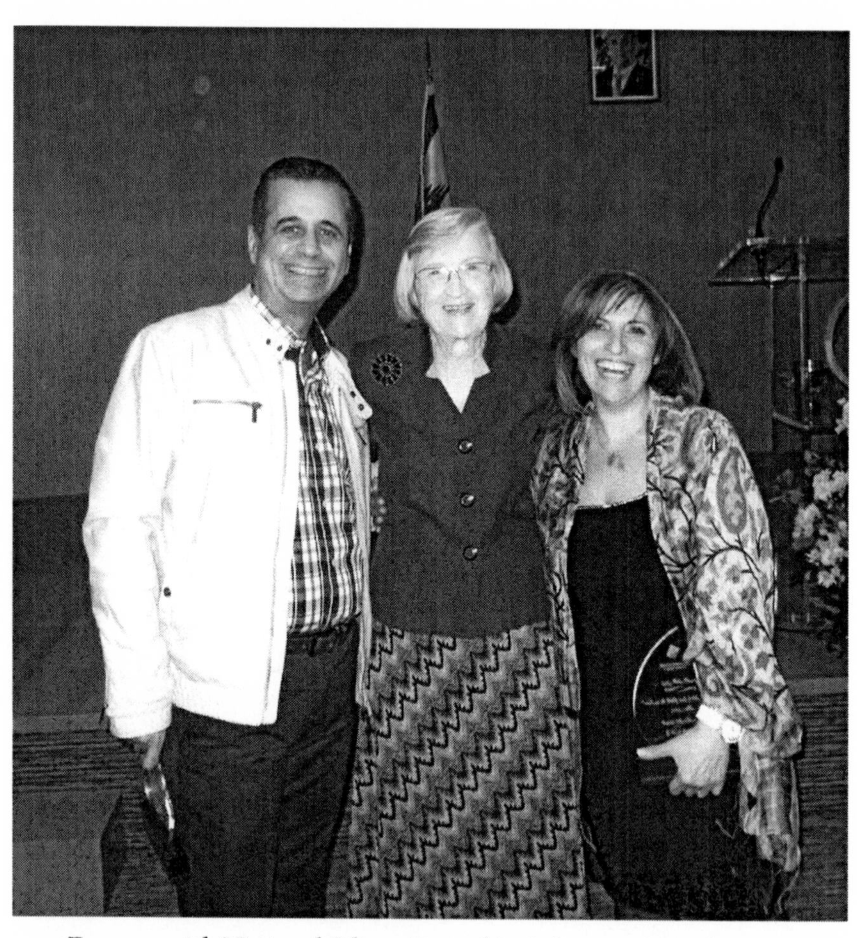

Frances with Naji and Siham Daoud in Lebanon, March, 2013

Intervals of Peace

Rendezvous in Larnaca

Jan was coming. This was scary, maybe crazy, definitely wonderful. I was meeting her in Cyprus. That's why I was on a hydrofoil boat speeding across the water, bumping the waves furiously. The passengers sat in rows of comfortable armchairs, facing the prow of the small craft and surrounded by windows. This was not a smooth ride. The sea was like a washboard, and the boat hit the top of each hard wave. The repetitive pounding was going to give me a headache. However, since the boat did not roll, or fall and lift like the ferries, I would not be seasick. Furthermore I had eaten lunch in Lebanon and would be in Cyprus before dinner.

In April, just when my hopes for Lebanon plummeted to an all-time low, Jan had declared her intentions. I had called her from the Broummana post office and talked for seventeen minutes, trying to dissuade her. This was the perfect time for a visit, she said. She couldn't plan according to conditions that might develop; she had one three-week window in June. I warned her that we might not be able to go anywhere, that shells might fall. I told her that Lebanon might not exist by June. I couldn't change her mind.

The country had a new government that incorporated a few changes but lined up the same old rivals. Karami, the prime minister, kept telling us we were "marching toward peace," while shells kept flying and people kept falling dead or wounded. In the first fifteen days of the new government, forty-five civilians died and two hundred and seventy-five were injured. A little boy we knew from church, a seven or eight-year-old, was one of those injured. Shrapnel cut a chunk out of his arm and left a marvelous puzzle to ponder—a hole in the front of his shirt and a hole in the back, with a healthy kid in between.

All parties claimed not to know who was responsible for the shooting, and no one seemed to benefit from the carnage. People clamored to know a reason. One radio editorial said, "If we are going to die, tell us who the executioner is."

Even Moussa ran out of explanations. Our official explainer actually said, "I don't know what's going on. No one does." Though I tended to be skeptical of explanations, I found Moussa's inability to rationalize one a terrifying sign; unreasoning and unreasonable forces must be in control.

In spite of it all, we wrote a letter to help Jan get a visa.

Then two more Americans were kidnapped in May. The career diplomat was one thing, but Ben Weir—a Presbyterian missionary, a friend—was something else. All of our family knew the Weirs. Their children had been classmates of our children at the American Community School. Ben, a man of peace who loved Lebanon, was seized on the street, hit on the head, shoved into a car and driven away, while his wife Carol chased the vehicle, screaming. The event became even more chilling when a radio station reported a call from Islamic Jihad, claiming that they were holding him and two other Americans and that they intended to leave no single American in Lebanon.

After that not only the American embassy but the Lebanese security forces asked that no male American walk on the street in Ras Beirut.

If any of this bad news had an effect on Jan, we didn't hear about it. She had determined to come to Lebanon, though she wouldn't explain why. She was flying Royal Jordanian Airlines and would get on the plane at JFK, though she had no reservation from Amman to Larnaca. "If I get that close, I'll hitchhike."

The very worst thing imaginable rarely happens, I've noticed, even in Lebanon, especially in Lebanon, which has a gift for wiggling out of messes without actually solving them. When the time came for me to travel to Cyprus and fetch our daughter home, Lebanon was still Lebanon, life was much improved, and a new spirit of hope had overtaken us.

I had business to do in Cyprus, and before Jan's arrival I would spend several days running around all over the southern, Greek part of this small island country. I hoped to arrange for a curriculum workshop high in the mountains, for writers from Egypt and Jordan, and to open a book depot in one of the major cities.

I sat beside a young man I knew who just happened to be taking the boat that day. Fouad and I talked, and the boat pounded the water, and the sun glinted off the sea. He was excited, too, because he was going to a conference in Korea, so we talked about happy things. It was the first time since January that I had been in a conversation that ignored the war.

Suddenly there was Cyprus, the city of Larnaca gray-white in the sun, the wheeling seagulls white, little boats with white sails running in the wind, the beaches narrow and bleached, all this whiteness surrounded by blue sky and sea. And Jan was coming.

Pictures in My Head

I have pictures of her visit, candid shots, mostly mental. In a war zone, carrying a camera is not a good idea, except maybe for journalists, and I had ceased to do it. But Jan brought a camera and smuggled it from place to place in a small bag with her underwear and pajamas on top of it.

* * *

In my living room with the stone walls and the white marble floor, in that corner between the arch and the entry to the dining room, she sits in a straight chair, her hair in a casual twist around her head. The room is full of other young adults, participants in what our church called "the youth group." In this, their first meeting after several months of fighting, their faces are happy and eager. They sing and pray and talk about their lives as Christians. Jan listens.

* * *

In Bourj Hammoud she has bought some gold trinket in a jewelry store, and we are on the way back to our car, when an explosion cracks the air and reverberates through the street. The sidewalks empty as people run toward entries and overhangs. We follow their lead and find a place to get some concrete over our heads. All the cars in the street are blowing their horns at one another in futility. Other booms shake the buildings. They seem very near. They are many.

Looking out toward the street, I tell her, "In the city, one boom sounds like six."

She says, "I know."

This is what I didn't want to happen. I am thinking that she remembers biting the dust, literally, on the playground in Amman, when the American school was caught in a crossfire, that she spent weeks in the Biqaa listening to the muzzle blasts of Syrian artillery as it blasted Beit Meri where she had just left us, that she will run away from a common fireworks display.

"Are you O.K.?" I ask her.

"Yep." She presses her lips together and nods.

* * *

At the gate of the Baptist Mission House in Musaitbeh two young men guard the neighborhood from behind a sandbag bunker. They look fierce standing there with automatic rifles in their hands and ammunition belts across their chests, but their fierceness is diluted immediately by curiosity. We say, "God give you strength," to acknowledge that they are doing their job, and they tell us, "You speak Arabic very well." They want to talk; they want to know many things and at the same time are reluctant to ask.

Jan wants to take a picture. "Sorry," they say, "that is prohibited." And she says, "*Ma'leish*," making it seem unimportant. Then they change their minds.

It's O.K., they say, if "the *bint*" (the girl) can be in the picture with them. So I take the camera and Jan stands with them in front of the gate of the house where she lived for a year when she was eight. They want her in the middle but stand at a prudent distance from her, in polite Muslim fashion. This is priceless—Jan smiling at me, in her white blouse and purple skirt, flanked by two armed men with stiff, emotionless faces.

Then one of the soldiers asks if they can have copies of the pictures. Jan says, "*Ma'loum*," (of course) but I add that it will be about a month, maybe more, before the pictures will come.

One soldier says, "Why?" disappointed or annoyed, and the other, with a quick glance at him and the nudge of an elbow, says, "They have to take the film to Paris and get it developed and send it back."

The elbow says everything. They need to pretend, he is saying to his companion. They must pretend not to know that we are Americans.

"Exactly," we agree. "It takes time."

Finding What Was Lost

Shortly after Jan left I went to a doctor about my stomachaches. He pressed on my tummy and made some remark about my colon being "hard like a pipe." Then he sat behind his desk and said, "Mrs. Fuller, do you know anyone in Lebanon who doesn't have a stomachache?"

Unprepared for the question, I did not think to say, "My husband."

He said, "We have two things that give everybody stomachaches—amoebas and falling shells." Then he asked me what I had been eating and advised me to stop eating it. I went home wondering if there could be a conspiracy between green vegetables and watermelon on one side and amoebas and falling shells on the other.

Wayne and I went to Kenya for the best vacation we had ever had, spending the whole time with dear friends. We watched herds of elephants come to the water holes, witnessed giraffes floating over a fence, light and graceful like deer, saw two leopards in one hour and a lake covered with flamingoes. We went to church with the Masai; Wayne loved the Masai. I smiled—and smile still—because a Kikuyu woman looked at me and said, "I'm sorry," when my friend told her that I lived in Lebanon. I began to feel better and ready to go home. Our friends thought maybe we were becoming careless, that we should consider doing our work somewhere else. I left them a note saying that Lebanon was our destiny, chosen or assigned, for better or for worse.

On the way home we stopped in Cairo and Amman to do work for BP, so we were away from home two months altogether, returning to a dusty house and piled up work, a tense Lebanon and all the problems we had left behind. We had lots of mail, too. Cynthia sent snapshots of her and Dwight. They now lived close enough to do things together. They went to concerts. She wrote that she wanted us to see her $2400 smile. That's what she had paid an orthodontist for her straight teeth. Dwight had a small mustache, like a Lebanese.

Jan's letter explained that before she came to visit she had been carrying a weight of anxiety and had lost all peace about our being in Lebanon. Then she was amazed, she said, to find us so calm and happy, going about our business. She had loved seeing our house full of young people and watching us in the office, producing books. She had realized finally that "staying in Lebanon is the kind of wisdom that looks foolish, because it is contrary to the world's way of thinking."

At the end she assured us, "I'm O.K. now. I've got my peace back."

It seemed a good idea, after all, to have visitors. And definitely a good idea to go out for a vacation—to be reminded of the wide, wonderful world. And to come home again—to realize again that Lebanon was home.

A Place to Be Together

It was a Sunday evening after church. When I came out and stood on the front steps of the building and looked down on Beirut, it was twilight. The sea was still brighter than the land, reflecting the glow in the west, and lights were coming on in the city. Except for the chatter in the vestibule behind me, all was quiet. I think that's why I had come outdoors; I was looking for the quiet and eager to go home.

I loved peaceful Sunday evenings, especially that time after church, when I could go home and do nothing—just put on a robe and slippers and feel that the next two hours were unscheduled and safe and mine. I had always liked this, but in 1984 I was "out of gas," as Wayne said, and needed all the pauses for refueling that I could get.

One other person came out to the steps, Nada, a very sweet and pretty girl, who was one of my favorites in the church. She was respectful and courteous. She was mature and responsible beyond her years. It was Nada who spent half a day with me scrubbing the upstairs bathroom before we moved into our house. It was Nada who always put fresh flower arrangements in the church. Sometimes we were shelled all night and everyone was exhausted, but the flowers were there, a small, graceful sign that we had not been defeated.

Nada and I smiled, spoke to each other and then just stood there, looking down on the green lot in front of us—a somewhat disheveled piece of ground, with a stand of bamboo canes—and beyond to the twinkling lights of Beirut. The air was warm and still.

"Aunt Frances," she said. She had been calling me that since she was a little girl. "Could some of us young people come up to your house?"

I turned to look at her, not yet understanding the question.

"See, we don't really want to go home now, because we want to be together. And we have no place to go."

Immediately I saw the whole problem. Of course, they wanted to be together, and where in a world at war would they do that? And of course, I did not want a bunch of energetic young people to come to my house, not now on Sunday evening. But never would I refuse Nada. And I was pleased that she could ask, though there was a gentle hesitancy in her voice.

I said, "Sure, Nada. How many of you will there be?"

She smiled, and her voice picked up a happy lilt. "Oh, maybe six or eight. But you don't need to do anything, Aunt Frances. We will stop on the way up and buy sandwiches and drinks. I'll go tell them. And my parents. Oh, thanks, Aunt Frances."

Eight of them came, boys and girls, bringing ten big hot sandwiches—chicken with garlic and salty pickles—and bottled drinks and happiness.

My kitchen came alive with movement and conversations—two or three at once, full of jokes and laughing. I made chocolate-oatmeal no-bake cookies, deciding to do it and measuring the ingredients and stirring them up and cooking them—sixty seconds, not a second more—and dropping them on the waxed paper all in fifteen minutes, and they sat there smelling good for another fifteen, and in the next five we ate them all.

The young people cleaned up the mess we made and thanked me a jillion times and shouted goodbye all the way down the slope to their cars. Wayne and I stood in the open door and watched them leave and he turned to me and said, "Kids need stuff like this. We ought to do it more often."

The next Sunday I didn't wait to be asked.

A Designer Shelter

Wayne had a small workshop in the semi-basement of the seminary building. The room was cluttered with tools and stacks of wood and old cans of paint and sometimes even dysfunctional appliances. I admit I never actually went inside, though once or twice I looked into it from its entrance on the backside of the building.

In this cramped space that smelled like grease and mold and wood shavings Wayne repaired broken gadgets, made most of his Christmas gifts, salvaged working pieces of broken-down washing machines, and probably did a lot of things I don't even know about. Out of this workshop came the miracle of cupboard doors. One day he just brought them home and began screwing the hinges in place. Each pair of doors he had cut from a single piece of oak, so that the grain made one pattern across the closed doors. They were the most beautiful cupboard doors in Lebanon. I'm sure of it. Equally perfect drawer facings came with the doors, and suddenly my kitchen was complete. Visitors could no longer see into my open shelves, and the room was transformed into a picture that belonged in *House Beautiful.*

Little by little we were completing our house. One thing I wanted Wayne refused to do. I wanted steps up the hill. The path was still rough, and I often pictured myself tripping or wobbling on one of those stones and tumbling down to the street. Wayne said that concrete steps would destroy the ambience. If I thought that concrete block room had violated the stone walls, wait until I saw steps up the hill.

Shortly afterwards I invited the mission to have the monthly meeting in our house. The occasion gave me opportunity to remind Wayne that Mabel Summers had vowed not to come to our house again until we improved the path to our door. So he spent a couple of late afternoons moving and digging and re-laying stones, so that they were flat and stable. His work was neat, and though people would still have to mount the hill single file, they certainly would feel more secure while doing it.

A few of the missionaries had not been to the house before and no one had seen the finished kitchen, so everybody spent the first half hour milling around, admiring details of Wayne's work, trying the drawers, exclaiming and complimenting us.

"I love your floors."

"I never imagined it would look like this!"

Someone wanted to know, "How much do you have to run the furnace?"

Wayne said, "On really cold days ten minutes, just to take the chill off when we come in from work."

"How many more years do you have? I want to live here after you leave."

We had put the bookcases back in their places and stacked sandbags, at an angle, in the entrance to the cave. (Michel had found them for us and helped Wayne fill them with sand.) The wall of bulging bags was much lower than the bookcases—just right for crouching behind—and blended right into the rocks of the room. I had added a green plant in front of them, to prevent the space from looking like a battle position.

Somebody said, "Old-fashioned stove, music, oriental light, cushions everywhere. This is what I call a designer bomb shelter."

Mabel Summers brought her camera and kept clicking and hopping sideways and saying, "This is a beautiful house! I can't believe how it turned out."

Emmett, the only one who had seen potential in the old stone stable the way Wayne did, said to the others, "Now, aren't you glad we bought it?" (Not quite, "I told you so.")

I made bran muffins, having borrowed extra pans so I could bring sixty muffins out of the oven at once and serve them hot at coffee break time. I laid out plates of assorted cheeses and poured up pots of tea and coffee, feeling grateful beyond words for the friendship of our colleagues, my genius of a husband, and the crazy, wonder-filled little house which was mine for a season. "A designer shelter" defined the whole thing.

Coincidentally, on the day before this meeting the Beit Meri municipality repaired the shell holes in our road and paved the whole two kilometers, so that our guests rode in on the cleanest, smoothest blacktop in the country.

Wayne was almost as funny as Mabel. He kept looking out the window and saying, "I can't believe they paved the road!"

Back then people got excited in Lebanon over small simple things, always with some incredulity about good fortune.

A Small, Momentous Decision

Sometime that November George Atiyeh came to my office to talk. George was our pastor, a young man with soft cheeks and hands and voice and manner. He did not like to confront. He could not be terse. In the pulpit or at the corner of my desk, he circled a subject, talking—softly, with a bit of a lisp—long after the picture was clear. He began this particular conversation with a lengthy preamble saying, "I appreciate all you do with the young people, inviting them to your home and all," and reminding me that he knew I was tired and had too much responsibility already, and he was sympathetic, but... He asked about Maria. How well did I know her?

Maria was a 27-year-old, a physical therapist whom we had been picking up for church on Sunday evenings. George had been praying for weeks, he said, about who would be her "big sister."

This terminology referred to our church's method for helping new believers become Christian disciples. The pastor usually appointed a church member to relate to the newcomer as a big brother or big sister, offering instruction and whatever support seemed necessary. "She is a well-educated young woman," he said. "I don't want to give her to someone who is less educated, and most of our mature women are."

Finally, he said that he had to ask me, because he felt I was the right one, maybe the only one.

Looking back on this moment when George sat leaning on the corner of my big metal desk, smiling slightly, as he always did—though his face revealed some anxiety about my answer, I see it as a scary intersection of life. Obviously, someone should disciple Maria. And I was afraid that George's assessment of the situation was right and his decision logical. But I really needed to say no, because I lacked the strength for one more thing. I tried to say no. I hesitated. I thought that George had a right, in spite of everything, to hope I would say, "I'll be happy to." I couldn't say that either. Instead I just agreed, reluctantly, to do what he asked, not knowing where I would find the energy or the time, or when I would learn to protect myself.

Of course I did not imagine that the decision would bring me in return the gift of a rare friendship, and I certainly did not suspect that it might save my life, besides.

Going Slow

When I suggested to Maria that we study together, I knew right away that she was not thrilled with the idea. We were standing in the small and poorly lighted vestibule of the chapel, after Sunday evening church, waiting for Wayne who was consulting somebody about something, always trying to kill one more bird with his stone. A few people were still milling around, putting on coats, saying goodnight.

Sounding unprepared for this suggestion and doubtful, she said, "What would we study?"

I said, "Well, probably we should study the basic principles of the Christian faith. There are some good books we could use."

She hesitated, her face now cautious, her big eyes wandering around. She pondered in silence. Finally, she said she would look at the books.

I took her up to the BP display room and showed her some of our options—materials in Arabic, French and English, arranged on a revolving rack. The French books were colorful and seemed less serious than the others, and since French was her second language I thought she might prefer them. I pointed out that I didn't know French but if she liked that set, I could manage, because we had them also in English. She took her time, weighing unstated issues, and then chose *The Survival Kit for New Believers,* which we had only in English—her third and weakest language. It presented the fundamentals—theological and practical—for a new Christian, in a workbook format.

We went down the hall to my office to talk, sitting on those black plastic chairs against the wall. The office was cold and we both kept our coats on. I asked her what she understood of the gospel. Shyly but surely she said, "Only one thing. Salvation is by faith."

Surprised to hear her state this core principle so well, I said, "That's enough for now, a good beginning," and didn't think she suspected that this was a blatant understatement. I added, "How did you come to that?"

"I read it in the Bible."

There was a whole story behind that, I suspected, but she didn't volunteer anything. Instead she said, "I want to go slow."

I knew that Maria was tired, too. Her job was strenuous; she left home at dawn, returned from the hospital in the dark and then received private patients at home. I told her that I didn't have much time either, and we could find our own pace. But then she said, "I told God if he wants to come into my life, he should come slowly, so I don't get scared."

She was like this—self-conscious and blunt all at once. Reluctant to look at me, then baring her soul.

It's reasonable, I guess, to be afraid of someone you don't know when it's someone as big as God, but I had never heard anybody say that, and I didn't quite know how to answer.

I looked at her. She had a long, slender neck and a proud profile like Queen Nefertiti—like those little alabaster busts the Egyptians sell to tourists—the inscrutable face with high arching eyebrows, wide eyes and mouth.

Her eyes darted around the room while the rest of her was very still, her hands in her lap—clutching the book, her feet together, and she explained, "I don't like big emotional experiences. I am uncomfortable if other people get emotional, like when they express joy in their faith."

She looked straight at me then and said, "I don't have joy. My eyes are not gleaming."

She was right; they weren't. They were heavy-lidded eyes, careful, maybe wounded, I thought, and it struck me that letting herself be happy was what she was afraid of.

This thought troubled me, but I decided to drop it and ask another question. I needed now, more than ever, to know if any changes had occurred in her life or had she raised her hand in church and gone away with nothing. So I asked.

After a pause to think about it, she said, "I am not angry anymore." She had been very angry, she explained—at life, but "now my anger has gone, replaced by... calmness. I guess it's... peace."

And I was certain, then, that something genuine was going on in her heart. I knew so many angry people. Everybody in Lebanon was eaten up by anger unless some work of grace had been done in their lives.

Rejoice with Those Who Rejoice

Tim telexed from Cairo. He had a visa and could come for three or four days on November 10 or any day until the 20th. For months he had been trying to get a visa. We had asked for it in Beirut and been denied. Then he had been refused in Washington and London, but now the consul in Cairo had been kind (or careless, or remiss).

Tim was on his way to East Africa. In the midst of a career change and expecting to be poor for the rest of his life, he had sublet his apartment in Berkeley, taken all of his money except enough for one month's rent, and started out on the trip he had dreamed of—to wander Africa, climb Kilimanjaro, see the wild animals, hear the music. When his money ran out, he would go home. Of course, Lebanon beckoned. He could not be so near and not see us in our rock house. I had warned him already that West Beirut was off-limits, that he could not go to Bisharri and see the Cedars or take off hiking across the hills.

On November 9 fighting broke out along the Green Line, and all crossing points were closed. I asked Tim to wait. Idil told me, "Don't let him come to Lebanon. *Abadan* (Ever. Never)."

Every day something happened to scare us, and then I sent a telex to Tim, through a bank in Cairo. Every morning he would leave some cheap little room where he was staying and walk down to the bank, and the manager would give him his telex from Lebanon.

Finally, I sent him an "all clear" and held my breath.

In spite of my not heeding Idil's advice, he went with me to get Tim from the Beirut airport on the afternoon of November 20. In the car he said to me, "When he comes, you grab one arm, I grab the other, and we put him in the middle here between us."

No one but passengers could enter the airport building. For years it had been like that. People who came to meet travelers had to stand outside behind a flimsy movable barrier—its integrity supported by an armed guard. At either end of this barrier was space for arriving passengers to walk around it. That day I stood—wary, observant, my eyes roaming—among these expectant people. The crowd was thin, everybody staring at the small door, straining for the one face that would make them glad. Just beyond the barricade, the guard sauntered back and forth. Another soldier paced farther away in front of the departure entrance, where a steady stream of vehicles stopped to drop off people and their luggage and then drove away.

A lot of men moved restlessly behind us—mostly taxi-driver types. Beside me a Muslim woman in black clothes—a tiny woman—glanced up at me now and then. She couldn't have been five-feet tall. I spoke to her, and she smiled and said, "*Ahlan.*" She had a dry, shriveled face and small alert eyes.

Travelers came out the door, one or two at a time, carrying suitcases and walking toward us. Some of them found family or friends and got kissed on both cheeks. Others whizzed off in taxis. Then a small river of people came out, none of them Tim. The time grew long, the crowd at the rail sparse. The Muslim woman remained; she watched me and the door.

Finally there he was, skinny and erect, fair and obvious, with his flaming hair and red beard, his hands free, a pack on his back. I forgot to be unobtrusive and clapped my hands together and laughed, and beside me the Muslim lady jumped and clapped her hands and laughed and looked from me to Tim and back, beaming. From this I knew she was a mother. I still love her for being happy with me.

We grabbed his arms the way Idil said and in a few seconds reached the car and pushed him in. We crossed the Green Line at Tayyouni, with Tim lowering his head and twisting his neck to see the buildings, full of holes like Swiss cheese.

Raising a Child

Tim stayed with us for six days. We celebrated Thanksgiving and went to visit Georgette, but not much else. I remember his standing at the front window, gazing at the deceptively peaceful view of the mountains, and saying, "I couldn't just walk down to the river? And maybe up to Ras el-Metn?"

The thought made my heart pause and then run to catch up.

He said, "I guess things fall unexpectedly."

"Yes." *And sometimes people disappear—Lebanese people, in cars, car and all.*

When he left I was sad, so sad that he was not there anymore, and relieved not to be scared that something dreadful would happen to him there, and reconciled, as never before, to the truth that my children could not live in Lebanon again.

After that Maria and I began to study.

At first we met in my office after the church's Wednesday night Bible study. Both of us were too tired to think by then. Sometimes she had not even had dinner, and exhaustion showed on her face and in her posture. So we moved our lessons to another night and sat in my cave by the stove, where our feet and our relationship were warmer.

She always came prepared. Not only had she studied daily and filled in the workbook, but she had brought some burning question to which I was supposed to have a correct and wise answer. She wanted reasons for everything—intellectually satisfying reasons. And she recognized spiritual truth when she heard it. She ate it like bread.

Knowing that salvation was a gift, accepted by faith, she wanted to understand the relationship between faith and living a good life. What difference did faith make? I told her that, with nothing to earn, we want to do right out of gratitude for the gift, and she replied, "That's a wonderful difference," sat and thought about it a while and then added, "I feel so free."

Our best discussions grew out of her questions. She didn't mean to be theological when she asked me, "Why are the believers always saying, '*Nushkar ar-rab*?'" I had never thought about it. "Thank the Lord," was part of the vocabulary of the church. We gave one another good news, and the spontaneous reply was "*Nushkar ar-rab.*" When a Christian was driving on the road and a shell landed just in front of him without hurting him, he would say, "*Nushkar ar-rab.*" If the same thing happened to anybody else, he would take the front of his shirt in his fingers and shake it, the way the Lebanese do to deny responsibility, and say, "I was so lucky." In an instant I thought all of this and said, "Because they know whom to thank."

She was satisfied, and I was glad she had asked. What a great thing to have someone to thank!

I remember her asking me, "What does the pastor do?" And after I listed some of George's duties, she said, "But I have seen other people in the church do all of those things."

This brought to light the treasured doctrine of the priesthood of the believer—we could all read the scripture and understand, we could all pray and teach and comfort the bereaved and bring God to one another. She loved it. She got prettier from understanding it.

We took every point in the book seriously—did every exercise, wrote an answer to every question, read every scripture, tried to memorize particular verses. One evening she read aloud, "if anyone is in Christ, he is a new creation; the old has gone, the new has come."

She paused to tap the spot where the words appeared in her Bible, 2 Corinthians 5:17, and said, "That's true. That's really true."

She grew confidential. "Remember when you asked me if I wanted to study with you, and I didn't want to at first? Well, I had just made a decision not to come to church anymore. I wasn't sure anything important had happened to me, and I thought that if I could drop out that would prove it was nothing."

I felt limp at the thought. She said, "You messed up my plan," and laughed.

A few times we talked about what had happened to Lebanon, and she reminisced bitterly, telling me about the pride, the idealistic patriotism that she and her schoolmates once had. That was all part of an innocent childhood. Now they were wise and cynical. The old despair would flicker across her face, and she would close her big eyes and open them again, and I would see profound pain. My own sense of the tragedy of Lebanon became more acute as I felt with her what it meant to be Lebanese and young, with the country disintegrating.

She studied ravenously, looked ahead in the workbook to know every subject that was coming up, asked questions before we got there, before I thought she was ready to be there. Then one wonderful day she said, "God can come faster now, if he wants to."

Watching her learn to pray with me was interesting. She would sigh heavily when it was her turn, like it was hard to get started and then she would say the kinds of brilliant and obvious things that children say when they talk to God or she would say, unconsciously, something as deep and true as what Jesus said in Gethsemane. Once she asked God for something, and added "We want this right away, but later will be O.K., too." And one day she astonished me by observing that, because we can pray, we are responsible somehow for everything that happens in the world. I think of her words often when the world goes wrong and I have failed to pray.

When our workbook asked her to write three things God had given her for which she was thankful, she wrote, "peace, self-control and joy." Joy? I could hardly keep track of the miracles that were going on.

Sometimes she was plain cute, like the afternoon she called me from Monsourieh. I was in my office, and she was hoping to see me. When I found her, standing near the pharmacy, she got into the car and, still closing the door, without even a Hi, she blurted, "Today I did a very bad thing!"

At first I wanted to laugh, but in fact she had suffered a real downer. While we were driving up to my house she told me. It all started with socks. In a rush to get ready for work in the morning, she had turned her sock drawer topsy-turvy looking for the pair she needed. They weren't there, because her sister had them on. Pressured by time, half-dressed and furious, Maria had shouted at Vivian—not very nice things, apparently. And that wasn't the bad part yet. At the hospital, trying to make life better for crippled young men, she had stayed angry. "I had a terrible day and didn't even think of God—not once."

Now she was mad at herself. Trying to tell me that she was a failure and a disaster, she suddenly observed, "But I always acted like that—my whole life. Why do I feel so bad about it now?"

I told her, "Because, Maria, you have the Holy Spirit in your life now. It's the Holy Spirit who isn't comfortable." I thought the whole story was a wonderful sign.

Furthermore I had been trying for a long time to get Maria to do her discipleship study—it was supposed to take twenty minutes—in the mornings before work, or at least to read the Bible for five minutes before going out to face the world. But she always told me that mornings were too rushed and hectic. Now my point had been proven.

I made her a cup of tea and produced a snack of some kind and told her, "This is a case of spiritual hypoglycemia. The way you're living is like going to work without any breakfast, knowing there will be no lunch. Eight or nine p.m. is too late to start taking nourishment."

And I came up with a plan, based on my personal policy of carrying peanuts in my purse for low blood-sugar emergencies. I suggested that every night when she studied she should find a verse of scripture that she wanted to take with her through the following day. "Write it on a slip of paper," I told her, "and put it in the pocket of the slacks or jacket you plan to wear the next morning. Read it on the way to work and whenever you get a chance throughout the day."

Before long her "peanuts in my pocket" were doing more than sustaining her. One day she took the little slip of paper out of her pocket and read to a discouraged patient: "I can do all things through Christ who strengthens me." This started a dialogue, giving her opportunity to tell her own story of faith. And after that, she often chose her verse for the day according to the need of a patient she expected to see. Many a young man got little treasures from the Bible along with his physical therapy.

Lebanon was a mess. Shells fell randomly, coming out of nowhere, often for reasons we didn't understand. Chaos prevented my getting ready for Christmas. I went to Bourj Hammoud to buy a few gifts, felt panicky for no known reason and came home barely in front of the rockets falling along the road behind me. All the Christian towns were shelled just as families were walking to their churches for midnight mass. And after Christmas, Americans in West Beirut kept getting kidnapped, another every few weeks. The value of the Lebanese lira dropped from 33 cents to 14. At my office, work piled on top of work and problems on top of problems. But Maria was a joy. From one week to the next she was different, like a flower budding and opening and expanding.

Discipling new believers is so much like raising children, I thought. You give them milk and pick them up when they cry and lose sleep over them and before you expect it they start reaching for the food on your plate and trying to walk all alone, and asking questions you can't answer, and knowing stuff that you didn't teach them, and you feel so proud and so consumed by love.

Houses of Clay

A Sorrowful New Year

On our first work day in 1985 the Green Line was closed, had been closed for five days already—not by fighting but by a demonstration. Families of kidnapped and lost people were demanding either the return of their loved ones or death certificates.

The rest of us were sympathetic with the demonstrators but still frustrated. Schools opened and closed again because so many teachers were trapped on the wrong side of the line. Mary called me and said, "I am stuck, just because I don't have a helicopter." None of our employees could come from the West side, including Charlie Costa, our new curriculum editor who was supposed to begin on that day.

I was almost too sick to care and went home with a heavy head, body aches and the highest fever I could remember having. For four days I lay in the floor of the cave, unable even to eat. "Dr. Fuller" gave me an antibiotic, lay slow-burning fires in the stove, left fluids and reading material beside my mat and went to work. I didn't move unless I had to. Wayne came home and told me that I was part of an epidemic; hordes of people were sick. Emmett Barnes had a theory that someone was using us in a biological warfare experiment. While I was sick, Lawrence Jenco, the American head of a Catholic relief organization, was kidnapped in West Beirut. A little restaurant that we liked very much was blown up, along with some customers and one of the owners. And the Lebanese lira—three to a dollar for years, a miserable seven before Christmas—fell to 9.14, then 9.40 (barely more than ten cents), on its way toward total disaster.

At the end of those four days I got out of bed to study with Maria. Wayne set up a small table by the stove and made us a hot drink. Tired and without any supper, Maria was still happy and relaxed, while informing me that I looked terrible.

The next morning, weary and hurting as though I had spent those four days moving rocks, I discovered that I had lost six pounds and looked pale and old. I dragged myself to the office. The Green Line had opened; Charlie came to work, and Abu Issam, but Abu Sleiman, our chief editor, sent a message that he had a headache and a drooping eyelid.

During the whole of the previous year we had searched for the right person to be our curriculum editor. We had taken applications and done interviews and prayed and agonized. Finally, we had chosen Charlie Costa. He was young, too young some people thought, but talented, smart, inclined to lead, and equipped with a strong vision of the curriculum we needed. Charlie had studied in the U.S., and after taking his university degree, returned to Lebanon, though his parents and brothers were still in America. I liked this commitment to his country and his enthusiasm for the curriculum.

We had agreed that Abu Sleiman (Rev. Jeries Delleh to some) would mentor Charlie and correct his work. Abu Sleiman's experience, his age, his spiritual authority and his beautiful Arabic style made him a wonderful teacher, and Charlie had told me that he was thrilled with the opportunity to work under him.

Now Charlie was there and would have to start without the coveted guidance. Abu Sleiman was seeing a doctor that day. Later we knew that a neurosurgeon examined him and said, "Come back tomorrow after I have had time to study the tests and read the x-rays."

That night Abu Sleiman collapsed. After surgery for a "cerebral accident," he lay in a coma for several days, not even breathing on his own. The doctors said his chances of survival were about 25 percent. These numbers didn't mean anything to me; I needed him too much. Though the work on his desk was urgent, I let it wait for him.

On the morning of the sixteenth, I felt the world wobble when I heard the news, "Abu Sleiman died early this morning."

Abu Sleiman was a Palestinian and lived in a West Beirut apartment building in which he was the only Christian. During artillery battles he sat in the basement with eight or ten Muslim families. Yasser Arafat had been an off-and-on neighbor, who had an apartment in the building and slept there occasionally—homeless because he had too many enemies and must sleep in a different place every night. Abu Sleiman's life experiences were impossible to replace on our staff. The years of war had created ghettoes; young people were not growing up with Muslim neighbors anymore. The people who came to me now, seeking jobs, knew the Muslims as enemies, and I assumed that the Muslim view of Christians also worsened every day, impacting our ability to communicate our faith to the majority population.

Besides all that were the intangibles for which I depended on Abu Sleiman. When deadlines and bombs crashed down on us, his perspective encouraged calmness. When we became agitated and talked too much, his silence made us simmer down.

I sat at my desk, wondering what to do now. Charlie was coping by helping with funeral plans, but he knew his own life had been changed. Abu Issam was weeping. The whole staff was upset, and except for time to go to the two funerals (one in the West, one in the East, so that Abu Sleiman's friends would not have to cross the volatile fire line), I could not give them the day off. It was Wednesday, and on Friday Wayne and Charlie had to leave for two curriculum conferences in Jordan and Egypt. (Larry and Georges, our faithful consultants, would meet them in Jordan.) Jeannette, our typist, was working overtime to finish a mountain of materials for use in the workshops. Charlie needed to proofread it all. Abu Issam was photocopying and assembling the pages. All day he walked back and forth between the copy machine and the collating table, with tears trickling down his face.

Abu Sleiman was gone. I would have given an arm to get him back.

Sharp Eyes

We were walking on the road through the village—Maria and I. The almond trees had dropped their blossoms, and the mountains were getting that smoky, hazy look common to the Lebanese hills in spring. The field in front of my house was an energetic green with yellow stones strewn through it; the *snobar* trees, cleaned by snow and rain, glistened in the sun. We had gone out for a deep breath of fresh air before our weekly study. Maria talked about how good it felt. At the hospital, she spent a lot of time on her feet, but mostly standing, and got tired of the indoors. She loved to walk among growing things.

By then I was calling her "Sharp Eyes," but not because she could see. Maria had several visual problems. She wore contacts all day and replaced them at home with thick heavy glasses, and she had especially poor night vision. "Sharp Eyes" was a nickname equivalent to "Longfellow" for a man who was four feet eleven. But it applied in a nicer way to some other kinds of vision she had. She was always spotting a particular weed and telling me some childhood memory related to it. That day a tiny green plant sprouting from the dirt bank beside the road caught her eye. She picked a twig and said, "I can take the wart off your finger with this."

She also saw clearly the problem I had, for which I had been making up excuses.

From my house, the road sloped upward, and my legs didn't want to go. Each step was harder than the one before, as though the road were changing its tilt, increasing the difficulty as I went. I tried really hard, I lagged, stopped talking to save my breath for climbing, then stood still, panting.

Maria said, "What's wrong?"

"I don't know. I guess I'm just out of shape." I gasped a little and said, "I spend too much time sitting at my desk."

Jaqueline, looking down from her patio and seeing us stop at the bottom of her stairs, shouted "*Ahla wa sahla*." Then I had to decline the invitation. If I wanted, how would I climb those steep steps?

Maria said, "Frances, I know you are a lot older than I am, but you should be able to climb this hill."

I was 55 and embarrassed. She was 27 and appalled. We turned around and went home. The path up the hill to our door had grown longer since yesterday.

Back at the dining table she said, "You need to see a doctor and get a thorough check-up."

She was right. In fact, my "annual" check-up was about a year overdue, though of course I had been to a doctor—about my spring allergy and my stomachaches.

"Maybe you're anemic," she said.

Anemia sounded like a mild, acceptable diagnosis to me, but she was smarter and more fearful. Possible causes appeared in her big eyes like shadows.

"I guess I never really got over the flu," I told her.

We studied and cooked a simple supper. Afterwards, opening the car door in front of her gate, she turned and pointed a finger at me, saying, "Tomorrow."

"What?"

"Call your doctor."

"O.K. I promise."

Ugly Suspicions

Our good friend Dr. Peter Manoogian found several things not quite right on my blood test. Interpreting, he said, "Well, yes, you are anemic, but..." running his finger down a column of mysterious numbers, "these readings also indicate illness, something gone wrong. They don't tell us what, but I suspect some kind of tumor."

Then I lay on his table, and he found the mass in my abdomen. I told him about my stomachaches and Dr. Habash's dismissal. He said, "But this is very low in your abdomen," then sent me for x-rays which revealed nothing and then on to a gynecologist.

Even the gynecologist said, "I don't know what it is or what organ it is attached to, only that it has to come out."

* * *

I had ten days to prepare myself, and others. A new sales manager had just joined us, and I had to make sure he was informed and organized. I ought to finish that editorial project on my desk. I needed type A blood donors. There was that curriculum committee meeting tomorrow. And people who had to know—my staff, my friends. I had to write to my children.

Wayne was calm and encouraging. "What can I do to help you get ready?"

I told Maria at the beginning of our weekly lesson, sitting at our table by the stove, with our Bibles and books in front of us. After a long silence, she said, "I'm sorry."

Later she said, "Frances, it could be really bad."

I said, "Or it could not be. And if it is, I have ten days to be ignorant and happy."

These words were partly bravado, but, in fact, I had learned not to borrow too much from tomorrow, especially not to mourn what I had not yet lost.

But I remember that the letters to my children—one duplicated letter, with private notes on each—were hard to write. I wanted to sound cheerful and unafraid, because I was. At the same time I wanted to say whatever those five precious people would need to hear, if something should go wrong and they never got another letter from me. Trying to do all that without scaring them silly, I realized that they had worried about me a lot already, thinking that a sniper would get me, or a kidnapper. They probably had not even considered the present situation. Nor had I.

So many times I had hidden behind the stone wall of our cave, listening to the heart-stopping screech of incoming shells, not suspecting that another enemy—silent and insidious—was growing inside my own body. *There are too many ways to lose,* I thought, and suspected that there must be just one opponent, a capital-E Enemy with endless faces, determined to uproot me from this place. While I was on high alert against external dangers, this Enemy had tunneled under the walls and invaded my life, knowing what I had forgotten—that without my health, everything I wanted would be lost. Being sick was a private thing, different from vulnerability to the perils of war. When a soldier died in war, I thought, this was like an execution. When a civilian died in war, this was like an accident, a parallel incident, like getting killed by a car while standing on the sidewalk. But this unknown living thing inside of me was very personal. For you, kiddo, nobody else, and no mistake.

Awake in the middle of the night, I easily found the hard mass in my lower abdomen. I remembered Dr. Habash saying casually, "Why is your colon hard like a pipe?" Eight months had gone by since then.

To the Edge and Back

A woman called my name. I was faraway and very tired, unable to answer. She called again and then slapped my cheeks, tearing me out of some desperately desired haven. I opened my eyes. She had the most beautiful eyebrows imaginable. That's all I saw—a green mask hiding her face, a cap covering her hair, her eyebrows thick, unplucked yet perfectly shaped, each black hair shiny black. I saw these eyebrows and slipped away again.

Unseen forces lifted me in a sling, threw me around—from one hard surface to another. I tried to scream but nothing happened. A wave of darkness rolled over me.

I had been flattened by a tank, or mangled by the olive press—my whole body crushed, broken, a useless weight, an obstacle—my inner self slipping over some precipice into oblivion. A lovely oblivion.

Wayne coaxed me with quiet, persistent talk. "Pies, can you hear me? It's over. You're going to be O.K."

I wished he would let me rest in peace. Maintaining consciousness was like swimming against a tide, losing it again like slipping underneath a warm sweet liquid—so attractive, so much easier.

Only after I was better did the pain localize—the sting in my side, the tear at the bottom of my abdomen, the pressure in my gut, the burning in my throat, the irritation on the back of my hand, the bruise inside my elbow, the cramps in my back, the agony of any fixed position, the torment of every movement. One by one, they surfaced, demanding dominance over one another.

Hands pushed me around, stuck needles in my hips, pressed little glass rods into my mouth, squeezed my arm, held my wrist, raised the sheet off my tummy, wiggled the tube that ran over the edge of the bed out of a hole in my side. A long time passed before I could wonder why I had this small stinging hole in my abdomen.

Some tiny, essential piece of myself withdrew to a dark corner and fought against aliens—chemicals perhaps, disguised as ideas in code, a code that only looked like some language I knew. My perceived mission was related to comprehension, so the violent dream was always a struggle with words—jumbled spoken words, mysterious written words, unformed but needed words. Each time the battle subsided, unresolved, my spirit lay like a rag in the bottom of its corner.

A man in a white coat, a slender man with a thin mustache, stood beside me asking questions. "Mrs. Fuller, before the surgery did you have any x-rays?"

I managed a movement of my head.

"Where?"

I formed the word "Here" with my mouth and heard a croak.

"In this hospital?"

Another nod, and he left suddenly.

Like a light on a dimmer, I folded by degrees into the darkness.

Again he stood by my bed, this time holding a sheet of film—black with transparent spots. He held the film in front of me and punched it with a sharp finger and said, "Here it is. This is your cancer. Those idiots down there couldn't see it."

I tried hard to see what he saw—not much—a blur, a shadow.

"That's why you went to the wrong doctor. That's why you weren't prepped. Why the incision was in the wrong place. Why they had to keep you anesthetized with your belly open 'til I could get here. I had a hard time. Now you're suffering, because some stupid guy didn't do his job. Blind idiot!" He left again suddenly.

I let it all go, let him be responsible for anger.

Once I came up out of the sticky, seductive liquid and saw Georgette. She was sitting against the wall facing the foot of my bed, staring at me.

She looked ghastly—her skin yellow with sadness, her eyes, with their dark circles, full of shock.

I knew I needed to assure her that I was O.K., but a signal from my brain got lost on the way to my hand, and I could not even move to acknowledge her presence. She faded before I could remember how to form words. When I opened my eyes again she was gone. Outside the hospital a noisy battle was going on—spitting, zinging, exploding sounds. Sirens, too. I knew I had been hearing these sounds for a long time—even when Georgette was there. I pictured her in the streets, running between the fighters. Later I knew that this picture was close to true, but when she got home she only told her children, "*Haram*. Mrs. Fuller is dying. In two days she may be gone."

Nazih Khater, one of my editors, came and sat by my bed quietly, like the gentleman he is.

Michel appeared in the doorway, looked like he was going to weep, turned his back and left. I didn't get a chance to remind him that I am a descendant of those people the Native Americans called "palefaces."

Lulu came, but I never saw her. She went back to the village and spread the word that my death was imminent, obviously.

Women friends, one at a time, stayed with me all night—sitting in the big chair sleepless, responding to my groans, talking to me, rubbing my thrashing limbs, trying in vain to make me comfortable, pressing a button to call for help.

One night I looked up and saw Anne Nicholas, amazed to see her big and strong. I was not accustomed to looking up at Anne. She was a dainty little thing about five feet two and under a hundred pounds, with bones like a bird. For years she had propagated the interesting idea that it was not fair of an airline to give her and a 300- pound man the same weight limit for luggage. Why not, she said, have one limit—say, 325 pounds—and weigh the passenger and her luggage together? Brilliant, I thought; only someone her size could think of it. I, who was capable of joining a team and playing basketball with men and boys in the seminary parking lot, would never have thought of it. But in the hospital, when I couldn't pick up my pillow, Anne stood over me and heaved that huge thing around like it was nothing. It was I whose bones needed feathers.

One day I complained to Wayne that my throat hurt. He told me I had a tube there. I didn't know. How could I have a tube down my throat and not know? Every day I discovered another hose or wire linking me to some apparatus.

My mouth felt swollen and moldy. For three days I begged for water and was refused. After that I could have tiny slivers of ice—like three at a time—flakes of cold that dissolved and left me greedy for more. My body smelled like rotting meat.

My room filled up with flowers and gift-wrapped boxes and friends. Like a baby I saw mostly colors and movement. I heard footsteps and voices, caught fragments of events, as in a dream. People-shaped shadows surrounded my bed, and I heard praying. I heard English and Arabic; "amen" and "aameen." I recognized voices. I knew the fervor of Ghassan Khalaf's voice, telling God, "We need her." And the calmness of Bill Trimble's, thanking God that He was going to heal me and bring me back to health. In my darkness, an awareness flickered—I was the paralytic, carried by my friends. They had broken the ceiling tiles and deposited me at the feet of Jesus. My own faith was not even necessary. They believed for me. Comforted, I felt free to sink under the warm waves one more time.

Some of my staff came, bringing messages from the others. Everyone was working harder because of my absence. They were designing covers and running a book fair and preparing materials for the next curriculum workshop. I was not to worry about anything.

A day came when I thought I was hungry, but a nurse told me that I couldn't eat yet. She didn't know how long it would be. All the same I had to get up and stagger to the bathroom, though it took two people to get me there, one of them dragging that tower with the swinging bottle.

Days and ages later a dinner tray appeared. Someone lifted the metal dome to reveal a bowl of lukewarm, odorless liquid. The spoon shook in my hand. Wayne took it and tried to feed me. My empty stomach revolted, though I had not swallowed yet. The tall severe nurse scolded me for not eating.

Mary Mathias came, with a gift in a tissue cloud. She paced back and forth the way she might in court and told me in detail about one of her cases. She said, "Think with me about this problem and give me your advice. How shall I defend this client?" I knew what she was doing—distracting me from pain, preventing my remembering that I had that scary disease—the C word. I tried to help her but ran out of energy to hear. I had never noticed before how much energy was required for listening. When she paused, I said, "Mary, I can't follow it." She fell silent, but I went away before she did.

Sometimes Wayne intercepted people at the door and told them I was too tired to see anyone. Later he would tell me who came. To Middle Easterners, visiting the sick is a duty. When they get to heaven Jesus is going to say to them all, "I was sick and you visited me."

Maria came. She had caught a cold and been sick herself, too sick to hitch a ride to Ashrafieh, too sick to get near me. She was very sad about something but didn't want to trouble me with the reasons. Instead, she took a scripture verse out of her pocket, one of those "peanuts" I had instructed her to carry around and read it to me. That was nice.

While she was there, the food cart arrived, and I got that faintly colored soup again, barely warm. It made me think of stagnant dishwater. Maria got sick just watching me try to eat it. She was the only one who took my side in that problem about the soup. She understood my fear of that nurse, too—the one who checked my tray before it could go back to the kitchen, the one who was going to give me a failing grade again. She told me, "She's a nun," as though that explained everything.

Maria had some illogical and funny quirks—an inability to survive the smell of food cooking before breakfast, a dread of pasta, a suspicion of nuns (not priests, just nuns), though one of her best friends was a nun. The roots of these peculiarities—like most of our hang-ups—were tangled out of sight, beyond the reach of other humans.

I only asked, "How do you know she's a nun?"

"Her hat tells me."

The nurse, the nun, was doing her job—like all the staff and employees of Jeitawi Hospital. Whatever happened outside the walls they were on duty, and that, in itself, was a marvel on some days. Though the windows shook from explosions, the cleaning people appeared, mopping my floor every morning, emptying wastebaskets. My doctor made rounds and did things to relieve my pain. He answered questions, telling me the truth—good and bad—about my cancer, even about what was happening in the streets. The nurses woke me with thermometers and bathed my face and made my bed fresh and responded to my bell, still speaking kindly. They even scrounged outrageous numbers of vases and kept my flowers alive.

When I graduated from soup to bread with yogurt, I thought I had received a banquet. The first two nibbles were wonderful. The third was too much to swallow. What the nurse said afterward sounded a little better than flunking, like maybe a D on my report card, and I found out that she wrote this stuff down.

One day when the doctor came I complained that my abdomen was bursting. I felt like a balloon that had been blown up to a dangerous tightness. With quick, gentle hands he pressed my tummy and vented the gas from my colon through the hole in my side. The smell that came up was like the stench of the Beirut sewer, and I felt ashamed. But then I saw his expression. He could have been a businessman signing a contract, or someone with no olfactory gland, and I said, "Oh, thank you. That's so much better."

Wayne brought a telex from Tim. All of his brothers and sisters were trying to call and no one could reach Lebanon. He protested the unfairness of my being sick in such circumstances. He wanted Wayne to bring me home; he offered to come out again. But none of this could happen. It was too late to travel to the States, and there was no way we could let him come. In the weeks since he had flown into Beirut, the situation had deteriorated further. While I was in the hospital, kidnappers in West Beirut had seized Terry Anderson, the Associated Press Bureau Chief. Later, when I was able, I wrote Tim that West Beirut was now worse than a jungle. "In the jungle each animal has only certain natural enemies and knows who they are." Maybe I should have included East Beirut, because it was there that two Christian militias had fought one another.

The possibility of leaving the hospital was both exciting and scary, as it became apparent that I could neither take care of myself nor climb up the path from the road to our front door. (My old negative prophecy had come true—Wayne would have a problem getting his wife into the house.) I could not even cope with the stream of visitors who would inevitably come to see me. A further complication was that Wayne had work to do outside of Lebanon and needed to be away for eleven or twelve days. As others realized our predicament, offers began to come from both Lebanese friends and missionary colleagues—offers to care for me in their own homes during my recuperation. Of all the loving things people had done for us during this crisis, none loomed so large as this, and I knew I would never forget such kindness, a generosity beyond "the second mile." In the end, I went to the Dunns' house, because their location was perfect and we already felt at home there.

Before I left the hospital, a date was set for a second surgery, to reverse the colostomy that had been necessitated by cutting my colon without preparation. I would have a month to recover first and was promised that the second operation would be a breeze.

Though Wayne drove slowly and carefully, our car seemed to have become a tin bucket and the streets a test run for automobile shocks. Every small jolt set off a wave of pain through my body. I had a slight fever (not apparent to people who learned in school that normal body temperature is 98.6) and later Maria discovered a little pus in one of my incisions and released it for me. Though I was so weak I had trouble holding myself upright, I was glad to see the city streets. The world looked warm and welcoming, a little damaged by shrapnel and fire, but raggedly old and familiar like a place I wanted to be.

With Wayne holding me up on one side and Maria on the other, I shuffled—bent over to favor my wounds—the twenty steps from the curb to the Dunns' front door, and the bed Pat had prepared for me felt wonderful.

Healing Our Diseases

Maria took charge of my physical therapy. She came almost daily to assess my progress and prescribe routines: breathing exercises performed while sitting on the side of the bed, long walks around the dining room table—building up to circular marathons through the study, the kitchen, the dining room, the living room and back to my bed. In a few days I advanced from receiving guests in my bedroom to sitting with them in the living room. Soon I was washing my nightgown in the bathroom sink every morning and hanging it on the clothesline in the backyard. I held committee meetings, propped up in bed.

Pat answered the doorbell and served coffee to all my visitors, while cooking meals for Wayne and me. It was a full-time job.

With the help of her beautiful and delicious meals, I learned to eat again. At first I came to the table overeager, then got full and exhausted and left while the others were still eating. But the more I ate, the more my appetite grew. I had lost so much weight I hardly recognized myself in the mirror. Bones protruded everywhere, and as my body tried to repair and rebuild itself, every cell cried out for nourishment. Not in my life had I been so hungry.

In the Dunns' study, a small quiet room with a table in the middle, Maria and I resumed our weekly study. I was feeling triumphant, though a little scared to celebrate. There had been cancer cells outside my colon—in the abdominal fluid, but all the other organs were clean. Having dodged a bullet, or maybe an artillery shell, I must keep my head down and listen for another. My angry surgeon had turned me over to an oncologist, a young Lebanese fresh from studying in Paris, with his office equipment still in boxes. He was the first doctor in Lebanon prepared to do fiber optic colonoscopies. Never again would the inside of my colon be a secret.

Maria's fragility was showing. She had been shaken by my illness and was still terrified that I would die, or maybe just leave. Not only had her spiritual guide fallen ill, but at the same time Lebanon's sickness had suddenly worsened. Whenever we talked about the new fighting—a senseless clash between brothers—and what it meant, she would begin to choke on her words. Once she told me, "This is not really a country anymore."

The scripture bathed our wounds, like a balm, and reestablishing good habits encouraged the feeling that life would go on, not because we were strong, but because some grace—mysterious and beautiful—had poured down on us.

* * *

Slowly, slowly I limped toward health, learning as I went the potential value of illness. I had been given an opportunity to learn things hard to learn any other way—like how to give up control and be quiet and let myself be carried for a while, and certainly I had experienced how good people are and how much they are eager to love somebody. I decided that it was important, actually, to experience for myself the humiliation of a stinking, diseased body and to let that instruct me about the nature of the world, my position in it, and the urgent need for another place to go. Finally, I noticed that when I could not function, the world got along very well without me.

Explosions of Grief

A bomb, carried in a butane gas delivery truck, exploded in the middle of a rush-hour traffic jam in Sin el-Fil on Wednesday, May 22, 1985. This happened in the morning, just after most men had left home for work, and the streets were full of vehicles and pedestrians. Faster than the eye could see, loose objects became flying missiles. Cars, people, store fronts ignited. Women and children died in an instant in the apartments along the narrow street, as the glass from their windows and sliding balcony doors blew everywhere, flames spurted into their homes and kitchen gas tanks exploded.

Fifty-eight people died in those first seconds, and 190 were wounded. The dead included the wives and several children of two brothers named Constantine. Some members of the Constantine family were Baptists—friends of ours, and the two decimated families sometimes attended our church.

The next day the Maronite Church of Our Lady held a mass funeral for thirty-two of the victims. This church was on the main street through Sin el-Fil, one block from the devastated street where the people had died. Wayne and Emmett attended the service. Not yet strong physically, I decided that I was unprepared to walk in that mass of people or to deal with the frenzied grief that would overwhelm them. LaNell also declined to go.

Afterwards Wayne told me that the crowd had been "emotional," but he did not elaborate. I read the papers the next morning. In the picture on the front page of the *Daily Star* I could see Wayne and Emmett, one gray head and one bald, near the foreground in a crush of people, as a coffin was lifted high into the air in front of them. Most of the service had taken place outside the church. The thirty-two coffins, draped in Lebanese flags—red and white with the green cedar in the middle—were carried through the neighborhood and lined up in the street.

The reporter wrote that women wailed and beat on the coffins and called out to their dead children and husbands. At times the crowd surged toward the line of draped wooden boxes and, when they were prevented, became unruly. Militiamen responsible for keeping order wrestled with mourners, while tears streamed down their own faces. Some of the crowd cried out for vengeance, though the banner hanging over the street read, "Father, forgive them, for they know not what they do." And even while funeral chants poured out of the loudspeakers above the heads of the grieved, the sound of exploding shells somewhere nearby reminded them of their own vulnerability. All day long church bells tolled every five minutes, and in all of East Beirut no one went to work.

Car bombs were not new. For years they had been a favorite tool for assassinations or attacks on particular businesses or offices. Most people had had at least one narrow escape. We had been there ten minutes earlier or tried to go down the street half an hour later and found it barricaded. The clean-up always started immediately, as soon as the ambulances were gone. Mangled cars would be dragged away, blood washed off the street, small debris swept up, glass installed, new displays arranged in the shop windows. By the next morning no one could see the damage, except maybe a blackened wall. And the trees. They couldn't put the leaves back on the trees.

It did seem that car bombs were getting bigger and more efficient and their stories more complicated. The Lebanese Forces believed that the Sin el-Fil bomb was itself an act of revenge and issued a statement blaming the *Washington Post*. The *Post* had published an article in April concerning a car bomb in a Muslim area, near the home of a well-known Muslim leader. That bomb killed eighty people and wounded 260. According to the article, the deed was done by an anti-terrorist unit trained by the CIA and had included both CIA and Lebanese intelligence personnel. Both the Lebanese Army and the CIA denied the story, but the Forces claimed that the *Post,* by publishing it, had incited revenge against the Christians. My thought was that the closer you are to a bomb, the less likely you are to have a clue. The hapless population lived in panic of car bombs, unable to function without going into the streets, and knew nothing—not who delivered the bombs, much less when or where the next one would explode, wasting the lives of people who just happened to be there. So we drove with suspicious eyes, feeling relatively O.K. so long as the traffic moved, but some people would experience extreme anxiety attacks if the cars in front of them stopped, or even if they had to follow a small truck or pass a worthless looking car—one they thought likely to be sacrificed as a bomb.

If we drove to an office building or a print shop, we would find parking non-existent, because cautious shop owners barricaded their curb-side spaces and would move the obstacles only for someone they knew well. They did not own the streets, but no one could blame them for being paranoid.

Explosions of Happiness

To be honest, the summer of 1985 was a terrible time. That was the summer that a TWA plane was hijacked and ordered to land in Beirut where it sat on the tarmac for days. The worst moment, I guess, was the moment in which the body of an American sailor fell to the ground from the door of the plane. I didn't see this, but in front of their television sets in America, millions of people—our children among them, and my mother—saw it. Trying to allay my mother's fears, I reminded her that all of that was happening in West Beirut. "I haven't been over there since just before Christmas and Wayne hasn't been for a couple of years. We are among Christian Lebanese here, and they hate what is happening over there as much as we do."

Then fighting broke out along the Green Line in Chiyah and Ain ar-Rommaneh. From my office window I watched the smoke go up in a ragged line and spread over the city, and even on the east side I refrained sometimes from going places I needed to go.

Shells fell in Beit Meri, too, and our little house got a front window broken without my knowing when it happened. Wayne was away at the time, and I wasn't sure what to do about it. Only a tiny piece of the glass fell out, but the rest of the pane was in about twenty fragments—long curved pieces with dagger shapes between them, like an imaginative jigsaw puzzle. Maria knew exactly what to do. On her way up for our evening study session she bought a wide roll of plastic made for such an exigency and covered the glass to hold it together. The stuff stuck like skin and held that windowpane in place for many weeks.

A few days later, Maria went upstairs to bed at her house in Ain Saade and fell asleep, while all her family were still awake in the lower rooms. Unexpected and sudden as lightning, a shell struck their next door neighbor's house, where there were people in every room except the one that was shattered by the bomb. In the Daouds' big stone house, every window broke—forty-two, to be exact, and the glass did not stay in the frames. The heat of the blast destroyed two of Mr. Daoud's fig trees, a grape vine and all their tomato plants. The damage to Maria was also significant. For weeks, every time she started to fall asleep she heard the sound of all that glass shattering and swishing down and breaking against the floors and concrete walks.

Lebanon's year-old "government of national unity" collapsed that same month. The prime minister resigned, saying to the people, "We are all lost and defeated. The enemy is the only winner."

Just remembering, I feel like crying, but I am hard-pressed to explain how I really felt, because I lived that summer with so much dread and so much joy. What did the prime minister's words mean? What would become of Lebanon? What would become of us all—the people who loved Lebanon? But when I remember the collapse of the government and the prime minister's emotional words, I remember too that July was wonderful, that all the things we wanted to happen were happening and were better than we imagined.

I realize that I can say this partly because no one in my family was hit by shrapnel, my son was not made to stand in the door of the airliner to be shot in the back, the shell that broke all the windows in her house and shattered her nerves did not kill Maria. But the relief I experienced about this was relative to the sorrow I felt over the very possibility of these losses. One could not live in Lebanon and escape being torn open in the middle by the cold knives of fear and grief, but sometimes the cavity was filled by some unexpected goodness.

My work had never gone better than it did that summer. We began receiving in installments the money we needed for the development of an indigenous curriculum. Charlie was in America taking training with the best curriculum experts I could find. We managed to have our international board meeting, in Cyprus as I remember. Dr. Ballenger, our Middle East director, was there, and one of the Lebanese asked him when Baptist Publications would have a building. He explained that, with the situation in Lebanon so precarious, the FMB was reluctant to put money into a building. The way I felt about that surprised even me. I said, "That hurts my feelings."

Dr. Ballenger, a caring man, asked what I meant. I said, "No one ever told me that I am too valuable to risk in Lebanon. If it's worth my life it ought to be worth the price of a building." Dr. Ballenger wrote in a little notebook and said, "I don't know if it will help, but I am going to quote you."

Shortly afterwards the wonder of all wonders happened. The board in Richmond released funds for a new international building. Both BP and the Baptist Center for Radio and Television would have a home. The plans had been ready for years, and we began construction almost immediately.

BP was close to finishing our comprehensive hymnal, the most difficult production of our lives, a book which included the classics long sung by the church and Arab songs often sung in their places of origin but never before notated or shared. We were reprinting some volumes of *The Picture Bible for All Ages* for the third time and in bigger quantities than ever. Though it had been on the market for several years, it was still the best-selling spiritual book in Lebanon, and Egypt was gobbling it by the thousands.

In June we passed our sales goal for the whole year, and we were doing this in the middle of an economic crisis. My new sales manager was a marvel, but that was not the sole reason. Lebanon had hit bottom emotionally, and everybody was looking for something spiritual, something that could not be blown up or burned or stolen.

Our church was growing, week after week, and in the process becoming a huge group of young adults. We had so many people between the ages of eighteen and thirty that I worried about what we would do for mature people to lead them all. Word must have gotten around that something was happening at the church, because young people none of us knew just showed up.

The early-evening English-language service was very popular, and from that service the youth came home with us to eat and hang out together and talk. The eight we had on that night several months earlier when Nada had said, "We just need a place to be together," had become twelve and then fifteen and now was regularly more than twenty. There was no program, no plan, no promotion, just a bunch of young people rushing to our house after church. Sometimes we sang around the piano; sometimes we didn't. Sometimes we put classical music on the record player and got quiet. Once Wayne showed slides of America, because somebody wanted to see the Grand Canyon and somebody else wanted to see the Golden Gate Bridge. Once I cooked in advance. One of the girls had asked me, "What is beef stroganoff?" The end of the conversation was that I promised to make some for the crowd, and I did the next week, using yogurt for sour cream and cooking the rice in my big spaghetti pot. We were twenty-five people that night.

Usually all we did was talk, and the talk was full of teasing and hilarity. On occasions it would be deeply serious. Often people would just start telling about things that were happening in the deep levels of their lives. A certain young man who, as far as I could tell, was all cynicism and jokes, leaned against one side of our stone arch one evening, his T-shirt tight over bulky shoulders, and told the group how he had believed in God irresistibly and woken up in a brand new world. Rima, not knowing the words to use, said she had been wandering and searching, and what she had found was the most important thing in her life. I was always touched by their desire for the intangibles and unchangeables.

Even when the talk was most serious, we would laugh a lot. I remember talking about roadblocks and laughing. If you have enemies standing in your streets at roadblocks, you save yourself from anger by noticing how funny they are and making up jokes about their stupidity. And we had a few serious discussions about what people really wanted their lives to be like, though they were not voluble on the subject. Planning was tricky, because we had to stay flexible. Dreaming involved an emotional investment, so it was scary. Maria had one idea about what she wanted. "Just a regular, ordinary, boring life." We all laughed, though we knew it was a lot to ask for.

I remember our talking about suicide. The young people were trying to understand why suicide was a major problem in countries like Norway and America while we rarely heard of it in Lebanon.

I puzzled with them about this very interesting question for a while, then complicated the issue by saying, "But we used to have more suicide back before the war. I remember that in Musaitbeh a girl with epilepsy made her cousin's wedding dress and then drank rat poison. And there was a boy who jumped off a tall building."

This sobered the group considerably, until Johnny Dragetsy—a 250-pound man with a sincere face and thighs the size of Maria—said, "Well, that was a long time ago, and it's logical that we wouldn't have suicide now, because... well, we don't need it." And the room exploded in laughter.

Whenever I think about that year and the opportunity we had to participate in the lives of all those fine young people, that moment comes to the top. Like a walnut shaken in a jar of beans, it presents itself, because even then I saw it as a shining piece of evidence that they would all survive. They would not in any way give up on life.

* * *

When I had my first colonoscopy, my earnest young doctor told me that the place where my colon had been put back together was so well-healed that he could not find it. He also assured me that there were no more cancer cells in my abdominal fluid. That was the best news of all. When I came home to tell it, I lifted my arms like a boxer who had knocked out an opponent. I was skinny, but I was well, and Wayne, feeling even happier and more generous than usual, took me to Bourj Hammoud and decked me out in a new wardrobe.

It's a Miracle

On the night of August 19, without warning or buildup or even premonitions, Beit Meri was attacked from two directions. We were preparing for bed when a few muzzle blasts barked at us from across the canyon, joined quickly by bigger guns far off in the direction of the Biqaa, and before we could think about what to do shells were slamming into the village at a terrifying rate.

As always we sat on the floor of the cave, leaning against the stone wall, to wait out the storm. Shells whistled and roared, one behind the other, striking the hillside everywhere—at the top of the hill, below us, to our left, to our right. We had sat in this same spot many times before, listening to in-coming shells, but the fury of this attack was unprecedented. It seemed that someone had set out to annihilate Beit Meri. If we ever meant not to die here, we should have gone before now. I survived cancer for this?

Feeling my desperation, Wayne tried to make me laugh, but the funniest thing he could think of was, "What did we say that they didn't like?" And I was too paralyzed to answer.

We could see nothing, not daring to go to a window, but hearing was enough. Clearly the village was being destroyed. I felt sick, believing that Boulos and Jaqueline had been hit again, as well as the Abu Jbreils who had given enough already and our next door neighbor, the anxious shepherd. Wayne and I gripped one another's hands and prayed for everybody we knew. I visualized their faces as we called their names and dreaded to see their houses on the ground, their crushed bodies inside.

Then a shell crashed down just above us, so near that its arrival was like a great silence in my head. I knew there had been an explosion, but all I could ever remember hearing was the sound of things falling—shrapnel, or the pieces of whatever had been destroyed, or a rain of stones that fell and kept on falling onto the roof. This shell was followed by another and another in the same spot, apparently in the lot above ours, mere feet from our roof, on our neighbor's house or in his beautiful garden. Again and again our little stone house shook with the impact, rattling like the bucketful of rocks that it was, and each time debris showered down on the roof.

I felt sicker then, knowing that we might die at any second. We would be fools then in the eyes of all—without sense enough to leave when we had the chance. We would abandon our children to find their own peace with the facts. I prayed for God to help them.

The explosions, the vibrating, the noisy clattering and crashing against the roof continued for an eternity. My fingers were hurting, squeezed so tightly between Wayne's. Each of us was thinking but not saying that if the soldier setting the sights on that gun made a change, lowering his aim by the width of a hair, we were gone. I prayed for that soldier.

Artillery battles never ended all at once. The gunners seemed to grow tired, to take more time reloading, to quit one at a time. In this manner the explosions thinned out until the guns fell silent, and we began to discover that we had survived. We relaxed our grip on one another's hands. Yes, we were alive—exhausted, stiff, hurting all over, changed in some not yet definable way, maybe alone in a burning village, afraid to move, but alive. A square of light, faint and smoky, appeared in the small window high in the north end of the little room.

Slowly we straightened our legs. All my muscles ached. Wayne looked exhausted. He started to get up, stopped and hugged me. Finally, we ventured together all the way to the front door where we could see the dim outline of the shepherd's house, surprisingly straight and whole. As the light grew we heard voices and raced up the steps to the roof, finding it completely covered with dirt, stones, broken concrete and jagged chunks of metal. Walking carefully through this debris, we turned around and around in the growing dawn, amazed to see that The Hara looked almost the same as on other mornings. For sure smoke was rising in all directions, but no roof visible from ours had collapsed, no wall had a gaping hole. Then we saw that the terrace above us, only two or three yards higher than our roof, was full of raw spots, like crude excavations. A giant prickly pear had toppled, metal pipes and pieces of fencing had been tossed about, but the big house up there appeared to be intact.

All over the area people began calling out, "*Al-hamdilla ala salaame.* (Praise God for your safety.)" We shouted it ourselves, seeing George down in the street and Boulos and Jaqueline on their patio.

George shouted back, "We thought you were dead and your house on the ground."

"We, too. We thought everybody was dead."

"It's a miracle," George said. "God loves us."

We went in to put on the coffee pot and scramble some eggs. I was dizzy from lack of sleep and an overdose of happiness. I was ravenous. I was shaken like Moses at the burning bush, afraid to say what I was thinking, careful of putting words in God's mouth, but ecstatic, because God had found ten good men and was going to save Lebanon.

Later in the day we heard statistics. Hundreds of shells had fallen on Beit Meri, a majority of them on our side of the hill, and only one house had suffered a direct hit—a house whose occupants had gone away for a while. All those shells had landed in empty fields, streets, gardens. Everywhere windows were shattered, trees decapitated, cars smashed and burned in the streets, roads pocked with holes, walls scarred in the cartwheel patterns of flying shrapnel, but no one had died. The fact defied logic and made "mathematical chances" a meaningless phrase.

Beit Meri el-Hara celebrated. Neighbors embraced. Men strolled up and down the streets calling out, "Praise God for your safety." Gawkers in cars paused to say it to people whose burned vehicles sat in front of their untouched houses. I went on a tour myself, on the upper roads where mangled automobiles littered the streets and businesses were open behind their stacks of sandbags. I greeted a woman who stood in her paneless window looking at the crushed car a few feet below, against the smoky wall.

Sometimes a miracle is just the only explanation for our lives.

Compromises

Even while the people of The Hara were celebrating their deliverance, shells kept falling on other communities, all of the East Beirut suburbs, and even some places that had rarely been shelled before, such as high in the mountains above Jounieh. And though it was a Tuesday we did not go to the office.

In the afternoon, I began to dread the night and to worry about my work, so I started talking about going down to the office to sleep in the basement. This looked like a camping trip without any outdoor beauty, but finally I persuaded Wayne, and we spent more than an hour packing the car with bedding, toiletries, clothes for a few days, and a little food.

We chose an inner aisle in the storeroom between the long stacks of books—a dark and airless space—and set up camp. At bedtime, which came early since we had not slept the night before, I lighted an anti-mosquito coil, made in China from animal dung. Though I couldn't live with pine pollen or walk among the wild flowers without sneezing and weeping, I could breathe that stuff. It was a mystery. Wayne, on the other hand, did not react to poison oak or fiberglass, but he ran from the smell of those Chinese coils. He dragged his sleeping bag to the far end of the aisle, where he sweltered from the heat and slapped mosquitoes all night.

It was Monsourieh's turn to endure a storm of shells, but I felt so secure with that big building above me—or maybe so exhausted—that I slept through the noise, waking only a few times when something fell really close. Later we knew that the people of The Hara lay sleepless all night again, listening to Broummana get a pounding like the one we had the night before.

We stayed for several days. Wayne brought my electric typewriter down, and I worked, ignoring bombardments everywhere. Anytime I went upstairs for air, I would hear more sad stories and retreat again to my workspace. Wayne went to his workshop on the other side of the basement and made the drawers and cupboard doors for our still unfinished bathroom. During lulls we took turns going up to Beit Meri to turn on the generator for an hour, trying to save the food in our freezer. On Thursday I found a piece of beef filet thawing around the edges so I brought it down to the office. Then I called Vivian and said, "I'll bring you a beautiful hunk of meat, if you will invite us for dinner." It turned out that Bill and Vivian were out of meat but had potatoes and vegetables and the potential for cupcakes. That was the first square meal we had eaten since Monday, and it definitely lifted my energy level. I lost two more pounds that week, pounds my body needed, but I gained them back on the weekend.

The next week, when I had staff and a window of opportunity, I sent two new books to the press, feeling smart and righteous because I was getting my work done.

* * *

The good and the bad lasted all summer—another car bomb, this one in front of a popular supermarket, a place I really liked to shop, the store where my dear friend Nadia normally would have been on a Saturday morning, but something caused her to vary the routine that day. So many people died—all the clerks, and mothers shopping with their children.

It seemed so beastly that I could not find a point. Maria told me that the purpose was to destroy the Christians economically and break their spirits so they would leave Lebanon.

* * *

In mid-September Ben Weir was released from captivity and two new missionary families arrived in Lebanon. Travelers brought us Brach's Rocks—a gift from Jan. And the gift of protection arrived again when needed. On a Saturday evening a rain of shells fell on the seminary campus, breaking twelve windows in the Kings' house, blowing glass into the sub-basement where the Trimbles were sitting, and sending shrapnel into the Barnes' home. One shell fell into the hole from which the new international building was beginning to rise. I considered it the christening of our building.

The next morning after this barrage of shells, the chapel was full of people, and two radiant young women, Maria and Pat, were baptized. The church was happy, Maria and Pat were happy, and my cup was running over.

In November I wrote a friend that it had been the happiest year of my life. I had been renewed on the inside, while, on the outside, I and everything around me disintegrated.

Affirmation and Warning

Ghassan Khalaf was the author of several Baptist Publication books and had compiled history's first *Greek and Arabic Concordance of the New Testament,* which we had published in 1979. Now, once again, he had come up with a work our market needed. *Lebanon in the Bible* was a detailed study of every biblical reference to Lebanon, its cities and rivers, events that happened in it, characters from Lebanon, the cedars and even the many references in which Lebanon or the cedars is a poetic image. We had produced it in hardback with a beautiful jacket, designed by Michel.

The publication of this book occasioned our visit to Dr. Charles Malik, professor emeritus of philosophy at American University in Beirut and an honorable statesman. Amin Khoury, the director of Eastwood College, a friend who had taken a helpful role in the work of Baptist Publications, went with Ghassan and me to the famous man's home.

Lebanon had many political personalities, most of them easily corrupted by the acquisition of power. They rose to prominence, enjoyed some popularity, created disillusionment, and when their power declined, left the country, usually—and sometimes mysteriously—rich. Dr. Malik seemed to stand in contrast to these. He had served the country in numerous capacities, always in appointed rather than elected positions. As Lebanon's first ambassador to the U.N., he had participated in writing the Universal Declaration of Human Rights. He had also been ambassador to the United States and foreign minister of Lebanon.

Though half the country had disagreed with his pro-western policies, though the tragic developments of the seventies were a painful disappointment to him, and though he was not being used anymore by the government, he was still in Lebanon. And I knew no one who thought that he had been corrupted by his prominence or diminished by his decline.

Dr. Malik was a Christian by birth, a member of the Greek Orthodox Church, and was a deeply religious man who mingled easily with evangelicals as well as with Roman Catholics and Maronites. He was much admired by the Baptists.

Our purpose in visiting him that day was to give him a copy of Ghassan's book, hot from the press, and to invite him to our upcoming presentation party. A local television station that featured book reviews and press conferences about new books had chosen *Lebanon in the Bible* for presentation. There would be journalists, cameras and a live audience. We wanted Dr. Malik to be the featured speaker.

He received us in his home, a modern Lebanese house, high-ceilinged, with spacious rooms. It suited him, for he was tall enough and broad enough to dominate a room, had a Mediterranean hooked nose, prodigious hair and eyebrows, and a natural dignity.

In the place where the four of us sat, the furniture had been arranged for small, informal groups. Mrs. Malik herself served us tea and cookies, stayed for a few minutes and then left. Dr. Malik handled Ghassan's book, read the table of contents and scanned a few random pages. "This is an important work," he said. "Our country needs this, especially now when our morale is so low." Right away, without any persuasion needed, he said he would be happy to read the book and make some remarks about it.

The purpose of the meeting already achieved, we munched cookies and talked, discussing some of those things the Bible says about Lebanon, and some present-day problems and needs of the country. I felt privileged to be part of an intimate conversation with a man of his stature and understanding. Then, to my surprise, he turned to me and said, "You are a brave lady to be here in Lebanon now."

Immediately, I explained or defended myself by saying that I was not alone but part of a large group—24 adults and some kids. Seeing that this caused him to lift his bushy eyebrows, I added that we even had five new people—two couples and a single man.

Clearly astonished, he said, "Your mission board has not given up on Lebanon."

"Not at all."

"I want to thank the board for that. Would you pass along my gratitude?"

"Certainly. I will."

"And I would like to meet these five new people," he said.

I told him that they would be thrilled to meet him.

"Be sure the invitation is serious."

And only a few moments later Dr. Malik said the words that blew up in my face. I don't remember how we came to this part of the conversation, only that, speaking with quiet authority, he expressed the feeling that Christianity was facing extinction in the Middle East.

I felt suddenly that it was harder to breathe, and noticed that Amin and Ghassan sat in front of Dr. Malik with somber faces. We were soldiers on the front line, being told that we were going to lose the war, being told this by someone whose word we respected and just when we had been experiencing success and encouragement.

"We have given up," Dr. Malik continued, "on the governments of the West. The only hope we have is in western Christians." It did not occur to me to ask whom he meant by "we" or what hope there had ever been in western governments. While I was still feeling stunned he turned to me again to say, "And in the U.S. there are just two really significant groups who can make a difference for us—the Catholics and the Baptists."

I left Dr. Malik's house with a new fear, but a distant fear, like the shock we feel suddenly when scientists warn us that an immense asteroid is on a collision course with earth. We visualize the cataclysmic impact, and then they say that it will not get here for another eight hundred years and maybe even then it will miss us. Suddenly we refocus on imminent dangers, like losing our job, like being kidnapped or cut by flying shrapnel. The asteroid is still out there, way out there.

I had been profoundly affirmed that day, too, and—putting everything together—believed more than ever that this time of turmoil in Lebanon was exactly the right time to be there and do my job. Maybe Dr. Malik was wrong about the future; he had probably been wrong before. And what if we could know that he was right? Wouldn't a fate so unacceptable have to be resisted? Extinction couldn't strike us like an asteroid; it would creep, an inch at a time, like erosion. We could stand and resist, an inch at a time.

The upheavals of the coming months prevented the meeting I promised to arrange with the new missionaries, Dr. Malik's health declined, and he died in 1988. By then, a great disaster had struck the Near East Baptist Mission.

Becoming Citizens

More than five years had gone by since Wayne found the little stone house. What a lot of living and learning had transpired since then. Every possession had proven to be fragile. Every aspect of work and life had been a struggle. But we had managed to hang in; our mission had hung in; God had stuck with us. And now the rewards were coming.

Lebanon appreciated us. That had not always been true. The Lebanese used to believe that foreigners who lived among them stayed because they liked Lebanon better than wherever they had come from—the climate was better, the fruits, the vegetables, the lifestyle. And we knew that some Lebanese—unable to understand the existence of servant types who spent their lives far from home—had convinced themselves that we had some big monetary reward coming at the end.

All of that had changed. Lebanon was not anymore a nice place to live, and foreigners had streamed out like water through a sieve. Now not even the Lebanese could imagine living there just for the promise of money if they survived. Responses to us began to reflect the new assumption that foreigners who stayed had special motives, either very bad or very good. Someone was kidnapping Americans, with the announced intention of driving all foreigners from Lebanon. And there were opposite reactions.

A stranger, a young man who worked for a computer company, said to me, "I love seeing you here. It gives me hope."

And a woman from another religious faith told me, "You missionaries can do anything you want in Lebanon. This whole country knows that when the world deserted us, the Baptist mission stayed."

The best part was being there for people who needed us. Lebanon is such a small country and people are so inclined to be nosy and socially judgmental that those who needed help often turned to the trustworthy foreigner. For instance, Pat Rabat, one of our young friends, knew an engaged couple who were on a spiritual search together and thinking of leaving the faith into which they had been born. They agreed to talk with us, so we invited them to our home for a meal.

After we had eaten and moved to the living room, our discussion was interrupted by a knock on the door. Another friend had brought a relative whose marriage was falling apart. So, while I stayed with Pat and her friends, Wayne took the second group into the cave. In about an hour he learned that the man's suspicious and always-present parents had caused him to lose his wife. That was an easy one for Wayne; he told him exactly how to get her back. A few weeks later, it was a happy young man who called Wayne and said, "I did it. I got another house, as far away as possible, and my wife has come home. We want you to bring your wife and come to dinner, because we want you to pray for our home."

As a group, we also had an important role. The fall of the Lebanese lira was bringing middle class people down to the poverty level, and the poor were barely surviving. Many children went to school with no lunch in their bags. The sick could not buy medicine. Urgently needed surgeries had to be postponed. And hospitals were known to turn away the dying who had no money. For the first time our mission had relief funds that we distributed through our churches, and we had asked our board for social workers, people trained to get a handle on the needs of a country, and organize an effective response.

The number of handicapped people in the country had multiplied. For every person who had died, several more had been crippled or paralyzed or needed therapy. The mission authorized me to do some research and find out what kinds of needs these people had. I learned that the biggest problem was the inability of the poor to get therapy. The worse they needed it, the less likely they were to get it. The existence of centers where therapy was free did not help those who were immobile, especially the desperately poor—the very people who lived in apartment houses with no elevators. At home on maybe a fifth floor, unable to walk, they were stuck. Expensive therapists who could come to them were unthinkable for families who could hardly eat. So the need was for a therapist willing to drive the dangerous roads and climb the stairs to their apartments and serve them without pay. And none of them could hope for that.

What they didn't know yet was that God had given us Maria. The mission asked her if she would be willing to become a home therapist, on salary from the mission, and she accepted. At the end of the year she would leave her hospital job and travel with us to the U.S. (1986 was to be a furlough year.) We had found opportunities for her to observe American methods, and afterwards, in the month of March, she would return to begin this new service. She would rebuild bodies and dispense love; that was her job description.

And then there was the professional woman I knew who brought Amal to me for spiritual nurture. Amal was a young woman who had learned to cope magnificently with her blindness after being shot at a roadblock several years earlier. I started driving down to Hasmieh on Sunday evenings to bring her to church. Amal knew English and loved the service, especially the songs we sang, and she made her own distinctive impact on the gatherings afterwards at our house. She made an impact on me, definitely.

I visited Amal in her home—an elegant apartment with details and furnishings that indicated considerable wealth. She played the piano for me there once—a baby grand in a large salon with beautifully draped curtains. Her mother sat with us—a tall, fair woman, very thin, wearing tights and a long blouse with artsy, handmade jewelry—not at all the person I expected. She looked like a European socialite whose life had turned tragic. On the piano stood a picture of Amal, before the bullet that blew her eyeballs from her head and scarred her cheeks and required the rebuilding of her nose. The music Amal played was called "Running Away," she told me. *Like my picture of leaving Beirut as it was being bombed.* She had composed it to express how she often felt. At the end she laughed and said that running away was hardly an option for a blind girl. Her glass eyes did not respond to the smile on her lips.

"Anyway," she added, "I would never leave Mummy," turning her face toward her lovely, despairing mother.

Another time Amal and I sat alone in a very small room with artistic blue and white tiles somewhere—on the floor, I guess, maybe the coffee table, besides. The Sri Lankan maid brought us refreshments. The electricity went off while we sat there, and when I needed to leave, Amal had to guide me out of the house and down to my car. I held her elbow as though I were the sightless person, and we both laughed.

On the way up to Monsourieh for church, I asked her something about her mother. Part of her answer was, "Life is so hard now for my mother. I'm her only child, and her summary of my life is that I could see and now I'm blind. I can't make her understand that really it is the other way around."

"What do you mean? Tell me about that."

And she explained to me that she had been shallow before, seeing only the surface of things, loving her own pretty face. "I was vain and had no religion. Everything I wanted was frivolous."

Her father had been born a Muslim and her mother a Christian. They left her free, and she chose to be a Christian.

The trip to Monsourieh was too short, and I never got to ask her what were the issues in her choice. All of our time was too short, because of another impending departure.

The necessity of furlough created a painful conflict of needs. Our children deserved to see us, and we could hardly wait to be with them. Jim had adopted David, so we had a grandson we hardly knew. Jan was getting married in May to someone we had never met. Mother needed to see me and be sure I had survived. And we had work to do in the U.S.—talking about Lebanon to anyone who wanted to hear, telling about all the pain and the absolutely wonderful surprises. But leaving was hard—deserting my staff with minimal guidance and the curriculum project barely on its way, trusting everything to the hands of a very young administrator, abandoning Maria and our weekly studies, leaving that joyful group of young people without a place to be together. Even leaving my little stone house was not easy.

The young people gave us a party on the last Sunday night before we left. Pat Rabat hosted the event in her home in Ashrafieh. I picked up Amal, and as we walked to the car, she asked me to stop at a certain bakery. I had no idea where it was, but she said, "*Ma'leish*. I can get us there."

So I drove, and she felt the bumps and the stops and somehow gauged the distance and said, "Is this...?"

"Yes."

"Turn left. See the pharmacy. Just beyond it."

The baker had prepared for her a huge chocolate cake, which the clerk now packed in a box and handed to Amal.

Everyone who ever came to the after-church parties at our house was at Pat Rabat's house, plus some people who never even came to church in the evening, because they did not know English. The pastor also honored us with his presence. I never knew how Pat managed all those platters of food on the big table, and so many chairs. The crowd filled their plates from the platters on the long table and then sat in the chairs, with the plates on our knees. Amal was sitting to my right, and Michel came and sat on the other side of her. He complained of being tired. He said, "I was drawing all afternoon, and my eyes are so tired they hurt."

Amal said, "When my eyes hurt, I just take them out for a while."

Michel looked stunned and then a little bit ill. His cheeks flushed. He got up as he said, "I need another piece of bread. Can I bring anybody else a piece?"

After dinner, Wayne and I were ordered to sit together in a certain place and presented with a gift in a flat package. While everyone watched, we ripped off the paper. Inside we found a folder, hand-made of sturdy construction paper. We opened the folder and saw that we had been given an out-sized replica of a Lebanese identity card, with both our names on it. The usual blanks for relevant information were all filled-in, handwritten in Arabic, some of the answers humorous, true but not quite factual. At the bottom were about forty signatures of the young people, in the space for the signatures of the General Security officers. And the final touch was the genuine General Security stamp, managed by one of the young men who worked there.

We found ourselves unable to express what we felt.

Helping us through our silence, someone called out, "Present it at the airport, instead of visas, when you come back."

Exiled

Love is the last thirty-pound bale. When you load it on,
the boat tips over.

Copyright, Coleman Barks,
The Essential Rumi

On Wednesday, January 7, 1987, newly arrived after furlough, I tried hard to work in my new office, but the effort was wasted. Because we had no electricity, my typewriter was dead and the room cold. My filing cabinet and my wastebasket had not arrived from the old building, so if I opened any of the stack of mail on my new cherry-red, glass-topped desk, I could neither answer it, nor file it, nor throw it away. Anyway, people kept popping in to welcome me back and talk for a while. Antoine Feghaly and Edward came from Heidelberg Press, plus a couple of translators who had done work for us, and a salesman from a computer company—none of them mentioning business. Some pastors came, too, and seminary students.

I've forgotten who was there when we heard the big explosion down in the city. Five minutes later one of my staff members, with a radio in his hand, said there had been a car bomb.

Coming back to Lebanon was like renewing contact with a chronically ill friend—learning the new symptoms, noting the deterioration. There was no bread in the stores. "A political problem," Chaanine said, "maybe tomorrow." The vegetables were not the usual quality, because the best were being shipped outside for cash, and beside the European pasta was cheaper stuff from Turkey. Prices were so strange that I had to stand between the aisles and ponder their meaning. Beef was 250 lira a kilo; it had been 60 when we left. In dollars there turned out to be little difference; the lira was simply fading away.

We had already heard an artillery battle. "Just to make you feel at home," our neighbor Bishara said. Even his handsomeness had deteriorated in some indefinable way.

Leaving our children this time had been difficult. On the last day we were there Tim cried off and on the whole day. When your grown sons cry, that's as bad as it gets. Tim said he had a premonition; something terrible was going to happen to us. I failed to say anything really helpful and finally told him that I was not afraid to die, only that he would be bitter about it if I did. A few minutes later he found a way to help us both when he decided, "Well, if it happens, my comfort is going to be that you did what you wanted to do with your life. I don't think very many people get to do that."

The kidnapping of Americans had created an unfamiliar mood in the States. Newspaper editorials were questioning the intelligence of Americans who stayed in Beirut. People who had admired us before now considered us fools. Even worse, they said we were putting our country in an embarrassing situation. An uncle I loved told me, "If you are kidnapped over there, don't expect me to send any letters to Washington."

And then the effort to get to Lebanon had been full of forewarning. We were stuck in Cyprus because the Israelis had blockaded the Lebanese coast and were turning back passenger boats. One captain said they accused him of bringing in Palestinian fighters. Since the Jounieh port was controlled by the very militiamen who hated the Palestinians, Wayne and I had given one another imitation laughs over that and walked the streets of Larnaca to get rid of nervous energy.

When we finally got there we found Lebanon looked like itself, acted like itself—sick but with strong life signs. Arriving at our little house in the early morning on January 5, having spent the night sleepless in the ferry's reclining chairs, we had been inundated almost immediately by neighbors and friends, coming to welcome us home. Jaqueline had lost two more teeth. Lulu still talked too loudly. The children still spun themselves around in my swivel rocker. My lovely friend Susanna no longer picked hindbi, because she had been very, very sick. As Jaqueline expressed it, "She was dying." Bishara had harvested for us a big bag of pine nuts, a thoughtful gift and worth a lot of money. Maria, who had done nothing for four days but go to the port and turn away disappointed, now took a day off work to stay with us and make coffee for our guests.

And though there were lots of problems to be sorted out at BP, and I knew it, we had gone to the office on Tuesday, seeing our wonderful new building for the first time, and had been honored by the staffs of all the international institutions with a big cake in the shape of a book with a ribbon marker. Its pages said, "Welcome back Wayne and Frances We love you." No one spoke of a problem or even work. I was supposed to accept attention, drink a lot of coffee, and relax for a few days.

Half an hour after we heard the car bomb, Maria appeared in my doorway, pale and shaking. I jumped up to lead her to a chair, and my visitor excused himself.

"There was a bomb," Maria said. Her voice came out in a breathless whisper, and she put a hand on her chest.

"Where was it?"

She managed to explain that she had an appointment with a patient on a certain street, had parked her car and was walking toward the bomb when it exploded. I told her, "Stay here. Just be still," and then went to the kitchen and made her a cup of tea.

When I came back to the room, she looked half-dead, her skin the wrong color, her eyes rolling. I put the tea on a table and took one of her hands. It was cold and trembling. She sipped a little tea, nibbled the cookie I had brought, and alternately took deep breaths and let her eyelids fall shut.

I tried to talk soothingly. "You're O.K., *habibti*. You missed it."

"By two seconds," she said, looking like she could still faint.

Gradually her hands quit shaking. Recovering some of her spunk, she said, "Look what you've come back to. Why didn't you stay in America?"

That didn't even sound like a real question to me, since not being in Lebanon was unthinkable, so I said, "I came to make you a cup of tea whenever you get scared by a car bomb."

And she said, with no mirth at all, "You're silly."

I went to see Susanna on Thursday morning, before I left for work. She was in bed, her abundant gray hair in disarray. When I leaned over to kiss her she clutched my head to her bosom and, holding me down, said, "Why did you stay so long?"

Just then I hated living on two sides of the world by turn. Susanna could have died while I wasn't there, like my Daddy, like Amal. (Yes, Amal had died of bleeding in her brain. The bullet that took her eyes had finally killed her.)

That day the employees began to come to me, each with something to tell, and all the problems of the past year began to surface. Everyone had done a lot of living since we left. That was plain. They had stored up confidences and couldn't wait any longer to talk. They had suffered through stressful situations, had done and said things they needed to explain. Our editorial and production staff had done a wonderful job, but several people had made mistakes, especially the young administrator I had left in charge. I listened. Before one person left, another arrived. Charlie Costa put his head in the door and said, "When do I get a turn?"

During one of those listening sessions, my staff member and I heard shells, moved to a window facing the city and saw a huge column of black smoke billowing up from the airport. A Middle East airliner had been hit just after the passengers and crew had left it. In the afternoon shells fell here and there in widely scattered Christian areas. Six people died.

I began making lists of things to do and at moments felt overcome with panic, because the list grew long and some of its items required the kind of wisdom I was not sure I had. Finally, I realized that I did not need to do it all in a week.

Problems related to poverty had multiplied. The mission received relief money and gave it away in a day. We were feeding children in various schools. All of us in the Lebanon mission were fully employed and none of us had time or expertise to deal with such needs, but help was not forthcoming. A couple had responded to our request for social workers, but the board had steered them in another direction.

Maria told me there had been burglaries and people were reinforcing their locks and putting bars on the windows. That same week, on January 20, Terry Waite, the British churchman who had come to Lebanon to try to free the foreign hostages, disappeared. Nothing that dastardly had been heard of in the whole world, I thought.

Life had such a strange feel to it—an enormous downhill momentum. The middle of an avalanche might feel like that. We did what we could to slow things down. I announced to my staff that Thursday was my writing day and stayed home. I knew I would not do much writing, but I wanted them to get used to the idea that I would not be in the office on Thursdays. That afternoon Maria and I resumed our studies together.

Two days later, on Saturday morning, four professors—three of them Americans—were kidnapped from the Beirut University College by men posing as police officers and wearing uniforms. If the foreigners couldn't trust a policeman's uniform, who was left to trust? The rest of us became even more fearful for our personnel in West Beirut.

An upcoming event was bothering me like a nettle under my skin. On the 28th of January the women of the mission were supposed to go to Cyprus for a retreat with all the other missionary women from around the Middle East. The time was bad for me—I didn't need a retreat, and BP didn't need me to leave. But I felt obligated. Johnnie Johnson, the woman in charge and someone I really liked, had asked me to lead a seminar for mission press representatives. I had made sketchy notes in preparation.

Jokes were flying around, being told by people like Wayne, about how the mission would fall on its face without the women, and most people had some genuine fear that the Israelis would blockade the coast again and we couldn't come back. Maria was upset that I had to leave again.

A shortage was complicating life for everyone, and the gas needle in my car was touching the red "empty" mark. For a whole weekend the stations had been closed. When I arrived at the gas station on the upper edge of Monsourieh on Monday morning they were pumping gas, using a generator, since there was no electricity, and I got in line. After half an hour I was the second car back from the pump, and my motor died and wouldn't go again. I had run out of gas while idling in the line. Then I had the problem that I couldn't drive up to the pump. I was using the brake to hold my car on an uphill slope.

The attendants solved that problem. They hung up the hoses, turned off the generator and told the waiting drivers that they could not give us gas, because "there's no electricity." I coasted backward into the street, after persuading several drivers to get out of my way because I couldn't go forward. Then I walked down the street to the Whites' house, and Jerree let me take their car so I could do my work. I had a morning appointment with Mary Mathias in Ashrafieh.

That day—it was January 26—some Lebanese radio stations broadcast reports that the U.S. State Department would order all Americans to leave the country. I didn't hear it. Maria did. She came to my office in the early afternoon extremely agitated. I told her that for years Washington had been saying that we should get out of Lebanon and reminded her that we often heard mere rumors on the radio.

The school committee, of which I was a member, met that day to make some decision that Jim Ragland had asked us to make. After doing that, we discussed the possibility that we should ask our four colleagues in West Beirut to cross the Green Line and join us in the Christian area. They were feeling a lot of tension. They were in danger, and they were tired. We could not tell them to come, but we could encourage them in love to do it. Some of us also felt that the presence of Americans in West Beirut and their vulnerability there was making it more difficult for all of us to stay in Lebanon. When it was time to vote, I lifted my hand and felt my eyes filling up with tears. It was their home. To them West Beirut was Lebanon.

The following day the Swensons and Dave Williams, personnel at the Home of Onesiphorous, received warning through a phone call from Minnesota that their home office was going to order them to leave Lebanon within 24 hours. The latest kidnappings were having a drastic effect in America.

That morning even the reliable BBC got behind the rumors that the American government had had enough. We women were packing to leave for Cyprus in the evening, and the BBC correspondent in Washington said that Reagan was considering various reactions to the holding of American hostages, including military action against West Beirut. Pressure was building on the State Department to order all Americans out of Lebanon and make the failure to comply a criminal offense. By the time I got to the office everyone was talking about it. I ran away from the conversations, because I had work to do, tons of work.

Maria came in, crying this time. I told her that God had put me in Lebanon and God would have to take me out. And I said I wouldn't cry until it was a fact, not a possibility. She left again, not comforted by my refusal to believe what was happening.

The mission's executive committee met and prepared a statement to circulate among the missionaries for approval. The statement was addressed to the Foreign Mission Board and asked them to communicate to the State Department the need to differentiate between West Beirut and the Christian enclave to the East, where no single foreigner had ever been kidnapped. It was such a reasonable letter. Surely it would make a difference. But, because the executive committee had seen the need to do this, I was afraid now, very afraid.

I wrote to my mother and told her that in West Beirut every kind of crime was rampant, but where we lived there was law and order and Americans were not considered enemies.

I tried to prepare for the seminar in that untimely retreat in Cyprus, but neither my heart nor my head would participate. I had never wanted to go to the retreat; now I was scared to go. If an order to evacuate Lebanon should come, I would have a fighting chance, I thought, so long as I was in the country. If I were outside, maybe I could not come back. It also worried me, of course, that I had promised Johnnie.

In the afternoon I went home and packed my small suitcase, putting my meager notes for the seminar in my briefcase. I tried to eat a sandwich. Wayne took me to the port, and all the way I kept telling him that I was afraid to get on that ship. It was one of the biggest boats on the Jounieh-Larnaca route and stood at the pier with steaming smokestacks. I hung far back near the street, staring at it, while all the other women said goodbye to the men and showed their passports and tickets to the soldier at the gate. Several of them glanced back at me and said things like, "Aren't you coming?" And I couldn't move my feet.

At the last possible minute I flung open my briefcase, handed the folder of notes to Jerree and said, "Give this to Johnnie; tell her I'm sorry."

In the car I felt so relieved to be going back home.

The next morning I woke not long after midnight and felt devastated, as though I knew that what I had feared for two days had happened. It was a fact—not reasonable, not believable, but a fact.

I could not even imagine what it really would say, this order that had been written, or what it would ultimately mean in my life. I simply lay there focusing on my presence in Lebanon, feeling myself lying on the floor in my house that was like no other house anywhere, in our "cave," surrounded by the lovely old stone walls. In the darkness I saw every inch, every detail, deliberate or mistaken, of my accidental house, saw it full of young people smiling, praying, saw the thorns on the terraces, the village, the faces of my neighbors, Sunnin covered with snow, the canyon filled with mist, the canyon full of battle smoke, the hills lavender at sunset, the *snobar* needles shiny with rain, my staff, our unfinished projects, our church singing *Halleluia* while the guns banged, Maria learning to believe, opening like a flower—and on and on. I saw Beirut torn down the middle. I floated down to Musaitbeh and Mustapha's friendly cluttered store and Ras Beirut, which reverberated with the voices of my children. I went to Nabay and climbed again the stone steps where Georgette waited for me. I saw the whole of Lebanon, heard it, smelled it, down to the gravelly beaches. I felt it around me. I was still in Lebanon. I belonged in Lebanon. The pure happiness that had filled my heart for years came from being in Lebanon.

* * *

At 6:00 a.m., as I was drinking coffee in bed, the voice from London told me. The reality was simple, simple like a wall falling, tipping and slamming down flat. As though I had to throw its weight off my body, I jumped to my feet and stood there. Later, overcome by grief, I would be perplexed that I could stand, that I had not cried out, that I could walk into the kitchen and say to Wayne, "Did you hear it?" But for the next hour I stumbled around my kitchen, not knowing how to prepare breakfast. I misplaced the spatula. I burst into tears. I went upstairs three times to get my coat.

Driving down the hill, I thought that I was altogether. They had given us thirty days. I could move a mountain in thirty days. I would start immediately restructuring my life to fit the facts. But when I got there everybody was crying—Um John, Michel, Pat, Elena, Abu Issam, and Fadia—the accountant/friend we had just hired. Charlie shut himself into his office for hours, and when he finally came out he looked like a child who was being deserted and said, "I'm in a panic. I can't do it without you."

Then Maria came, looking as though she might collapse. The two of us went out to her car, because a carpenter had come to work on my office door, and she cried uncontrollably. I just hugged her while she cried. There were no words to be said. She cried. I hugged her. We were sitting in a public place but were past caring what anybody thought. When she finally said she had to go somewhere to take care of a patient, I thought I should pray before she left. Praying always calmed her. While I was praying my own tears started. They ran in a river off my nose, and she wiped them for me and stopped crying.

* * *

That night the mission met to discuss our predicament and what to do. David and Bill had been to the embassy to talk with the consul, who was brusque and emphatic. He blamed them and our mission for being there, for staying through the years, in spite of the embassy's repeated advice that we leave. About the women traveling to Cyprus, he first said that they could not come back, but he softened when he learned that some of them had small children. If they kept the spirit of the law and returned only to get their belongings, he decided, they would not be prosecuted. He did tell David and Bill, however, that exemptions might be obtained from an office in Washington.

The group made several decisions related to this news: First, we would ask the Foreign Mission Board to get exemptions for the whole mission—24 adults. Second, in case this request was denied, we wanted to try for exemptions for five couples, those who were involved in running the international ministries. Third, in case both of these requests failed, we would ask for exemptions for two couples: the Barnes and the Fullers. I felt hopeful, then, because if anybody stayed, I was going to stay. Surely we would win something.

The mission asked me to write a letter to Assistant Secretary of State Richard Murphy. He had become a friend 20 years before in Jordan through our children who were in school together. We wanted him to understand the role of our mission in Lebanon and the reasons why we thought we were safe and would not embarrass our country. Finally, we all agreed to pack and be ready to leave, in case we had no options.

Just as we were finishing the meeting, a reporter called from the Foreign Mission Board's press office. Because I was the press rep, I went to the phone to tell him what we had just done. And because I was the secretary of the meeting, I also talked with Dr. Ballenger. He listened as I read our decisions and told him that we were united in our wish to stay in Lebanon. Then he told me some things that he was already doing to help us, and I felt encouraged and happy to relay this news to the mission.

The next morning I gathered my staff for prayer and told them, "Yesterday we cried; today we work." I assured them that I would not desert BP, and we would find a way to do our job. Afterward, making lists of what had to be done before I could leave again left me overwhelmed. I began to realize the impossibility of accomplishing this list while packing up my house in preparation for leaving. At the top of the list was the letter to Richard Murphy, so I wrote that, then drove up to Broummana and sent it to Dr. Ballenger by telex, asking him to mail it to the State Department. Wayne and I, as well as the Barnes, decided not to pack our possessions. If we had to go, we would leave everything we owned as evidence of our intentions.

The embassy called Bill Trimble and told him to instruct our people in West Beirut to meet embassy personnel at the Riviera Hotel at 7:30 a.m. the next day for evacuation to the Christian area.

We began to hear more about exemptions. Of course, people who had both Lebanese and American passports would not have to leave. Then all the Americans who were married to Lebanese. Red Cross workers and journalists. Anybody on U.S. government business. Even the families of hostages were exempt. So who had to leave? Any professors left at the universities. And missionaries. There was nobody else. I started to feel used and angry.

I raged at Reagan, or rather, I raged at other people about Reagan. He had been elected in the first place, I told Wayne, because Carter looked so weak when he couldn't get the hostages released from Tehran. Now he had to be seen doing something, and so he was threatening a bunch of missionaries with jail.

We invited Maria and Michel to eat supper with us and spend the night. After work Maria and I went shopping for the food. On the way, we saw some of our youth group walking by the road and pulled over to talk with them.

One of them said, "We have decided to kidnap the missionaries."

Another, "We will bring you in chains to the pulpits on Sundays and make you preach to us."

I thought this was very funny.

"We're serious," they said, "Your government is willing to let kidnappers win."

They began to compose headlines for the American newspapers: "Missionaries Kidnapped by Lebanese Baptists and Held Captive in the Churches."

They imagined the threatening letters they would write to Washington. "We love them. We need them. Say they can stay, or we'll kill them."

They stood by the road waving their arms and getting happy as they got more and more outrageous ideas. They would send pictures of us, blindfolded, with guns at our heads. They added, "We can do more than that. We can say that if any missionary gets on the boat to leave we will blow it up."

By the time Maria and I drove on toward the store, I felt the world had been set right again. When we got home, Wayne and Michel were already there. Michel scrubbed the potatoes. Maria created a salad. I cooked the meat. Michel set the table. Wayne built a fire in the cave. While we were eating, we worked on more and more ridiculous variations of the kidnap theme. Maria's idea was that kidnappings were unnecessary. "All we need is news releases. Let the missionaries go on with their work. How will Reagan know?"

After dinner we had tea and cookies by the stove and then played Rook. Wayne and Maria beat Michel and me.

The men slept upstairs, Michel in the bedroom, Wayne on the floor in the hall. Maria and I slept in the cave. We sat on our mats and prayed for our people in West Beirut, the Raglands and Mabel and Nancie, because I knew their hearts were broken. And at the end I begged God to let me stay in Lebanon.

After we turned out the light we held on to each other and cried. Trying to get us both calm, I began quoting scriptures, passages that had been meaningful to Maria. I repeated the 23rd Psalm and when I came to "He prepares a table before me..." the meaning of the words came to me as bright as a sunrise. I had never really understood (maybe because I had not admitted that I had enemies) that God meant to honor me in front of those who hated me. I would be God's guest at the table. This was happening already, and I told Maria, "The love of my friends is a feast God has spread for me in the presence of my enemies."

In the morning Maria claimed that I had a new line on my cheek and said, "*Haram*! This pain is making you old." She tried to make me laugh, and then told me, "When you smile now, nothing happens in your eyes."

Wayne found out that we were awake and brought two cups of coffee to the cave.

Maria said, "How do you get a husband like that?"

I said, "You don't. You take a silly 24-year-old and you teach him."

She said, "Oh, no! It's already getting late for me to marry a 24-year-old."

And so began the third day of the thirty days we were given to live in Lebanon.

* * *

At church the next morning George Atiyeh talked a long time and solemnly about the order from our government. He said that all the Lebanese Baptist churches were writing letters to the State Department, asking for the missionaries to stay. They were backing up their letters with an organized day of fasting and prayer. The Lord's supper was a healing experience, reminding me that I was part of a community, and the community cared about its members.

Afterwards some of the people wiped tears as they told us they were praying. Several said they thought God was working things out, but everyone was inviting us for meals, and I thought that their urgency about this meant they expected us to leave.

* * *

That evening I became aware of the great chasm opening up inside of me. In our five p.m. English-language service, one of the missionaries got up at the time of prayer requests and said, "We want God's will to be done." I was surprised, first because she said it and then because I could not say it. The words sounded silly to my own ears. Of course Jesus taught us to pray for God's will to be done on earth. But why should God's will be in question? When I thought I was going to die for it, God did not release me from this commitment to be in Lebanon. Why should he release me now because Reagan was in trouble? My tears began to fall as I realized the conflict between the orders from the U.S. government and the orders I had been living under all those years.

David Swenson sang a solo. "Be strong and of good courage; I am with you and will not forsake you." And I thought about the young militiaman who said to me, "When I take my gun and go to Ain ar-Rommaneh to fight, I can't ask God to go with me." Because he knew he was wrong, he couldn't ask. David sang, and I cried. "Be strong, I am with you," was only a silly platitude. I was not strong, not strong enough to violate my own inner sense of what was right, and God would not help me do that. The tears streamed down my face.

Wayne and I were sitting on opposite ends of the pew, with several young people between us, Maria next to me, then Pat Rabat. I knew that Pat was somehow disturbed because I was crying; she said something to Maria, who touched me to show concern, but I could not stop.

Dennis Hilgendorf, a Lutheran friend, preached. He used the passage about Jesus coming to earth in the fullness of time and talked about all the glorious periods of history that had not been the right time and all the interesting, important places that were not the right places. He described Palestine in the time of Jesus, and it was cruel and chaotic like Lebanon at that moment in 1987. And when he finished, God had assured me for the one thousandth time that I was in the right place at the right time, but the knowledge could only make me weep. I knew that if I got on the boat to leave, I would go with a crack in my soul. Maybe I would lose the dearest thing I had ever had.

At the back of the church, as we were going out, I asked Dennis if anyone else could push me out of my time and my place, and he thought about it and said, "Frances, I don't know."

* * *

After that I did not cry as much. I worked hard at the office, talking things out with our administrator, helping Nazih over some rough spots in the editing of Survival Kit, planning with Charlie, approving some of the design work Pat and Michel were doing, writing blurbs for our catalog, adding tasks to the list of things to be done. All the time I was thinking: What does Reagan know of my destiny? What right does he have to interrupt the voice of God in my life? What right have I to obey him? These questions were tearing me apart, and I didn't think I could leave without some answers. Still I was calm. I told myself and others that the final word had not been spoken. Maybe even the State Department would rescue me from this trial. Maybe... many things. I was willing to wait.

But in my dreams I was drowning. The water was like a dark river, its level almost up to my eyes. I couldn't breathe or find anything to grab, but ahead of me was a little arched bridge, a stone bridge with water lapping at the underside of the arch. As the current moved me toward this bridge, my only hope, it crumbled and collapsed into the water.

Maria came to my office very sad. She had just been with the Trimbles and said that Bill was near tears. Something Dr. Ballenger said on the phone had made our position seem hopeless. I prayed with Maria, quietly, without tears, asking that we would all behave like Christians, whatever happened.

At times I remembered that I was not the first missionary to face such a crisis. Other missionaries had left China and Vietnam and Ethiopia. I wondered if any of them had left their place without feeling God's blessings on their leaving. I wished that some of them would come and help me.

For a long time I had known that the presence of Americans in their country gave hope to many Lebanese, but now I was astonished by the reactions of some of our young friends. One said, "I can't imagine this place without you." And another declared, "I can't stay, if you go." Some felt that the decree was a judgment of them, rather than us, and asked, "Why are they punishing us?" Suspicion of Washington's intentions also surfaced. "Are they taking you out, so that we can be attacked?"

Newscasts lent credence to these suspicions. The BBC correspondent in Washington kept mentioning the possibility of military action, dispelling the notion that America might hit Iran, though Iranian groups were thought to be behind the kidnappings. The newsman said that attacks against "facilities" in the Biqaa and West Beirut were more likely. He even reminded us that the U.S. could bring enough firepower to reduce Lebanon to rubble. It seemed cowardly to me that America would attack Iran in Lebanon. It required about as much courage as sending missionaries to jail.

I felt bold and plotted defiance. I would not go. Let them arrest me, I thought. Probably it would not happen until I arrived in America again. They would nab me as I entered New York or Detroit. I would be 60 by then. I wondered what American Christians would do if a 60-year-old grandmother were jailed for standing by her missionary task. I was not afraid to try it.

By this time, messages were arriving from our children, all of them boosting our morale and making us proud. Tim said, "I can't imagine what you will do, but I know it will be right." Dwight said, "If you feel you need to stay and go to jail later, I will be proud of you, as I have always been." All their messages carried sadness over the loss of home and puzzlement that West Beirut, in their memories a place in which they felt free and secure, had become a symbol of strife and terror.

I called the American embassy and spoke with Joseph Karam on the phone, visualizing him with his wounds, his sightless eye, remembering the appointment I never kept, the day the embassy was blown up. His voice was soft and respectful. I told him how much we wanted to stay in Lebanon, described our difficulties in leaving so many big ministries on such short notice and asked if he had any suggestions. He told me that the mission should write a letter to the consul. "We will send this letter to Washington, and then we can wait for a response. This will at least buy you some time."

When I reported this to the mission, I reminded them of the efficiency and courteousness with which this man had served us through the years, and the mission asked me to write a letter to the consul commending Joseph on their behalf. I enjoyed writing this letter and sent it by hand to the embassy. Later Joseph called and thanked us for that.

Dr. Ballenger kept in touch, and once I got the chance to ask him the question that was on my mind. "What would happen if I just simply didn't obey the order? What if I just stayed here and went on doing my job?"

He was silent for a long moment before saying, "Frances, if you stay and the Foreign Mission Board has not given you permission to do that, then they will have to take you off salary."

So, was it going to be about money in the end? About making a living?

I mentioned to some of my friends that if I stayed I would have the problem of how to buy groceries and all of them claimed immediately that they would feed me like a queen.

Somehow we were alerted to receive a phone call at the Kings' home early in the morning. Wayne and I arrived by the appointed time and found a small group of missionaries sitting with glum faces. The call had already come and was finished. It was not Dr. Ballenger but Keith Parks, the president of the Foreign Mission Board, who had called. What he said was, "It will be very embarrassing for me, if you are not out of Lebanon by the deadline."

The Foreign Mission Board had thousands of representatives all over the world and had to deal every day with the State Department. The embarrassment was about that, about jeopardizing trust and hurting our colleagues across the world.

I leaned against the wall, limp with despair. After they gave us the message, no one found anything else to say. All of us respected Keith Parks. We had believed for many years that he was God's man in the right place at the right time. If anyone had spiritual authority over us, it was Keith Parks who had troubles enough already without our weakening his position.

One by one people dragged themselves off to do what they had to do. I had never imagined that it would happen like this.

* * *

We left the country in two main groups on succeeding nights, boarding ships bound for Larnaca, only a day or two in front of the deadline.

Anticipating that our departure would attract attention from the local media, the mission had asked me to write a statement that could be given to journalists. I requested that Jim Ragland help me. One Beirut television channel gave twenty minutes of its half-hour evening newscast to the departure of the Baptist mission, filming the first group as they boarded the ship, and reading this statement in both English and Arabic.

"We, the 24 members of the Near East Baptist Mission, are leaving Lebanon in obedience to the order of the U.S. government. Some of us have been here for thirty years, some for only two. All of us feel that our hearts have been torn out and left in Lebanon.

"We do not fully understand the intention of our government in forcing us to go. If it is to protect us, we are dismayed, because in gaining protection, we have lost our right to obey God as we understand His will for us.

"If it is to punish Lebanon, we are sorry, because Lebanon is dying. Punishment is not appropriate for the dying. The dying need urgent and intensive care. We believe that our educational and spiritual and benevolent work is part of that care. We are sure that punishment, revenge and isolation are not the answers to Lebanon's problems.

"We ask the American people to understand that Lebanon is a hostage, that Lebanon is fractured and battered and helpless to free itself from forces that are leading it toward certain death. We plead for a policy of fairness and compassion, a policy that will attempt to remove the causes of terrorism and to heal the wounds of Lebanon.

"As Americans, we uphold the necessity and rightness of obedience to the law, and we hope never to embarrass our country. As Christians, we believe it is our duty to stand by these people in their time of trouble. As conscientious citizens and servants of God, we plead for the freedom to make our own decisions and take our own risks for the sake of our Christian purpose.

"Finally, we promise the people of Lebanon that we will speak always, everywhere in your behalf, that we will pray for you constantly, and that we will come again, as soon as we are permitted, to share your life and reclaim our hearts."

It must have been obvious to everyone who read or heard this letter that we had been undone by love and our boat had tipped over.

Epilogue

Lord, you establish peace for us;
all that we have accomplished you have done for us.
O Lord, our God, other lords besides you have ruled over us,
but your name alone do we honor.

Isaiah 26:12,13

Leaving Lebanon without believing that it was right was the worst thing that had ever happened to my life. It was a discontinuity beyond my imagination—not only an interruption, not only an exile from home, but a separation from part of myself, a personal disaster.

In Cyprus, Wayne and I borrowed a lot of houses. We found ways to do our work—traveling in and out of Lebanon, riding a lot of boats, running greater risks and enduring more stress than when we lived in Beit Meri. We missed so many events and developments in Lebanon, including another conflagration in which the people of The Hara thought they would die. And I was not there for Maria when her mother died of cancer.

The mission's ministry to the handicapped was a great success. Maria became a true healer, bringing love and hope into many of the poorest and saddest homes in Lebanon. An American journalist wrote a story about her, calling her "the angel of Beirut." Later, with her position threatened by the lack of funds, she studied for and passed the California physical therapy licensing exam and got a great job offer. She lives in California, just three hours from us, and is a loved and valued member of our family.

BP finished the *Faith and Life Curriculum,* and it has enriched the churches of the Middle East for more than 20 years.

With Mary's help I formed two companies and obtained two publishing licenses, one in the name of Baptist Publications, the other as Dar Manhal al-Hayat (House of the Source of Life). This second name opened numerous markets and became the primary imprint.

Elena married, but the marriage was unhappy and ended in divorce. Eighteen years after the deaths of the Marines, I talked with her about John, and she wiped tears.

Michel obtained a student visa to the U.S. after leaving Lebanon on a laissez passer. When his travel permit expired, he became a man without a country. Studying constantly to keep his visa and avoid deportation with no place to go, living on peanut butter sandwiches and faith in God, he obtained a doctor's degree in commercial art and, finally, the right to seek American citizenship. Almost weeping, he told me recently, "Your house was a refuge. We could express our anguish there and pray and laugh."

Though it took years, Adeeb, still stateless and restless, obtained a travel document and, from the consulate in another country, a visa to America. After a brilliant university record, he went to work for a major corporation where he has found the success he deserves. I feel good about helping him have a home, a country. Once he visited us in California. At the dinner table he said, "I saw my life going down a hole. I don't know how you did it, but you yanked me back up." I told him, "I had *wasta.* Without Joseph Karam, you were gone."

Wayne surprised me totally by having a heart attack, which turned a large part of his heart into scar tissue. The rest of it, however, is still strong and generous.

The war in Lebanon ended in 1990. It ended probably because everyone was so tired of fighting and everyone had lost. Foreign investment and a building boom followed, altered the landscape for both better and worse, then came to a screeching halt. Unemployment, economic duress and the loss of hope created a continuing exodus. The churches consequently suffered the loss of members and financial resources. Conflicts throughout the region have added to this trend, and the Christian minority in the Middle East continues to decline.

In November 1994 Wayne and I came to America to retire. We had already been here for years when the State Department lifted its ban against Americans living in Lebanon.

A couple of years after our retirement the Foreign Mission Board began withdrawing support from its institutions around the world. As part of this strategic move, they closed the publishing house in Lebanon, firing my wonderful staff, stopping all editorial projects and interrupting the flow of books to the Arab world. A lot of hearts were broken, a lot of damage done to ministries and relationships. Worse for me than leaving Lebanon was the feeling that what I built had been destroyed.

But the Lebanese Baptist community rose up in indignation and self-defense and refused to lose its publishing house. After negotiation, the FMB gave them the building, the stock and the publishing licenses. With these assets and their innate Lebanese resourcefulness, the community began to rebuild the program, using the foundation already laid. What they have done is proof that we built with stone, not straw.

In 2013, while I was on a personal visit to Lebanon, the publishing house honored me and my former staff at a beautiful gathering of nearly four hundred people. The theme of the program was "Publishing Remains." Their work and their words have brought healing to my heart.

As for the little stone house in Beit Meri, it survived everything and was bought by Ghassan and Hanni—not to live in but for an investment. They put concrete stairs up the hill, like I wanted long ago—the result proving that Wayne was right—and a tall iron railing along the edge of the terrace and around the roof. These additions made me sad but brought the house suddenly from the nineteenth to the twenty-first century. It will be there when everyone who remembers this story is gone.

In California our family helped us build a house—a place big enough for all of us to come together (we are 24 with Maria) with beautiful details reflecting the loving motives of the builders. I like living in this house so much that I don't want to leave it for a week, but I do—sometimes for months—knowing that attachment to houses is a useless emotion, for all of them are borrowed.

The happiness I enjoy here near my family has been now and then overwhelmed by a familiar but unspecified grief, whether the pain of living in Lebanon or the pain of leaving I cannot tell. I accept both as a fair price for all I learned, however slowly.

Maybe there have been, and will be, better times to be in Lebanon, or even better times to be alive. But none of us can choose our time; it is given. Regret is destructive and envy useless. When I consider the failures and trauma and dangers of those days in the war, I remember also a shining joy and know that this was pure gift, the reward for nothing but staying in my life. I know, too, that many people could have done my job better, achieved more and maybe lived more gracefully, but they were not there. So I did the best I could, and now, having borrowed a house, I give it back to its gracious owners, saying "Thank you," as I go.

The End

Acknowledgements

I am deeply grateful to the many people who gave the encouragement and help that this work required.

Tony Wales asked me to write a memoir long before I was ready, and published my short stories instead.

Bob Klausmeier read my memories when they were raw and rambling without concluding that the case was hopeless.

Larry Brook pushed me to complete this project when I was discouraged.

Mark Carpenter requested the rights in Portuguese (very nice, though he was joking).

Robert Reekie made countless contributions to my work in Lebanon and then recently to my memoir.

My son Tim read the manuscript again and again, astutely, lovingly every time.

Some of my Lebanese friends knew I was writing about them and trusted me to do it.

My long-suffering husband tolerated, while I was writing, my absence from places like the kitchen.

Other professional and incredibly busy people took time to read my book and write commendations or helpful observations, including Pat Alexander, Colin Chapman, Jeanne Larsen, and Aliki Barnstone. I am lucky to have such a list of friends.

Finally, as I wrote this book, I experienced the work itself as an expression of gratitude to God for a life full of wonder and richness. I have dared to hope that by putting part of my story into words I might share a bit of the blessing with someone else.

About the Author

Frances Fuller was born Frances Anderson in Wynne, Arkansas, and holds degrees from Louisiana Tech, Golden Gate Baptist Seminary and Hollins University. For twenty-four years she was director of a Christian publishing house in Lebanon, and her husband Wayne was a member of her staff. Together with their Lebanese colleagues at Dar Manhal al-Hayat, they trained writers and produced in the Arabic language numerous historic works, including scores of titles basic to a Christian library. While engaged in this work, they lived through several wars and witnessed many headline events in Lebanon and the region.

The Fullers, who have five children and ten grandchildren, now live in the foothills of the Sierras.

Frances Fuller is also the author of:

- *The Chameleon's Wedding Day* (short stories), Lion Publishing, Oxford, England.
- Portraits of Women in the Bible (8 articles), New Lion Handbook to the Bible and Zondervan Handbook to the Bible.
- *Pictures of Jesus* (in Arabic), Baptist Publications, Lebanon.
- *How to Read the Bible* (in Arabic) Baptist Publications, Lebanon.
- *The Spiritual Foundations of Freedom* (in Arabic), Baptist Publications, Lebanon.
- Articles in: *The Commission* magazine, *Interlit* (David C Cook Foundation) and in Baptist state papers all over the U.S.

CPSIA information can be obtained at www.ICGtesting.com
Printed in the USA
LVOW08s0327150114

369405LV00001BA/83/P